BOLIVIA

Oxford University Press, Amen House, London E.C.4

GLASGOW   NEW YORK   TORONTO   MELBOURNE   WELLINGTON
BOMBAY   CALCUTTA   MADRAS   KARACHI   LAHORE   DACCA
CAPE TOWN   SALISBURY   NAIROBI   IBADAN
KUALA LUMPUR   HONG KONG

First published 1954

Second edition 1955

Third edition 1964

Reprinted 1965

Set in Great Britain by
The Broadwater Press Ltd
and reprinted lithographically by
Ebenezer Baylis and Son Limited
The Trinity Press, Worcester, and London

BOLIVIA

A Land Divided

HAROLD OSBORNE

Third Edition

Issued under the auspices of the
Royal Institute of International Affairs

OXFORD UNIVERSITY PRESS

LONDON   NEW YORK   TORONTO

CONTENTS

Contents

PREFACE

THIS is the first general survey of modern Bolivia to be published in England. It is one of a series of studies of the Latin American republics which are designed to give a concise but comprehensive picture of the political, social and economic conditions in those countries for the benefit of the non-specialist reader and student. If it succeeds, therefore, in bringing the Bolivian scene before the eyes of a wider audience than the Latin American experts both vividly and with accuracy, it will have achieved the purpose for which it was written and commissioned.

Bolivia is not an easy country to know. Its affairs have attracted little public attention now or at any time, and to many people it is no more than a name. It is difficult of access, internal communications are bad and travel away from the main air routes savours rather of pioneering than of the milder forms of tourism. Indeed it is commonly—and truly—said that few even among Bolivians themselves know more than a small part of their own country well. It is one of the few remaining countries in the world which contain areas still awaiting exploration. For these reasons, and also because the physical conformation of the land has exercised a paramount influence on its history and economy, the regional geography has been described fairly fully.

The internal history has been turbulent and explosive. But as this is likely to hold little interest for the general reader, only so much has been said as is necessary for an understanding of present problems and tendencies. A separate section on the history of the tropical lowlands has been included because, although they cover more than three-fifths of Bolivia's territory and offer many of the richest prospects for future development, they are neglected in the standard histories and text-books. A very abbreviated survey of Bolivian mining is also given both for its intrinsic interest and because of its crucial importance in the life and social structure of the Republic over three centuries. The sociological picture is coloured by the conflict of interests between a backward and unadaptable Indian population on the one side and a small controlling minority of European stock on the other. Some account has therefore been given of the psychology of the highland Indian and his stolid resistance to assimilation into the modern economic state.

In the economic chapter an attempt has been made to present the economic difficulties which are endemic to Bolivia side by side with an indication of its vast untapped reservoirs of natural wealth, to portray both its enormous unexploited resources and the extraordinarily difficult problems of development which stand in the way of their utilization. The important social and economic revolution of 1952 has been described in some detail.

Owing to limitations of space educational and cultural aspects have been touched upon only incidentally. Bolivia has seven universities—at La Paz, Sucre, Cochabamba, Potosí, Santa Cruz, Oruro and Tarija. It has several Escuelas Rurales Normales training teachers for the education of the rural Indian populace, and the author was pleasantly impressed by the keenness and enthusiasm which he saw when he visited those at San Lorenzo outside Tarija and at Santiago de Huata on the borders of Lake Titicaca. But the provision is still woefully inadequate, and any country which admits 70 per cent of its population to be illiterate has obviously most of the way still to go before achieving a sound measure of general education. Bolivia has made no significant contribution to contemporary Latin American movements in music and the arts. Although it has its poets and writers—rather surprisingly many in proportion to the small reading public—it has none who has attracted international attention.[1] The origin of the Press in Bolivia goes back to 1823, two years before the foundation of the Republic. There is a large number of local journals of very limited circulation and of the two national dailies one, *La Razón*, could confidently invite comparison with any paper in South America for the high level of its international news and its cultural supplements. It was, however, owned by mining interests and was suppressed at the revolution of 1952.

With regard to survivals of native customs and folklore, languages, beliefs and handicrafts, Bolivia contains a wealth of varied ethnological material unsurpassed in any other country on the continent. This is too vast a subject to be even summarized within the confines of the present short study, but the author has already touched upon certain isolated aspects of it in his larger book

[1] Dudley Fitts in his *Anthology of Contemporary Latin-American Poetry* (Norfolk, Conn., 1942) includes selections from the work of only two Bolivian poets, Yolanda Bedregal de Cónitzer and Raúl Otero Reiche—a choice which must have given some surprise in Bolivian circles. Franz Tamayo alone of Bolivian writers ranks indisputably among the great creative poets of our time.

Indians of the Andes.[1] Specialized studies are available of the native
music, languages and literatures, social institutions, and so on,
and considerable work has been done on the archaeology of parts
of the region. But there is still a place and superabundant material
for a comprehensive work of research to be done.

The statistics used in the text are taken from the official publications of the Dirección General de Estadística in the Ministerio
de Hacienda and of the Banco Central de Bolivia. But it is admitted on all sides that Bolivian statistics, particularly vital and
production statistics, are both partial and inexact. For this reason
direct acquaintance and personal impression count for more here
than in most countries and the author considers himself fortunate
that he was able during his years of residence to travel to regions
rarely visited as well as to the better known centres. He is heavily
indebted to previous writers on Bolivian matters and even more
to the many Bolivian friends whose courtesy and frankness en-
abled him to acquire an understanding of the country and its
problems, its many merits and its great shortcomings, in the only
way in which such knowledge can be acquired. Further, the
author wishes to record his gratitude and appreciation to Mr
Thomas Ifor Rees, formerly H.M. Ambassador at La Paz, to
Coronel Angel Telleria Gutiérrez, former Bolivian Consul-General
in London, to Professor R. A. Humphreys and to Mr H. S.
Lambert for reading the manuscript and for making many help-
ful corrections and suggestions, and to the Antofagasta (Chili)
and Bolivia Railway Company Ltd and The Peruvian Corporation Ltd for information. He is particularly indebted to Mr C. F.
Geddes, formerly General Manager of the Banco Mercantil,
Bolivia, for the benefit of his extensive knowledge of Bolivian
economy and finance. The author must, however, make it clear
that he takes sole responsibility for all opinions and statements in
the book.

June 1953

PREFACE FOR THIRD EDITION

THIS book was written shortly after the author's return from a
period of service in the British Embassy at La Paz, when impressions of the people and the country were vivid in the forefront of
his mind and some first-hand knowledge of recent political and

[1] H. Osborne, *Indians of the Andes* (1952).

economic predicaments could be claimed. Much of what was then written is as valid now as it has ever been. The physiognomy of the country does not change. In so far as they arise from climatic and geographical diversity, physiographic regionalism and the sheer physical difficulties of arranging adequate communications, the basic economic exigencies and sociological intractabilities persist with undiminished urgency. Inherited cultural patterns have great durability and the ecological situation does not change its face with transient political propaganda. Changes in social, economic and political behaviour come slowly in a culture where the family is little assisted by state agencies in providing the fundamental training for the child. But to set against this, the revolution of 1952 meant much more than a mere swing of power from one political group to another. The Nationalist Government came into the saddle committed to radical social and economic reforms which had been unrealistically debated for a very long time. Their accession brought hurried and not always well considered modifications to the fundamental structure of the body politic, whose immediate result was widespread disruption and the exacerbation of many difficulties. The intervening decade has been a record of economic collapse, social unrest and hand-to-mouth survival by means of palliative assistance from abroad. The country now stands at the commencement of a Ten Year Plan of radical reconstruction upon whose success or failure national survival may well depend. But lest the reader should be tempted to assume too hastily that the revolutionary Government have gone about their business with insufficient adroitness, it should be remembered that they came to an already teetering economy, in which the elements of self-sufficiency were lacking, and to a country where basic reforms were long overdue. The magnitude of their task and the intractability of their material can scarcely be exaggerated.

In view of the critical nature of the years which have supervened, the preparation of this third edition of the book has represented much more than patchwork and addition. Besides the correction of some errors which have inevitably come to light the historical section has been brought up to date and a new assessment of the revolution and its resulting reforms has been attempted. The economic material has been completely rewritten with main emphasis upon the critical decade between 1953 and 1963, leading to a review of the situation which the Ten Year Plan was devised to meet. Some attempt has been made to gather together the rather contradictory indications as to the consequences of the Agrarian Reform in the years following 1953 and to trace the effects of nationalization on the mining industry. The section on the Beni has been expanded and a completely new section has been devoted to Santa Cruz, which has been the scene of the most successful recent efforts towards agricultural revival. Some account has been given of the limited boom of the petroleum industry in this area and elsewhere. Something is said about the endeavours of the National Government towards improvements in rural education, national health and other social services and very tentative hints are suggested in the direction of an appraisal of the realities of social changes behind the façade of political propaganda. But the author has not visited Bolivia since 1951 and pressure of other preoccupations has prevented him from keeping the affairs of that country under continuous survey. Apart from a contribution on Bolivian economy to the new edition of the *Encyclopaedia Britannica* his interests have been drawn largely elsewhere. Bolivia is a country difficult beyond the usual to assess from a distance, and the lack of opportunity to renew first-hand contacts during years which have seen such momentous developments must necessarily diminish the value of what he says about them. The reader is therefore advised to treat the parts of the book which are new to the third edition with somewhat more caution than the rest.

I wish to record my gratitude to Professor R. A. Humphreys for his encouragement and advice at a time when I was hesitant about undertaking the task of making this new edition of a book which belonged to my personal past and the particular debt which I owe to Mr C. F. Geddes, who read again the whole script and made many valuable suggestions and necessary corrections. I am also vastly indebted to His Excellency Señor Manuel Barrau Peláez, Bolivian Ambassador at the Court of St James, for his friendship and encouragement over the years and for the alacrity which he has shown in making available information and statistics. I must also mention my obligation to Mr N. L. Weatherall of the Antofagasta (Chili) and Bolivia Railway Company Ltd for supplying information and my special indebtedness to Miss Katharine Duff of the Royal Institute of International Affairs for her patience and meticulousness in bringing order into an all too disorderly manuscript and for reading the proofs.

May 1963. H. O.

NOTE

The revision for this edition and the extensive re-writing mentioned in the Preface were executed in 1962 and the early part of 1963, when the text was finalized for the press. Since Bolivia was at that time going through a period of change and unsettlement sometimes verging on crisis, a cut-off date had to be determined. It was therefore decided to make 1960 the target date, since this would allow for the fact that many statistics become available in definitive form a year or even more after they are compiled and usually refer to the year preceding that of their dating. The intention therefore has been to present a reasonably balanced picture of the state of Bolivia at about the beginning of the 1960s, although exact precision in the various fields touched upon has not been attempted.

Since 1960 the political, and to some extent the social, situation has remained disturbed. Improvements in agriculture and production generally have been claimed but the period has been too short and the evidence is too partial for it to be possible to postulate with assurance such a definite change of trend or modification of the general picture as could warrant a new edition in 1965. The present reprinting therefore still substantially presents a survey ending with the assessment of Bolivia's economic and social condition in 1960. Its value will be as a background to which later reports may be related.

CHAPTER I

THE COUNTRY

VISITORS to Bolivia are still told the tale of the British Minister Plenipotentiary who fell into the bad graces of a Bolivian President and was run out of the capital unclothed, undignified and seated on an ass; whereupon Queen Victoria ordered a ship of war to La Paz to demonstrate her shocked displeasure off the Bolivian coast. On learning that Bolivia no longer had a seaboard and that La Paz lies well beyond the range of any ship unaddicted to mountain climbing, the Queen, it is said, had the guilty country expunged from the map, condemning it to geographical extinction with a regal stroke of the pen. Whether this story is any more than an allegory told to account for the average Englishman's ignorance of Bolivian geography is unimportant. What is certain is that there is no other country of its size which contributes so little to the general stock of information of the reasonably well-informed. Anybody will tell you that Bolivia is the Switzerland of South America and that in it tin is mined; and with that the fountain of knowledge runs dry. Even in the neighbouring countries there are few among the general public who know or wish to know more of it than fanciful and slightly malicious gossip. As the writer travelled across the continent from Buenos Aires over the Andes to Santiago and up through Chile to Antofagasta on his way to La Paz, the moment of shocked silence which invariably greeted the announcement of his destination was more disconcerting than the commiseration that followed. *Un pobre país*—a poor country—is the stock formula for Bolivia throughout South America. Most people can add that La Paz is situated at a height at which no normal man can breathe in comfort, amidst towering and barren mountains where the inhabitants are uncivilized and rude. And there too the average knowledge ends.

Most even of this meagre information is false or half-truth. Bolivia is not a small country as we are accustomed to measure size, but is as large as France and Spain combined. It is the fifth largest republic in South America, coming after Brazil, Argentina, Peru and Colombia. It certainly contains some of the most formidable mountain territory in the world; but over more than three-

I

fifths of its extent it embraces tropical forests and savannas of the
Amazon and La Plata basins, which are no more than a few hundred feet above sea level. The country is now poor. But in Colonial
times it was a major source of the fabulous wealth which crossed
the Spanish Main and it remains today a land rich in unexploited
and largely unexplored natural resources. Bolivia must certainly
be classed among the backward and undeveloped regions of the
world; yet few countries have been endowed by nature with such
an abundant diversity of essential raw materials. In one of the
picturesque phrases with which the Bolivian will describe his
country,[1] it is 'A beggar sitting on a chair of gold'; and the *Report
of the United Nations Mission of Technical Assistance to Bolivia* (1951)
agrees that the phrase is justified 'by the contrast that still exists
between the relative poverty of the people and Government on the
one hand and, on the other, the unquestioned richness of Bolivia's
heritage of natural resources.'[2] If the extraordinarily difficult problems of exploitation and communications could be solved—problems which are certainly beyond the country's own unaided resources—Bolivia could, there is no doubt, become more than self-
sufficient in most primary essentials and still over and above that
retain an important export of minerals. In practice, however, it is
largely dependent on importation for almost its every necessity,
while its own lavish endowments are allowed to waste unfulfilled.
And in this world of ever tightening economic pressure so large
an area left unproductive draws to itself the eyes of envy, sets in
motion expansionist forces probing as into a vacuum, and may
even endanger the tranquillity of a continent.

Bolivia is situated between 57° 29' 40" and 69° 33' 36" longitude
west and between 9° 34' 50" and 25° 13' latitude south in the east
and 10° 56' 40" and 25° 0' 05" latitude south in the west, lying
roughly within the same parallels as Madagascar. It is bounded to
the north and east by Brazil, to the south by Argentina and Paraguay, to the south-west by Chile and to the north-west by Peru. It
became an independent republic in 1825 with a territory stated
to have covered 904,952 square miles. By cessions and wars it has
since lost areas amounting to 492,155 square miles of these—
46,333 square miles, including all its seaboard, to Chile in the
War of the Pacific (1879–83), 189,353 square miles to Brazil,
65,924 to Argentina, 96,527 to Peru and 94,018 to Paraguay as a

---

[1] A phrase which originated with the French explorer Alcides d'Orbigny.
[2] p. 1 (*UNMTA Report* in subsequent references).

2

BOLIVIA: GENERAL

3

result of the Chaco War of the nineteen thirties. The dangerous
precedent of annexation was established to its detriment almost
from the beginning of its independent career and each of its neighbours has since taken its toll. Yet it remains with the not inconsiderable estimated area of 412,800 square miles. At its greatest
length it measures about 950 miles and it is about 900 miles across
at its widest. In general outline it is like a single-headed axe with
the haft towards the west, land-locked in the heart of the South
American continent.[1]

It is a land of violent contrasts, excessive in everything, and
language inevitably runs to superlatives in describing it. In physiographic characteristics it is three countries and not one. There is
the country of mountain and plateau, the country of high valleys
and gorges, and the country of the tropical lowlands. The face of
the land alters with elevation; temperature, rainfall and productivity depend upon the sudden changes of altitude rather than on
distance south of the equator, and the western part of the country
presents the anomaly of a frigid climate within the tropical zone.
La altura is as common a phrase in Bolivian conversation as the
word 'weather' in Great Britain. The French scientist-explorer
Alcides d'Orbigny called Bolivia the 'microcosm of the planet',
because within its frontiers every type of scenery and every variation of climate from steaming jungle heat to more than Alpine

[1] Owing partly to the difficulties of physical survey, statements of Bolivian
topographical data show considerable variation among themselves. Of sources
most readily accessible in this country the *Concise Oxford Atlas* (1952) gives
the total land area as 415,000 square miles, *Collins Graphic Atlas* (1952) as
507,000 square miles, *Bartholomew's* (1947) as 514,400 square miles, the *South
American Handbook* as 419,470 square miles and the *New World Guides to the
Latin American Republics* (1943) as approximately 510,000 square miles. (One
may suppose that the higher figures neglect to take account of the depletion of
territory which resulted from the war of the Chaco.) The report of the U.N.
Mission referred to above accepts the figure of 411,127 square miles. The 1963
edition of the *Encyclopaedia Britannica* gives the area as 424,162 square miles. The
writer has relied in the main upon Jorge Pando Gutiérrez, *Bolivia y el mundo*
(1947) and Abel Peña y Lillo Escóbar. *Síntesis geográfica de Bolivia* (1947). But
Bolivian authorities also differ, and although these two works were published in
the same year and are generally taken as authoritative in Bolivia, the former
gives the area of the country as 1,078,000 square kilometres, the population as
3,400,000 and average density as 3·2 per square kilometre, while the latter puts
the area at 1,069,094 square kilometres, the population at 3,787,800 and the
average density at 3·5 per square kilometre. As certain sections of the frontier
are still under survey, no figure can in any case be definitive to within a few
hundred square miles.

cold alternate in unnatural juxtaposition with the suddenly
changing altitudes. From the cool, sun-swept capital La Paz,
straggling up the ragged slopes of a deep ravine twelve thousand
feet above the sea, you may drive in a couple of hours to Chacaltaya
which boasts the highest ski-run in the world at 16,500 feet, or you
may board a plane and in less than an hour immerse yourself in the
lazy heat of Amazonian forest at Rurrenabaque on the river Beni.
In the mountains of Potosí, which stands more than a thousand
feet higher than Lhasa, you look downwards when you hear the
sound of an approaching plane, and along the cayman-infested
tributaries of the Mamoré, or at Guayaramerin, terminus of the
Madera–Mamoré railway, you swelter through the tropical night
to the pulsating orchestration of cicadas and frogs. It is a strange
and secret country, whose frigid mountain uplands nurtured the
earliest civilizations of the continent and whose vast low-lying
jungles have not even yet been fully explored.

The importance of altitude as a factor determining climatic
conditions in Bolivia may be gathered from the following table,
which gives latitude, mileage from La Paz, altitude, mean annual

	Latitude	Altitude* (ft)	Mileage by air from La Paz	Mean annual temperature (°C.)	Mean annual rainfall (mm.)
La Paz	16° 30′	12,130	—	9·8	622·4
Oruro	17° 58′	12,160	143	8	580
Potosí	19° 35′	13,255	296	6	608·5
Cochabamba	17° 23′	8,392	177	18	506·5
Sucre	19° 02′	9,460	320	12	650·3
Tarija	21° 32′	6,250	513	17·55	406
Santa Cruz	17° 46′	1,476	370	15·3	1359·7
Trinidad	14° 45′	950	401	26·2	1425
Riberalta	11°	564	454	27·5	1579·7
Cobija	11°	853	646	27	1770·4

* In all these altitudes authorities unaccountably, and one would think un-
necessarily, differ. Trinidad, for instance, is given as 126 metres by Jorge Pando
Gutiérrez, *Bolivia y el mundo*, on the authority of the official *Revista de Agricultura*
(La Paz), June 1943, as 320 metres by Dr Juan Manuel Balcazar, *Epidemiología
boliviana* (La Paz, 1946) and as 236 metres by Abel Peña y Lillo Escóbar,
Síntesis geográfica de Bolivia. The *UNMTA Report* takes the last figure (p. 121).
In the case of La Paz, a city with no level streets and very steep gradients,
very considerable variations in stated altitude would be expected unless the
central Plaza or some other point of reference were generally agreed. But similar
considerations do not hold for lowland towns.

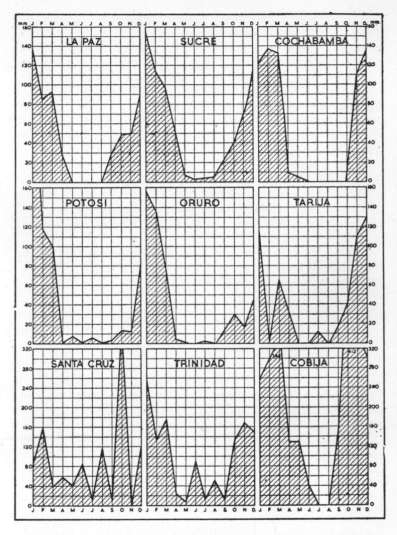

SEASONAL VARIATIONS IN RAINFALL IN DEPARTMENTAL
CAPITALS FOR THE YEAR 1945

Based on Abel Peña y Lillo Escóbar, *Síntensis geografica de Bolívia* (La Paz, 1947)

6

temperature and rainfall of the main towns of the country. The high seasonal variability of rainfall is indicated by the graphs on page 6.

the graphs on page 6.

THE ALTIPLANO

The whole western side of South America is dominated by the Andes, the most extensive orographical system in the world, which sweep north and south for four thousand miles along the Pacific coast from the eastern end of the Isthmus of Panama to the Magellan Straits, terminating in southern Patagonia and the islands north of Cape Horn. And it is owing to this massive range that South America, despite its enormous jungled plains, its low savannas and parching pampas, contains a higher proportion of land over ten thousand feet in elevation than any other continent. Through the greater part of their extent the Andes do not form a single compact wall but run in series of two, or sometimes three, parallel folds, which unite from time to time in complicated knots and then divide again. Enclosed at a great height between these parallel ridges are the long and narrow tablelands, the *punas* or *mesetas*, which, in the centuries before Columbus, cradled the pre-historic civilizations of the continent.

The western territory of Bolivia is occupied by two chains of the Andes, which divide at the knot of Vilcanota or Apolobamba (lat. 14° south) in southern Peru and run bifid through the whole territory of the Republic to the Pass of San Francisco (lat. 23° south) in the frontier region between Bolivia, Chile and Argentina. The western of these chains, the Cordillera Occidental, along which runs the frontier with Chile, stands as a bulwark between Bolivia and the Pacific coast. The eastern chain, named the Cordillera Real, runs first in a south-easterly direction, encircling Lake Titicaca, and then almost due south through the middle of Bolivia—a stupendous granite wall which justly merits the title 'Royal'. And between the two is enclosed the high plateau of the Altiplano on which the main life of the country has traditionally unrolled.

The Cordillera Real is a group of Palaeozoic massifs resting on a granitic core and has been very incompletely explored. The Cordillera Occidental is built of Quaternary volcanic rocks and the peaks are the summits of former volcanoes. Both the eastern and the western Cordilleras are broken into segments, also called Cordilleras or serranías, set end to end or partially overlapping.

7

The Cordillera Occidental is divided into three sections, the Cordillera of Pacajes and Carangas in the north, the central serranías of Huatacondo (which lies in Chilean territory) and Sillicaya extending south as far as the Pass of Ollagüe, through which runs the Antofagasta–Bolivia railway, and the southern chain of volcanic peaks. The whole range is said to average 16,500 feet in altitude and is dominated by the central mass of Sajama, which rises to a height of 21,420 feet above sea level. There are copper deposits in the sector of Pacajes, exploited mainly at Corocoro, and in the volcanic section there are deposits of sulphur which are not exploited.

The Cordillera Real is divided into five sectors. The most northerly extends from the Peruvian frontier to the Pass of Luribay, below La Paz, and averages 18,000 feet of altitude for over a hundred miles. It contains the most majestic individual mountains in the country: Cololo (19,394 ft), Illampu (21,522 ft) with its flat, truncated crest still one of the highest peaks in the Andes, Chachacomani (20,528 ft), Huayna Potosí (20,407 ft), Mururata (15,763 ft) and Illimani (21,325 ft), which overlooks La Paz.[1] The whole sector is capped with snow all the year round, although in general snow is not perennial except on isolated peaks of the Andes, and it is impossible to imagine a more impressive spectacle than these gigantic crests rising up into a pillow of adhering cloud from the vast arc of static brilliance which fringes the horizon against the unflecked azure of the highland sky. The range is rich in non-ferrous mineral deposits, though they are most of them very difficult of access, and is mined for tin, tungsten, zinc and lead. South of Luribay comes the Cordillera of Tres Cruces, from the southern extremity of which the Cordillera of Cochabamba juts out laterally towards the eastern plains. It is mined for tin, antimony, lead and silver. South again of Tres Cruces is the sector of Azanaques, which lies east of lake Poopó and contains the former Patiño tin mines, and the Cordillera of Los Frailes, in which is situated the famous Cerro of Potosí, once the richest known silver deposit in the world. In this sector are now mined tin, antimony, lead, wolfram and silver. Below Los Frailes extends the Cordillera of Chichas, in which tin, antimony, zinc and lead are mined. Finally the sector of Lipez

[1] Bolivian altitudes are particularly unreliable and it is no exaggeration to say that there is the utmost difficulty in finding any two writers whose figures agree. In the above I have followed in the main the indications given in the *Boletín de la Sociedad Geográfica de La Paz* (1948).

8

curves westwards in two parallel arms towards the Cordillera Occidental. It has no great economic importance.

The orographical configuration of western Bolivia, which may be seen schematically in the map on p. 35, is of primary importance in the life of the country, since it determines both the distribution of the mineral deposits on which the national economy has for centuries relied and also the internal transport system and lines of communication with the outside world.

Within the oval described by the two Cordilleras is enclosed the Altiplano, a surprisingly level tableland (*puna, meseta, altiplanicie*) at an elevation between 12,000 and 13,000 feet above sea level, the Kollasuyu of the ancient Inca empire and the Collao of the Spaniards. It tends north and south with a slight bias north-west and south-east, and a very slight tilt, for a distance of 520 miles and averages eighty to a hundred miles across. Its total area has been calculated at about 50,000 square miles, of which some 38,000 square miles lie within Bolivian territory. Despite its frigid climate and its aridity it has for centuries been the most densely populated part of the country and now contains about 70 per cent of the total population of Bolivia.

The Altiplano has the forsaken aspect of a landscape on some vaster and more ancient planet where life has long been obsolete. 'A land where no one comes, nor hath come since the making of the world.' It is a harsh inhuman land, inhabited by a dour, unsmiling, toiling race; a high, bleak, barren, wind-swept tundra with the paradox of a tropical sun blazing through frigid air. There are no trees. Except in the brief season of the rains there is no green. The small centres of habitation, the scattered patches of hard-won cultivation and the occasional flocks of llamas dwarfed against the limitless flatness of ochreous grey, serve but to exaggerate the greater desolation of the whole, as though they were symbols of man's puniness in face of inorganic forces too mighty for him to master. An immense dreariness of solitude stretches incredibly to the eternal barrier of the mountains on the horizon like the scene of a nightmare dream. Yet in the very magnitude of its implacability there is a grandeur which humbles and turns one to admiration of those men who for centuries have made it their home.

The monotonous surface of this plateau is built of sedimentary water-laid deposits. Originally an intramontane chasm, it was filled up to the level of the existing floor during the glacial and inter-glacial periods by debris of red sandstone, clay, conglomerates and volcanic ash brought down from the encircling mountains. This process of sedimentation is still going on more slowly, less now by the action of rivers and glaciers than by the medium of the wind which year in and year out carries down clouds of fine dust from the mountains onto the surface of the *meseta*. The thickness of this geologically recent sedimentary filling is not exactly known, but in the gorge of La Paz, where it has been eroded in places down to the original floor, it is possible to measure a depth of about three thousand feet. Where it has the appearance of rock it is in fact simply hard compressed sand, clay and gravel and is as a rule readily friable in the hand. It is peculiarly liable to erosion. Where it is in fact open to the action of the weather, it is often eaten and worn into fantastic configurations of machicolated walls, pinnacles and colonnades, which give it the unreal air of a stage setting. La Paz itself seems like a city set against a background created by the unbridled imagination of a lunatic in love with beauty. But the soil lacks stability and firmness. Landslides and subsidence are a constant menace and roads have no permanence. Because of its loose and spongy texture there is no limit to its capacity to absorb moisture and the inadequate though violent rains which fall in the short season from December to February drain rapidly away, leaving the top-soil permanently thirsty and parched. Nothing of use to man grows there naturally. Agriculture is burdensome and unrewarding.

In the north of the Altiplano and half within the territory of Peru is situated Lake Titicaca, which boasts of being the highest navigated lake in the world. The surface of its water is 12,500 feet above sea level. It extends between 15° 20' and 16° 35' latitude south and between 69° and 70° longitude west and is 138 miles long and 70 miles across at its widest. Its total area, including its thirty-six islands, has been calculated at about 3,500 square miles. The level of the water and the area it covers fluctuate seasonally as melting snows from the neighbouring mountains drain into the Lake and cause the waters to rise. The shores of the Lake, particularly in the south, are very jagged and irregular, as if the agonized rock had been twisted and tortured into grotesque deformity by stupendous geological upheavals of the past. It is pinched almost in half by protruding tongues of land, the promontories of Yunguyo and Achacachi, and the two sections are united only by the mile-wide Straits of Tiquina. The main commercial route into Peru runs by this way and the traffic of lorries is ferried across the straits on flat-bottomed Indian boats.

The water of Titicaca is of exceptional diaphaneity and reflects the intense blue of the sky with extraordinary depth and purity. Its serene beauty in the midst of the parched dreariness of the *meseta* has won for it an almost mystical significance in the minds of the Indians and a mass of legend has gathered around it. In ancient cosmological myth the Lake is the birth-place of the sun and from it the Sun-god created the races of men in the days of primeval darkness. With Lake Titicaca also is associated the origin of the legendary founders of the Inca dynasty. There exists too to this day a tenacious belief that the Incas threw into the Lake fabulous stores of gold from the temple on the Island of the Sun and the palace of the Ñustas on the island of Coati in order to avoid the rapacity of the Spanish Conquistadores. Efforts at recovery have been without result, however, and even serious writers have alleged that at its centre the Lake cannot be plumbed. In fact its maximum depth is about 1,500 feet and in few places is it more than 900 feet deep. It is fed by twenty-five rivers and streams which draw their waters from the snows of the mountains that fringe it. The most important of these are the Umanata, the Suches, Calvario, Khecka, Colorado, Tiahuanaco, and the Ilave, Juli and Pomata in Peru. None of them is large and some are seasonal only. Its only outlet is the Desaguadero in the south, as famous in Andean history as the Rubicon in the history of Rome. It has been estimated that the amount of water entering the Lake is more than could be accounted for by evaporation and the drainage of the Desaguadero; and yet the Lake is steadily shrinking.[1] From the conformation of the land on its borders one can readily see that at no very distant period its bed extended much farther than its present limits, and some ten miles south of the present shore lies the hamlet of Tiahuanaco, the site of the most extensive megalithic ruins of pre-Inca civilization, which is thought to have been originally built as a port on the edge of the Lake. In 1550 Cieza de León said that the Spanish and the Indians of his day thought that the waters bored their way through the rock by underground channels to empty into the Pacific. The probability is, however, that the water is being constantly drawn

---

[1] The Lake is subject to annual high and low water levels with sixteen to seventeen year and—probably—fifty year cycles, the maximum extreme difference of levels recorded being sixteen feet.

off by seepage into the parched and absorbent soil of the Altiplano.

There are two modern ports on the Lake, Guaqui at the southern extremity and Puno in Peru. Navigation between Guaqui and Puno was begun in 1873 and is maintained by the British-owned Peruvian Corporation as an integral link in the railway system which connects La Paz with the Peruvian coast. The first steamer to navigate Lake Titicaca was the 200 ton *Yaravi*, built by Cammell Laird in 1862. It was brought from England to Peru under its own steam, dismantled at the coast and as the railway up to the Lake had not yet been completed, it was hauled up over the incredibly difficult country by mules. There, on the borders of the Lake, it was reassembled by Indian labour under the dour supervision of a Scot who knew no Spanish and never succeeded in mastering the difficult Indian languages. It is now converted into a motor-driven vessel and is still giving efficient service. For the transport of passengers and cargo the Peruvian Corporation have three steamers of 1,200 tons, 900 tons, and 600 tons respectively.

The river Desaguadero, which drains Titicaca to the south, was aptly described by Mulford B. Foster in *The National Geographic Magazine* as 'a lazy, thirsty, shallow river that looks as if it had never had a really good drink'.[1] It is 200 miles in length and flows into lake Poopó which lies almost in the centre of the Bolivian Altiplano. Poopó is much smaller than Titicaca. It is fifty-six miles long by twenty miles wide and its area is estimated at about 1,000 square miles when the water is low; but owing to the shallowness of its bed and the flatness of the surrounding land it is apt to flood extensive areas on its margins during the season of the rains. It was explored in 1903 by a French scientific mission to Bolivia and its altitude was established by Neveu Lemaire as 12,140 feet above sea level. Although the surface of its water is lower than Titicaca, it is very shallow, rarely more than ten or fifteen feet, and its bed is correspondingly higher than the bed of Titicaca. While Titicaca is a fresh-water lake, Poopó is intensely salt and heavy salt deposits in its vicinity vitiate the soil. It has no outlet except the small stream Lakajahuira, which disappears underground after three or four miles. South of Poopó again are large deposits of solid salt, the *Salares* of Uyuni (3,220 square miles) and Copaisa, Empexa and Chiguana, which exceed Titicaca in their total area.

Some geologists have believed that all these lakes of the Altiplano are the relics of an inland sea which once occupied the

[1] *National Geographic Magazine*, Oct. 1950.

intramontane chasm and emptied itself through the gorge of La Paz into the Amazon basin; but this has not been substantiated. Nor is there any convincing evidence for the view put forward by certain archaeologists that in prehistoric times the Altiplano had a benign climate and a fertile soil. Although it is situated within the torrid zone, its climate is now cold and arid. The easterly rain-bearing winds are checked against the barrier of the Cordillera Real and deposit their moisture on its eastern slopes. The total annual rainfall on the Altiplano averages between 400 and 700 millimetres, but in much of the section south of Oruro is as low as 250–350 millimetres. The greater part of the scanty rains are precipitated in heavy storms during the months of December and January and owing to the absorbent nature of the soil are rapidly dissipated, leaving the land parched and arid for most of the year. There is very little rain at all in the winter months from April to October. Except in sheltered declivities the Altiplano is swept by strong cold winds, which carry with them fine dust from the mountains and are highly unpleasant. The average temperature through the year ranges between 7° and 9° C. There is, however, an unusually high variation of temperature between day and night and at Uyuni night temperatures of 20° below zero are recorded in June. The altitude reduces organic resistance to cold and on the Altiplano itself it is virtually impossible to keep warm at night. One may sleep in layers of pullovers and poncho beneath a pile of blankets and still shiver with cold. But by day the sun is strong and despite the coolness of the air it is often necessary to wear only a light vest as a protection against burn. For the actinic power of the Altiplano sun is unusually high and it burns quickly, although in the sweltering tropical heat of the Oriente both sunburn and sunstroke are unknown. There are few experiences more stimulating than this strong sunlight through the cool keen air of the Bolivian highlands. There can be no doubt that it is owing to its natural heliotherapy that the Indian population has survived in moderate health through centuries of malnutrition and economic depression.

Owing to the thinness and dryness of the air the luminosity and diaphaneity of the atmosphere are unequalled and the intensity of the light is increased by reflection from the snow-capped peaks. Nowhere else is seen such beauty of light and clarity of colour. The blurring of outlines and dimming of hues upon which the sense of visual distance depends are reduced to a minimum by the purity of the air and the limit of vision is the sheer power of the eye to see. One sees for unbelievable distances with absolute sharpness and precision and it is almost impossible to estimate distance by the eye. The hills of Lima are blurred and hazy in the moist dim atmosphere of the coast; but on the Altiplano everything is brought as it were sharply into focus. It is only here that the natural powers of the eye can be realized.

Many people are deterred from visiting the Altiplano and La Paz owing to a widespread belief that the altitude causes sickness, headache, lassitude and digestive disturbances in those who are unused to it. Basing himself mainly upon the findings of an Argentine scientific mission which studied the physiological effects of altitude in Bolivia in 1937, Dr Juan Manuel Balcazar claims that this belief is a popular misconception with little or no basis in fact.[1] Physiological reactions, he maintains, are an effect not of altitude in itself but of atmospheric pressure and the oxygen content of the air. Because the Bolivian Andes are situated within the tropical zone, atmospheric pressure there is greater than it is at an equal height above sea level in, say, the Alps. Physiologically La Paz at a height of 12,000 feet (barometric pressure 490·4°) is equivalent to an altitude of about 5,500 feet in the Alps. In the Alps the limit of forestation is reached at about 6,500 feet and the line of perpetual snow at 10,000 feet. In the Andes forestation extends up to 13,000 feet and the perpetual snows do not begin much lower than 16,000 feet and contrary to the usual reports the notorious mountain sickness, called *sorojche*, does not manifest itself much below this level. The slight physiological discomforts which many people experience on the Altiplano are mainly due to a combination of suggestibility and a too rapid change from the atmospheric conditions of the Pacific coast, where the air is denser than on the coast of the Mediterranean, to conditions analogous to those which cause little inconvenience to holiday-makers in Switzerland. Whatever truth there may be in these claims, it is certain that most people suffer some discomfort, rarely severe, on first reaching the Altiplano and that there are few who do not succeed in acclimatizing themselves in a week with reasonable precautions against over-exertion. But strenuous bodily exercise always remains exacting and burdensome beyond the usual.

It is also stated that the Indians native to the Altiplano have become physiologically adapted to the altitude and are now un-

[1] *Epidemiología boliviana.*

14

able to acclimatize themselves to life at lower levels; but this too seems to be of doubtful validity. In pre-Colonial days Aymara colonies existed in the coastal region and today both Aymaras and Quechuas live comfortably in the semi-tropical conditions of the Yungas. The writer has seen Aymara Indians satisfactorily settled on the Yapacané, only about 1,600 feet above sea level, and Quechuas have been brought to the Chapare and other low-lying districts of the eastern territories. The Indians are, however, strongly attached to the Altiplano by centuries of tradition and are not immunized against tropical infirmities; nor do they adapt themselves readily to a different diet and way of life. It is for these reasons that there is always difficulty in transplanting them from the highlands to the sparsely populated lowlands of Bolivia.

The flora and fauna of the Altiplano are peculiar to the Andean high plateau country. Except in large tracts of the south, where nothing grows, the Altiplano is sparsely covered by *ichu* (*Stipa pungens*), a coarse bristly grass called by the Spanish *paja brava*, which grows in clumps to a height of a foot or eighteen inches and is dingy brown in colour. It can be eaten only by the llama and is used by the natives chiefly for thatching and packing. Large areas are overgrown with certain hardy shrubs, the *tthola* (*Lepidophyllum quadrangulare*) and the *yareta* (*Asorella biloba*), which are used by the natives for fuel. The *kenua* or *ckeuna* (*Polilepsis tarapacana*), a stunted and misshapen tree now found only in the most solitary districts around Mt. Sajama and here and there in the Potosí area, was once more widespread and was the main source of fuel for the natives of the *puna*. Various cacti flourish in the shallow declivities and up the sides of the hills and certain of them are cultivated by the Indians for fodder. Here and there grows the *kishuara* (*Budleya incana*), called the 'wild olive of the Incas', and every native hovel has its *khantuta*, a flowering shrub which has become the Bolivian national emblem. Lake Titicaca is thickly bordered with a pliant bulrush called *totora* (*Malacochaete totora*), which is used for thatching and matting and by the native fishermen for building their *balsas*. In ancient times by an astonishing feat of workmanship a permanent bridge of *totora* was maintained over the strategically important river Desaguadero. In the last fifty years the eucalyptus has been introduced and flourishes in more sheltered regions, in the gorge of La Paz and around the borders of the Lake. But the most striking feature of the open *meseta* is its complete bareness of trees.

Of domesticated crops the potato is the most important. The Altiplano is the original home of the potato and potatoes are still the staple food of the native population. It is said that more than 240 distinct varieties had been cultivated on the Altiplano before the Spanish invasion, besides several varieties of *oca*, an edible tuber which has not been introduced into Europe. Both potatoes and *ocas* are eaten mainly in the dehydrated form known as *chuño* or *tunta*. The tubers are first soaked in water for a week or so and then exposed in the open to the alternate heat of the sun by day and frost by night. After some ten days of this treatment, when they begin to pulp, the remaining moisture is trodden out with the feet and they are left in the open for three or four weeks to dry out. The resulting product is quite hard and dry, about the size of a walnut, and is said by the Indians to keep indefinitely. When Redcliffe N. Salaman, the great authority on the potato, in his Presidential address to the anthropology and archaeology section of the British Association on 4 September 1950 spoke on 'The Influence of Food Plants on Social Structure',[1] his references to *chuño* provoked the mirth of *The Times* leader-writer, who facetiously hoped that *chuño* would not come to the notice of the Ministry of Food. As a matter of fact *chuño* is pleasanter to eat than the unprocessed potato, has the consistency of a cooked chestnut and a distinctive and agreeable flavour.

Of the cereals which were introduced into the New World by the Spanish, wheat and rye have never done well on the Altiplano, but some barley is now grown. Maize, which was probably first domesticated in the Andes from a pod-grass brought from Paraguay,[2] does not do well on the Altiplano itself but flourishes in the lower and more sheltered valleys of Cochabamba, Chuquisaca and Tarija. The cereals native to the Altiplano are *quinoa (Chenopodium quinoa)*, a kind of millet, and *cañahui (Atriplex cañahui)*, a smaller and darker grain, and these are not cultivated at lower altitudes. *Quinoa* is a staple food of the Indians who live on the *puna*, as maize is of those in the high valleys. It is eaten by them in the form of a soup or porridge called *ppesche* and from it is brewed the national intoxicant, *chicha*. Both *quinoa* and *cañahui* are said to be extremely nutritive and are claimed to be richer in vitamins than any other

[1] British Association for the Advancement of Science, *The Advancement of Science*, vol. VII.
[2] This view is gaining acceptance over the older belief that maize was originally domesticated in Central America.

known cereals, but exact studies have not been undertaken.[1] *Cañahui* is little eaten except by the native population and *quinoa* is not produced in sufficient quantities for general consumption.

The indigenous fauna of the Altiplano is equally sparse. High up in the mountains are found the chinchilla (now becoming scarce) and the vizcacha, a long-tailed rodent of the chinchilla family, which is prized for its meat. The *mara* or Patagonian hare and the cavy (guinea-pig) are also indigenous to the highlands. Most characteristic of the region and most closely bound up with the life of the people are three animals of the auchenid family, between sheep and camel, the vicuña, the alpaca and the llama. The vicuña has not been domesticated and will not breed in captivity. It is highly valued for its very beautiful skin but despite protective laws is becoming rarer except in the most elevated and inaccessible mountain regions. The alpaca and the llama are domesticated and the llama, in particular, is the traditional transport animal of the Andes. It is still used extensively by the natives for this purpose and a flock of llamas is a common sight in the streets of La Paz. The llama is the cheapest carrier animal known and is particularly valuable in mountainous country because it is slow and sure-footed, can support itself on the meagre pasture as the mule cannot, and like the camel can go long distances on its own resources. In his *Historia natural y moral de las Indias* Father José de Acosta naively remarks that God gave the Indians this animal, which costs them nothing and serves them instead of sheep and mare, 'because He knew they were poor'.[2] It is at any rate true that the llama has been for centuries and still is the main stand-by of the native agriculturalist. Its wool is woven into garments, its hide is made into leather for harness, its flesh is eaten and even its dung is burned as fuel.

Lake Titicaca contains three or four varieties of edible fish which are traded, fresh or smoked, over the northern parts of the Altiplano and recently salmon-trout have been introduced commercially. Curiously enough the Altiplano is rich in bird life. The region of the Lake is abundantly stocked with gulls, duck, geese, widgeon, woodcock, grebe, plover, coot or gallinule, avocet, ibis,

---

[1] A Bolivian farmer informed the writer that when offered a choice poultry will take *quinoa* in preference to maize and *cañahui* in preference to *quinoa*.

[2] José de Acosta, *Historia natural y moral de las Indias* (Seville, 1590). Eng. trs. by E. G[rimston], 1604. Reprinted with notes by C. R. Markham, Hakluyt Soc., nos. 60, 61.

and even the humming-bird. Curlew, plover, and snipe are found
in the swamps that border the Lake. The Altiplano is the home of
the condor, which breeds at heights between 10,000 and 16,000
feet. In the south the ostrich is far from uncommon.

The usual European farm animals were introduced with the
Spanish conquest and donkeys, mules, sheep, goats, pigs and
poultry are produced wherever the conditions allow. Good local
mutton is available and eggs are not scarce. But only in relatively
few places is there pasture suitable for cows and milk is almost
unknown to the native population. Four domesticated animals indigenous to the region are the llama, the alpaca, the guinea-pig
and the muscovy duck.

Such then is the animal and vegetable life of a region no more
friendly to animal than to man. Yet more than half the total
population of Bolivia is concentrated on the Altiplano and the
region around the Lake is the most densely populated agricultural
area in the country. But compared with the English countryside
it is still a solitude. The native villages and hamlets are many
leagues apart and the landed estates few and scattered.[1] One can
drive the whole day through with little variation in the grandiose
monotony of scene except for the slowly changing contours of the
hills and the range of snow-capped peaks on the horizon. Occa-
sionally one may pass a small cluster of adobe huts marking an
Indian settlement amid the waste, crouched under the lee of some
rising ground for shelter against the winds. Here and there stands
out a small square of bright green barley, an untidy patch of red-
brown *quinoa* and acres of sad potatoes. But these serve only to
emphasize the dun drabness of the landscape and the works of
man seem but a nibbling at a vastness too great for human endeavour. Ever and again one meets a solitary Indian plodding
tirelessly and endlessly with his donkey or his llamas or one may
pass a small group of men and women patiently scratching a
pathetically tiny strip of stony ground amid the boundless waste—
the men like grey ghosts of a bloodless past, the women more
solid and real with their brightly coloured skirts and broad vital
faces. It is a land infinitely contemptuous of man, a land which
dwarfs and elevates the spirit together, but a land which having
been known can not be forgotten.

[1] Since the Land Reform in 1953 few landed estates remain on the Altiplano.

THE HIGHLAND TROPICS

Yungas, an Aymara word, is the general name given in Bolivia to the semi-tropical mountain valleys of the eastern slopes of the Cordillera Real. They are also referred to by the word *montaña*. Together with the more open 'high valleys' of the upper Río Grande and Pilcomayo they embrace something like one-tenth of the country's total area and carry about a third of the population.[1]

Between the western and the eastern slopes of the Cordillera Real is the difference as between two worlds. In the west the snow-topped peaks rise naked and sheer from the dun desolation of the Altiplano beneath the brilliant light of a cloudless sky. The eastern slopes descend more gradually in lateral spurs and ridges running down towards the wide eastern plains in an inextricable tangle of intersecting hills and gorges. They are seamed with deep valleys, eroded in the glacial and inter-glacial epochs and gouged ever deeper by swift torrents fed from the cascading waters. The moisture which is denied the Altiplano is deposited upon these eastern slopes as the rain-clouds are condensed against the barrier of the Cordillera. Humidity is high and the climate sub-tropical. The upper reaches are veiled in a constant pall of cloud through most of the year; lower down the air is sodden with heat and moisture, rich with warm organic smells like the atmosphere of a conservatory of hot-house plants. The slopes are thickly forested and the valleys exuberant with lush vegetation. The summits of the ridges are sharp, the valleys deep and narrow. There are rarely three acres of level ground and all cultivation is pitched athwart the steep slopes of the hills. The inorganic grandeur of the west has suddenly changed to a riotous lusciousness of life.

The journey from La Paz to the nearest Yungas is the experience of a lifetime. The road begins to climb immediately on leaving La Paz and within seven or eight miles mounts from 12,160 feet above sea level to 15,250 feet at La Cumbre—the Crest—where one is in the region of perpetual snow and it is difficult even to breathe. Here there is no life or movement except the lonely station on the railway which the Bolivian Government began to build

[1] The areas of the Provinces of Nor Yungas and Sud Yungas in the Department of La Paz (which do not comprise more than a part of the Yungas country) are given as 1,590 and 2,728 square miles respectively. When irregularities of elevation are taken into account, the actual land area is estimated in *La Paz en su iv centenario*, vol. 1: *Monografía geográfica* (1948) at 2,040 and 3,590 square miles. Their estimated populations were 29,740 and 40,970.

from La Paz through the Yungas, and an occasional flock of llamas etched in black against the fields of snow. After crossing a flat table some five hundred yards across one drops over the edge and descends with even more frightening abruptness. The road winds down sheer slopes with hairpin bends every two hundred yards, wide enough for two lorries to pass only at the turn, until it reaches Unduavi, 10,725 feet above sea level and twenty-eight miles from La Paz. Here it is still chilly, but one can see the deep blue haze of forest spread out below and already one can taste the new scent in the air. From Unduavi the road soon enters thickly wooded country and winds among orange and banana groves, coffee plantations, and orchards of papaws, avocado pears, soursops and so on. It becomes hotter and hotter until Puente de la Villa, thirty miles from Unduavi and about 4,000 feet in elevation.[1] The descent from the Altiplano to the valley of Sorata or to Ayata and Chuma is even more abrupt. When the writer visited Ayata the bends of the road were so sharp that the lorry had to back up in order to get round them.

Precipitation in the Yungas is about 700 millimetres (Chulumani) or 800 millimetres (Coroico) annually, the months of heaviest rainfall being December, January and February, and the climate is semi-tropical with a mean annual temperature varying from 16° to 18° C. Despite a high humidity the Yungas are not unhealthy, for the valleys range from 3,000 to 6,500 feet above sea level and most inhabited areas are located on the hillsides above them. Chulumani, the largest town in the Yungas, is the most popular health resort of Bolivia and tourist hotels have been established by the municipality of La Paz both there and at Coroico.

---

[1] 'The physical barriers to roadbuilding in the Yungas may be well imagined when one recognizes the fact that, of the approximately 72 miles from La Paz to Chulumani, capital of the Province of South Yungas, 60 miles are along the side of canyon walls that, for long stretches, lie at from thirty to forty-five degree angles from the horizontal. One who has not travelled the road can hardly imagine the innumerable sharp curves and steep descents in the road, which, over this distance, falls from above 15,000 feet to 4,000 feet. One would hardly exaggerate in stating that there are no two points along the road, 100 yards apart, that are on the same level. Landslides, especially during the rainy season, are of such frequent occurrence and magnitude as to keep more than a hundred workers occupied in freeing the road from fallen dirt and boulders.' Olen E. Leonard, *Bolivia* (1952), p. 21. The present writer was on one occasion held up for five hours by such a landslide which had cut the road at three separate points, one below the other.

The vigour and variety of plant life in the Yungas defeat the imagination and are hardly to be believed even while one moves in their midst. These mountain jungles—for that is what they are in truth—have nothing in common with the bare forests which screen the hills of Europe, but are rather like the true jungles of the tropics where every tree is clothed with liana and every space dense with undergrowth and lichens and ferns of every kind. The variety of vegetation is hardly less than in the true *selva* of the plains. The timber includes cedar, mahogany, walnut, box, laurel, jacaranda, ceiba, caucho, *guayacan* or lignum vitae, the cinchona which is the source of quinine bark, and many kinds of palms including the hard iron-wood or *chonta*; the red arnotto or campeachy and many other dyewoods; innumerable medicinal and aromatic trees and shrubs such as the sarsaparilla, saffron, maguey, the boldu, the copal, the 'incense tree', the *vilca* shrub which yields tannin and was used as a stupefacient in Inca days, the *sacha* which keeps fleas at a distance and is used by the natives as a piscicide, and a profusion of others whose properties have yet to be investigated. It is a wild but manageable region, a region in which one can sense the possibility of coming to terms with nature. Fruit and vegetables grow for the asking. Here there is no necessity to coax reluctant crops to meagre life but rather to restrain their brash exuberance, and agriculture wages a ceaseless war against the rank undergrowth which will swallow up a clearing almost in a night. In the upper reaches grapes, peaches, figs and apples are cultivated desultorily. But below 6,000 feet one enters the true paradise of semi-tropical fruits. The citrus fruits, first introduced by the Spanish into South America, now include many varieties of oranges, limes, grape-fruit, lemons, sweet lemons, and tangerines. Of bananas there are six staple varieties, from the tiny *guineo* with its delicious savour to the large floury kinds which are cooked and eaten in place of bread. In addition there grow pineapples, avocado pears, chirimoyas, papaws, pomegranates, soursops, melons, cantaloups, quinces, medlars, mangoes, persimmon, guava, opuntia or Indian fig, and many more with only local names—the *lacayotes, jocos, pacayes* and others. The most typical vegetables are the sweet potato or *camote*, the cucumber, and yucca or sweet manioc, which throughout tropical Bolivia takes the place of bread. Ground-nuts, called *mani*, and *aji*, a chilli pepper, grow freely and a sauce of *mani* flavoured with *aji* is one of the typical dishes of the region. From prehistoric times the Indians of the highlands have delighted to season their very monotonous food with *aji* and before the arrival of the Europeans it was a major item of commerce between the warm valleys and the uplands. Today the highlanders of Spanish descent have adopted the taste and use *aji* as a matter of course with all their dishes, either as a flavouring in the cooking or mixed with chopped tomato as a piquant sauce. It is said to stimulate a flagging appetite, and to this the writer can subscribe. Father José de Acosta, who seems to have been the first European to write about the Peruvian *aji*, said in his *Historia natural y moral de las Indias*: 'When this *Axi* is taken moderately, it helps and comforts the stomach for digestion; but if they take too much, it hath bad effects, for of its selfe it is very hote, fuming, and pierceth greatly, so as the use thereof is pre-iudiciall to the health of young folkes, chiefly to the soule, for that it provokes to lust.'

Sugar-cane, tobacco, cacao and coffee grow readily in the Yungas, though the first two have been little cultivated there. Tea has been tried only on an experimental scale but there seems no reason why Bolivia's small consumption of tea should not be supplied from this source. Potentially the most important product, however, is coffee. Alcides d'Orbigny, after visiting Chulumani in 1830, described the coffee of the Yungas as the best in the world, and his judgement has since been confirmed by others. Bolivian coffee is of the mild variety which is in high demand in the world markets and the United Nations Mission of Technical Assistance recommended that the high quality coffee of the Yungas should be intensively cultivated for export. The obstacle to this suggestion is transport and until the problem of Bolivian transport, internal and external, has been solved, no project of agricultural export from the Yungas could be economically realistic. It is indeed characteristic of the whole situation in Bolivia that the great and obvious possibilities of the Yungas, a region which cries out for planned agricultural development with proper safeguards against soil erosion, remain largely unexploited. Part of the market of La Paz, a city of some 300,000 persons, for fruit and garden produce is supplied from there; but for this no intensive cultivation is needed. Indeed one might rather speak of passive acceptance than of active cultivation. Some fraction of the spontaneous abundance is gathered and sold; the majority is consumed locally or left to waste on the ground. Nor indeed would a farmer who cultivated his land intensively find an outlet for his produce. It is the problem of transportation to markets of consumption which here, as throughout the length and breadth of Bolivia, hampers initiative and holds progress in check.

There is, however, one important exception to the general indifference and one crop which is seriously cultivated and with such good returns that it encourages the neglect of the rest. This is the coca, the plant from which cocaine was derived. From times immemorial coca has been the cherished and almost the only indulgence of the natives who inhabit the Andean uplands. The leaves of the plant are masticated from morning to night and the juices extracted from them produce a feeling of euphoria which contributes something to alleviate the harsh conditions of their lives. It is the one luxury which they retained under the Conquest, and remains today a daily necessity of their lives. Every adult Indian of either sex requires his daily ration of coca. The commerce in coca was of economic importance in Inca times. When La Paz was founded in 1548 as a half-way house for the caravans of llamas carrying silver from Potosí to Arequipa and the coast, its rapid rise to prosperity was materially aided by the traffic in coca which passed through it in the opposite direction from the Yungas to Potosí. And the industry remains to this day an outstandingly important item in Bolivian internal economy.

Coca requires a warm and moist climate and flourishes best at an altitude of 3,000–5,000 feet. It is cultivated by highly specialized methods which are understood by the Indians from centuries of tradition. Carelessness and negligence are fatal. It is grown in plantations prepared in stepped ridges and furrows up the steep slopes of the hills and with proper attention a plantation will last for forty or fifty years. The care of the plants and the processing and packing of the leaves is a delicate and expert process, but the coca plant has a life of some forty years and gives three or four harvests in a year, so that once a beginning has been made it is a very lucrative crop. This industry is the life of the Yungas. Scattered irregularly over every hillside, visible from afar against the surrounding vegetation, are the characteristic ribbed patches of the *cocales*. Eighty per cent of the revenue of the Yungas derives from coca and in comparison with it other crops are of very secondary importance. Without it the Yungas would have remained unpopulated and abandoned. For coca was in the first place the sole inducement to settle there and its proceeds have paid for the building and upkeep of the roads which connect the

Yungas with La Paz and without which no other produce could be moved. And even today without coca few fincas could pay their way.

In addition to the Yungas there are around Cochabamba and in the Departments of Chuquisaca and Tarija more extensive high valleys, less closely hedged in by the buttressing spurs of the mountains. The Cochabamba valley is 8,000–8,500 feet above sea level. The climate is of semi-arid Mediterranean type, with a mean annual rainfall of 450–600 millimetres and a mean annual temperature of 17°–18° C. The Tarija valley is somewhat lower and warmer, Tarija itself lying 6,250 feet above sea level. Most of the rain falls from November to March and in the winter months the land, lacking adequate irrigation, suffers from drought. From these valleys comes the majority of the wheat, maize, barley, grapes, and ground-nuts which are produced in Bolivia. Apricots and peaches are grown and tobacco is cultivated in Chuquisaca and Tarija. Cochabamba has long been known as the 'granary of Bolivia' and the appellation is deserved. With adequate irrigation, modernized methods of agriculture and a suitable use of fertilizers these valleys of the upper Río Grande and Pilcomayo could, along with the Yungas proper, supply the main agricultural requirements of the present population of Bolivia.

THE LOWLAND TROPICS

The eastern lowlands of Bolivia extend from the foothills of the Cordillera Real eastwards to the region of the Matto Grosso on the Brazilian frontier and from the rivers Madera and Abuná in the north to the *llanuras* of the Gran Chaco in the south. In all, the Oriente contains about 70 per cent of the total territory of Bolivia. The land slopes gradually from an altitude of about 1,500 feet on the edge of the Cordillera to 300 feet or less in the east and north. Over the greater part of it the rainfall is high but seasonal and enormous stretches suffer each year from alternate flooding and drought. The town of Trinidad is hemmed in every year by very extensive floods beginning in March or April, and in exceptionally bad years the town itself may be under water; yet in the summer months water is brought from the river eight miles away and sold on the streets. The climate of the *llanos* is hot, with a mean annual temperature ranging from 23° C. or 25° C. in the south to 27° C. in the north. Occasional cold winds blow from the south, bringing with them clouds of sand and dust and causing a drop of 15° C.

or 20° C. in a few hours. They are called locally *surazos* and last from three or four days to a week.

The Oriente consists of dense tropical forest of the Amazon basin, vast natural pasture lands, and open forest and savanna in the south. It is underpopulated, underdeveloped, very deficient in means of communication especially in the northern and larger section, and is in danger of becoming economically isolated from the rest of the country in consequence. Transport within the Oriente itself is conducted largely by the rivers, which play as important a part in the east of Bolivia as the mountain systems in the west.

The tall tropical forests lie mainly in the north and the east. The northern forests occupy the whole Department of Pando, following the courses of the rivers Beni, Orton and Madre de Dios, and cover the Provinces of Caupolicán in the Department of La Paz and Vaca Diez in the Beni. In addition a broad belt of forest runs from near Santa Cruz in a north-westerly direction to the Beni and joining the northern forests extends to the Peruvian frontier. Rich in a bewildering variety of deciduous and evergreen tropical hardwoods, with often a superlative development of individual trees, this forest has been exploited for Para rubber, quinine and Brazil nuts. But these industries are now in decline and difficulties of transport have so far prohibited the development of a lumber industry. Among the most important hardwoods are the *cuchi*, the *almendrillo*, the *mara*—a mahogany used for furniture—and the cedar.

A hardly less extensive belt of rather lower and drier forest lies along the rivers Guaporé and Paraguay and in the Province of Chiquitos. It has become familiar to many through the popular travel story *Green Hell* by Julian Duguid. In all, Bolivia's share of Amazonian forest, most of it still in virtually primeval condition, is calculated to cover some 200,000 square miles,[1] and constitutes not the least important of the country's assets for the future when the problem of exploiting the natural resources of the Amazon valley is effectively tackled.

In the south are the rolling savannas and open woodland of the Chaco country, grazed by herds of cattle and goats, which range over them in a wild or virtually wild condition. As a whole the Chaco now suffers severely from drought during seven or eight months of the year and districts of cultivation are few and small.

[1] *UNMTA Report*, p. 65. This estimate is too high.

From Yacuiba on the Argentine frontier northwards to Santa Cruz there runs a broadish belt of dry forest containing walnut, *tajibo* and quebracho, which is irregularly traded to Argentina. The whole area of the Chaco is subjected to recurrent plagues of locusts, which spread northwards and have been known to penetrate in isolated units as high as Cochabamba.

The open plains occupy the centre. They are covered by rough pasture, swamp, scrub and occasional belts of woodland. The Santa Cruz plains extend from the Río Grande, west of Santa Cruz, eastwards to the Brazilian frontier at Corumbá, with medium heavy forest in the east. Around Santa Cruz conditions are good for the cultivation of sugar-cane, rice, oil plants and citrus fruits.[1] The plains to the east of Santa Cruz are mainly grazing land with small areas under cultivation for yucca, maize, rice and fruit. The northern plains of Mojos in the Beni are far more extensive and together with the northern forests cover more than half the whole area of Bolivia. They are the most important cattle region of the country and the herds which range wild or semi-wild over them are estimated at up to a million head of cattle. But the Beni is even more seriously isolated from the main centres of population than the southern part of the Oriente and its present population is inadequate for any serious projects of development.

The centre of the Beni was once occupied by an inland freshwater sea which geologists have named Lake Mojos. Originally covering some 3,500 square miles of territory, its remains are still recognizable in the lakes Rogoaguado and Rogagua and the extensive swamps which lie between the rivers Mamoré and Beni. The waters which poured into it from the Cordillera on the west and the mountains of the Matto Grosso in the east were denied exit by a low barrier of granite in the north until, whether owing to a gradual rise in the level of the bed or to erosive action of the pent-up waters, an outlet was found at the present channel of the Madera and the lake emptied itself into the Amazon. But the one northern outlet is inadequate and its capacity is reduced by the remains of the rock barrier which still lie across the channels of the Madera, the Beni and the Mamoré between 9° and 11° latitude south, impeding outflow like a partial stoppage in a drain-pipe and obstructing navigation by a series of rapids called locally *cachuelas*. The plains of the Beni are an alluvial cap built up on the

[1] In the last ten years this has been one of the most successful development areas in Bolivia (see pp. 99–101).

ancient lake bottom, which can now be detected at a depth of some thirty or forty feet beneath the present surface of the soil. The whole region is very flat. Eighty-five per cent of the land is alluvial and for hundreds of miles there is no hill, no stone, no gravel to be seen. The writer has seen loads of gravel shipped up the Mamoré from Cachuela Esperanza on the lower Beni to lay a road in Trinidad. The land is still in process of formation by the action of the rivers, whose waters come down a deep chocolate brown from the mountains and are constantly building up new layers of sedimentary deposit along their changing courses. For this reason the hydrographical system of the east is as important to the life and economy of the country as the orographical system in the west. The rivers are almost the only channels of communication and transport, determine the location of the populated places, are responsible for the configuration and the habitability of the land and bring with them the scourge of the floods to the detriment of man and beast.

The barely discernible watershed between the northern and the southern plains is usually considered to be marked by the course of the river Parapetí, which has its headwaters in the central sector of the Cordillèra Real, in the Department of Chuquisaca, flows eastwards through the Department of Santa Cruz, passing beside the petrol-bearing region of Camiri, and disappears in the marshes of Izozog to re-appear later flowing northwards as the San Miguel as far as Lake San Luis and then, as the Itonamas, into the Iténez. The southern and drier sector of the Oriente is drained by the Paraguay and its tributaries. Of these the Pilcomayo, whose headwaters spread widely over the Cordillera of Los Frailes, flows south-eastwards through the Chaco and enters the Paraguay outside Bolivian territory. Its total length is about 800 miles but its lower reaches fall within the territory ceded to Paraguay. It is a river even more phenomenally rich in fish than the other rivers of the Bolivian Oriente, and when its waters recede after flooding shoals of fish are left piled up to rot on the ground. In the season fish are so plentiful that they are scooped out of the river in buckets. The writer has known lorry owners who used to make the heroic journey from Villa Montes across the Chaco and the south-eastern foothills of the Cordillera, driving twenty-four hours without pause to bring them to market in Tarija. It is only the difficulty of transport which prohibits Bolivia from utilizing effectively the abundant stock of fish in the Oriente; but owing to the present impossibility of rapid freightage from the east fish are imported to La Paz by air from the Pacific coast. The Bermejo, another confluent of the Paraguay, flows wholly within territory ceded to Argentina in 1889 and only its upper tributaries are now within the borders of Bolivia. The most important of these is the Guadalquivir, or Río de Tarija, which skirts the town of that name. The Paraguay itself does not rise in the Cordillera but in the mountains of the Matto Grosso and flows due south, marking the southern sector of the frontier between Bolivia and Brazil, to unite with the Paraná at the frontier of Paraguay with Argentina.

The northern section of the *llanos* is drained by a triple configuration of waterways, all of which debouch into the Madera at the north-eastern corner of Bolivia. The central and most important river of the triple system is the Mamoré, which is in effect one with the Madera but changes its name at the frontier. It originates in a complicated fanwork of tributaries flowing down from the central sector of the Cordillera. The most southerly, the Río Grande or Guapay, has its headwaters in the Cordilleras of Cochabamba and Sucre and one of its many sources is the Rocha which flows through the town of Cochabamba and into the Guapay after uniting with the Mizque. Starting out due east, the Río Grande is then deflected northwards and again to the north-west and after describing a great curve of two-thirds of a circle over a distance of more than 600 miles, debouches into the Mamoré a few miles below the juncture of the latter with the Chapare. It was once an important river, but owing to the gradual silting up of its bed it has degenerated over large stretches into marsh and lagoon and is considered lost to navigation. It is a prime cause of inundations which on occasion spread as far north as Trinidad. Its most important tributaries are the Yapacané and the Piray, the latter of which skirts the town of Santa Cruz. The river Ichilo, which runs along the base of the Cordillera, is in effect one with the Mamoré as the Mamoré is one with the Madera. And into the Ichilo flows a series of tributaries—the Ichoa, the Izarsama, the Sacta, the Chimoré, the Chapare and the Secure, with many smaller streams between—all running down the deep valleys cut into the eastern slopes of the Cordillera and entering the watercourse which flows along their base. From the edge of the mountains to its juncture with the Madera the Mamoré sets its course due north for a distance of about a thousand miles, skirting the town of Trinidad half way and taking in various tributaries

28

as it goes, the most important of which are the Ibare and the Yacuma, which rises between Rurrenabaque and San Borja and flows through the rich cattle country of Santa Ana south of Lake Rogagua.

In the northern sector of the Cordillera Real rise the many confluents which converge into the river Beni, among them the Choqueyapu, the river of La Paz, once famous for the gold panned there, the Bopi with which it unites in the Yungas before joining the Beni, the Mapiri which rises in Illampu and flows through the gorge of Sorata—the route followed by Colonel Fawcett on his first expedition into the Amazon basin—and the Tipuani where gold was panned by the former Aramayo mining interests. It is one of the more peculiar features of the land that among the sources of the Amazon are rivers originating in the mountains of the Altiplano, so much nearer to the Pacific than to the Atlantic. As one transacts one's affairs in the modern office buildings of the Avenida Camacho of La Paz the imagination boggles to think of the immense distances of tropical, fever-laden jungle which the feeble stream below—now but a trickle of water over the stones of its deeply-cut bed, at times swollen into a swift torrent threatening roads and bridges—must traverse on its long journey to the Amazon and the Atlantic. The Beni itself flows to the north-east through densely jungled country and is united at Riberalta with the Madre de Dios, which rises on the slopes of Vilcanota in Peru and is navigable up to the Peruvian port of Maldonado, and a little lower down it is entered by the Orton. To give some idea of the size of these lowland rivers, the Madre de Dios is 780 yards wide at its juncture with the Beni and the Beni itself rather more. These two rivers converging through high jungle, with the small wooded island at the point of confluence, are a sight of surpassing beauty and there can be few towns at once so finely and so inaccessibly situated as Riberalta, on raised ground by the right bank of the Beni. From Riberalta, after passing Cachuela Esperanza, the rapids where the once famous rubber firm of Suárez Hermanos had its headquarters, the Beni joins the Mamoré at the frontier town of Villa Bella. From Villa Bella they continue northwards as the Madera, marking the frontier until the convergence of the Abuná; and the latter river, flowing in from the west, marks the northern frontier of Bolivia with Brazil as far as the town of Cobija, capital of the Department of Pando.

The third finger in this riverine complex is formed by the Iténez or Guaporé, which is the longest river in Bolivia. It rises like the Paraguay in the mountains of the Matto Grosso and flows to the north-west, marking the frontier with Brazil until its juncture with the Mamoré a few miles above the frontier town of Guayaramerin or Puerto Sucre. The Iténez is a very beautiful river and its waters flow limpid clear into the brown sediment-laden stream of the Mamoré, so that for some miles below the confluence you can still distinguish the two constituent streams. In ancient times it was the scene of protracted frontier conflicts between the Spanish and the Portuguese. Now it is practically untravelled and unknown.

One might well write the story of Bolivia in terms of water. In the western uplands it is lack of water which brings barrenness to the land and aridity into men's souls. The ancients fought it by marvels of intricate irrigation, now derelict and lost. The modern *kolla*, or highlander, so craves the relief of freshness that his highest ideal of natural beauty is a perennial rill bordered by an oasis of green. In the east, however, where men live in perpetual dread of inundation, over-abundance of water is no less serious a scourge than its lack in the highlands. The Beni is flat and formless, without natural contours to channel the waters. From Puerto Grether, at the extreme limit of navigability of the Ichilo, for a distance of 950 miles to Villa Bella the difference in altitude is only 308 feet. For this reason the rivers are slow, sluggish and shallow. They move in continuous horse-shoe loops and sinuosities so that seen from the air against the dark grey of the forests they look like smooth oily intestines doubled within some gigantic belly. From the launches which ply upon their surface they appear as a series of enormous curves, one following another with no straight stretches between. On the outer edge of each curve the banks rise sheer for anything from six to twenty feet and the heavy timber comes right down to the water's edge. Each year the river cuts a little deeper into the bank and great trees are loosened and fall, to add to the debris which blocks the channels. All along the banks one sees these giants of the forest which have crashed and are waiting to be floated off in the next hurricane or inundation. On the inner sides of the curves are vast *playas*, or sedimentary beaches, sometimes extending for ten or fifteen miles and running back four or five miles from the channel. Flat and featureless, they represent the new land which is being built up by the annual deposits. Gradually they become covered with thickets of a bamboo called *chuchío* and expert pilots of the river can estimate the age of a *playa* by the extent and type of its *chuchío* and in this way gauge the movements of the river. Sometimes when the river makes an immense horse-shoe loop, bending round and back almost to the point of departure, it will in the course of a few inundations cut for itself a direct channel (*corte*) through the neck of land at the head of the loop and the loop itself will become separated from the parent river and remain as a vast lunar lagoon of stagnant water, called *curiche*, where mosquitoes breed and caymans bask.

The rivers are rich in fish. The largest of these, called by the Benianos 'Coronel' and 'General', run to eighty or a hundred pounds with thick layers of fat enclosing the meat. The most delicious are the *corbina*, or blue-fish, the *pacú* and the *surubí*. The river dolphin may be seen almost as high as Puerto Grether on the Ichilo, while caymans are hunted throughout the course of the rivers. The dreaded *piraña*, which will strip a man or beast to the bare skeleton in minutes, is not common in the Mamoré. The only danger is from a large flat fish called *raya*, which lies on the mud bottom and can inflict a serious wound with a ferocious saw-edged sting in its tail. Large and small river turtle are plentiful. Along the banks can be seen the *capybara*, or swimming river-hog, whose flesh is a delicacy, the *londra* or river seal and the *coypou* and otter. The forest is the home of the jaguar and the wild pig, monkeys, squirrel, badger, peccary, ant-eaters, ocelot, armadillo, tapir, opossum, sloth, and many other creatures. Bird life includes wild turkey, parakeets, hornbills, fruit pigeons, toucans, touracos, partridge. King and black vultures range the skies; gulls, herons, and wild duck abound. Salamanders, frogs, lizards and toads are very plentiful. But the Mamoré is bare of human life except for an occasional isolated *chacra*, or homestead, cultivating a little coffee, yucca, bananas, sugar-cane and oranges. The Ichilo is entirely desolate of human occupation and is the least travelled and least known of all the rivers of the Amazon complex.

The Mamoré is navigable by wheel steamers as far as Trinidad during the season of high water. Above Trinidad it is navigated up to the mouth of the Chapare by shallow draught motor launches, which pull large flat-bottomed *remolques* or barges, one on each side. Navigation is made difficult and dangerous by the large trees (*palos*) which become anchored to the bottom and against which masses of lesser debris collect to form snags (*palisadas*). Navigation is easiest in the summer months when the water is deeper, but the danger is then greater from concealed obstacles which, if they lie just below the surface, may rip away the bottom from the boat. Many learned and painstaking studies have been made of the means to salvage and improve the navigability of the rivers of the Beni.[1] But as things are now, all such studies are doomed to frustration; for this whole system of waterways leads from nowhere to nowhere, blocked at one end by the *cachuelas* and at the other by the Cordillera. In the north it is necessary to tranship at the *cachuela* of Guayaramerin on to the Madera–Mamoré railway which runs at prohibitive cost to Puerto Velho in Brazil. In the south Puerto Grether on the Ichilo is separated from Santa Cruz by 125 miles of forested country intersected by rivers and streams. The Ichilo runs along the base of the Cordillera but there is still no practicable route through that immense barrier to the markets of the more thickly populated Altiplano above. The river Beni is navigable as far as Rurrenabaque at the foot of the mountains; but from there the only means of reaching the Altiplano is by air.

In 1832 Alcides d'Orbigny, realizing that Bolivia's most pressing need was for a practicable commercial route between the Altiplano and the Beni, set out from Cochabamba to find a way through the mountains to Trinidad. Helped by friendly Yuracaré Indians he came upon the Secure, built a raft and sailed down it to the Mamoré and after travelling for forty days reached Trinidad so emaciated that his friends were unable to recognize him. And such a link with the east is still Bolivia's most crying need today. The route at present in use is that of the Chapare, but it is barely practicable. The Chapare is a more swiftly flowing and

[1] For example by Professor E. Harrison, whose services were made available by the British Government in 1942 to investigate and advise on the agricultural possibilities of the Mamoré region. In his unpublished report, which is still preserved in Bolivian government departments, Professor Harrison wrote: 'As a preliminary to the awakening of this vast area, transport routes must be opened and must be worked cheaply, and should reach as many centres of population as possible. From the map it will be clearly seen that the northern corner of this area is connected by rail from Guayaramerin, in Brazil, to Puerto Velho, and thus by river to the Atlantic Ocean. Also this area is much traversed by rivers, which, if they could be navigated readily, would connect this huge tropical country with the Guayaramerin outlet in the North and with the road system of the Cordilleras and the Altiplano to the South and West.' In sad and sober truth, however, both these outlets are illusory. The Madera–Mamoré railway, constructed at a time when the fantastic revenues of the rubber trade brought the most wildly impracticable undertakings within the realm of possibility and constructed, it is said, at the cost of a human life for every sleeper, now carries but the barest trickle of trade.

capricious river than the Ichilo, changing its course from season to season, badly silted up with many shallows and dangerously impeded by obstacles. Even during the months when it is in water small launches have to unload as many as four or five times to get through the worst patches. From Todos Santos on the Chapare a lorry road runs for 125 miles to Cochabamba, crossing the Cordillera by a pass at about 1,600 feet. Its lower reaches, around San Antonio, are made impassable by flood-waters for four or five months in the year; and as the Chapare is navigable at all only during the months when the road is flooded, it is not surprising that this route has proved defective. The present writer sailed the Ichilo in 1949 with Señor Eracleo Melgar, Government Delegate of the Chapare, and Yuracaré Indians to prospect for a more feasible link between the Beni and the Altiplano. A route was thought to have been found at the Sacta, a higher tributary of the Ichilo, from which a road free from flooding could be constructed to debouch upon the completed portion of the Cochabamba–Santa Cruz highway. Further exploration from the landward side has been undertaken under the auspices of a United Nations mission, although whether or when the route will come into operation it is impossible to say. But until this problem is solved, Bolivia will remain cut in two and deprived of its main sources of natural wealth in the east.[1]

The second and hardly less serious problem of the Beni is inundation. The shallow channels of the slow-flowing rivers are inadequate to contain the volume of water which pours into them from their mountain tributaries at a time when they are already swollen by local rains. The surface of the land is so uniformly devoid of natural undulations which could canalize and direct the flood-waters that they spread shallowly over a very great area and are slow to subside. For several months of every year, between February and June, the land looks from above like a vast lake with water extending to the horizon in all directions. Although the flooding is not deep, it is sufficient to deprive the animals of grazing and the mortality among the livestock is estimated by *rancheros* in a bad year at as high as 30 or 40 per cent. Both wild life and

[1] It was announced early in 1963 that the National Bureau of Roads and Rivers planned later in the year to send an expedition under Jaime Taborga, the Bureau's chief of river navigation, to determine whether the river Ichilo is suitable for commercial navigation and that the Bureau had hired a New York firm of consulting engineers to plan a new road from the Ichilo to Montepunco with the object of linking the cattle regions of the Beni to the markets of the uplands.

33

cattle perish each year of inanition, starving by the thousand in the midst of a drowned land where no islands of fodder rise above the surface of the waters. Nor is this the end of the matter, for the flood-waters turn rotten with putrefying vegetable matter, sour the land and when they recede the rank pasture which springs up within days is without nutrient properties and unable to fatten the beasts which survive. Rational projects have been devised for miti-gating this curse of inundation in the Beni. Among them it has been proposed to deepen, clean and straighten the courses of the rivers, to blast away the *cachuelas* in the north in order to allow the water a more rapid exit, to construct artificial canals to contain and limit the floods, as was done by the natives in pre-Colonial times, and to construct raised corrals (*potreros*) wired and sown with good pasture, to which some part of the cattle could be driven when their natural pasture is under water.[1] All these devices would in some degree palliate the worst effects of inundation, but all would involve expenditure far beyond the unaided resources of the country.

COMMUNICATIONS

Bolivia is, then, a country of heterogeneous geophysical char-acteristics, a country of many diverse regions very imperfectly in-tegrated, and a country virtually cut in two by the divide of the Cordillera. Violent contrasts of climate and differences in way of life have encouraged the growth of regionalism to a dangerous de-gree. The Altiplano is as a foreign country to those who live in the tropical lowlands and few of the highland dwellers know more of the rest of the country than the fringe of the Yungas. The people of Santa Cruz and the Beni affect to look down on the highland *kollas* as a people of mixed blood, while resenting the superior development of La Paz and the persistent disregard of the central Government for the economic needs of the eastern provinces. The

[1] Professor Harrison in his unpublished report devoted most of his attention to the clearing and straightening of the courses of the rivers. José Gonzáles Arze of the Bolivian Directorate of Highways—whose knowledge of the country is un-surpassed—realizing that the clearance and straightening of the rivers could have no other effect but to increase the rapidity with which their beds are being silted up, and therefore actually make worse the dangers of inundation, unless the waters were given a more adequate outlet, has drawn up a detailed project for the blasting away of the *cachuelas* which block the northern channels. The third device, which could at any rate control and direct the worst of the flood-waters, has been studied by Medardo Solares of the firm of Suárez Hermanos.

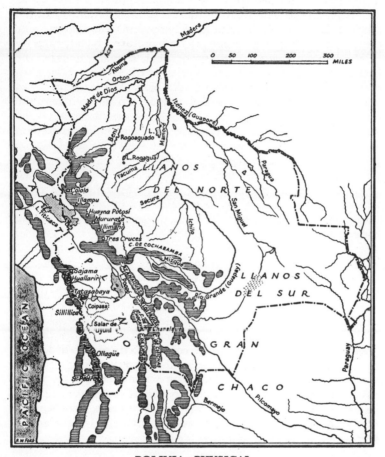

BOLIVIA: PHYSICAL

Government, located in La Paz, has by long tradition tended to give prior, if not exclusive, consideration to promoting the welfare of the Altiplano, contenting itself with unrealistic and unrealized projects for the rest of the land, and the city of La Paz in particular has expanded out of proportion to the rate of progress in the rest of the country. And while there are many Bolivians in and out of office who have devoted serious thought to the integral development of the country as a whole, all such considerations tend too often to be based upon imperfect knowledge and are doomed to remain abstract and theoretical by the physical barriers to communication between one region and another. For as has been indicated, the problem of communication is vital to any uniform and planned economic development of Bolivia as a whole and it is the lack of communications which causes economic stagnation in precisely the regions whose recovery would contribute most to the country's well-being. Owing to the high cost of internal transport Argentine meat is cheaper in La Paz than meat from the Beni, in many parts of the country Peruvian petrol is cheaper than Bolivian petrol, sugar is imported from Peru and the United States, while the sugar-cane of Santa Cruz was for many years used only for the production of alcohol. A bottle of beer costs six times as much in the Beni as in La Paz and consumer goods in general, imported through Pacific coast ports to La Paz, are prohibitive when transported by air to the east. All the many projects for increasing the production of essential raw materials on Bolivian territory must presume that conditions will be created which would enable them to be placed at economic prices in the main markets of consumption. Unless the problem of transport is solved, all projects for increasing production outside the Altiplano are foredoomed to economic fiasco. In discussing transport we are, then, discussing not one problem among others but the one problem upon which all else depends. In this situation it is encouraging to learn that with help from abroad the present regime has been able to do something to revive the former prosperity of Santa Cruz and to develop some at least of its potentialities. (See pp. 94–104.)

Air Transport

Bolivia is well served for air transport. Two international air lines, Braniff and Pan American Grace Airways (Panagra), connect La Paz with Lima, Arica, Santiago, Río de Janeiro and Buenos Aires. At the beginning of 1953 an air service was established between Bolivia and Argentina by agreement between the Bolivian national line, Lloyd Aéreo Boliviano, and Aereolinas Argentinas. Lloyd Aéreo Boliviano serves most of the larger towns in the country, and some places of even minor importance. It is excellently run and has a very fine record for safety and efficiency. The Army Air Force provides official transport and certain private companies run cargo planes but private commercial flying has not justified itself and the number of privately operated commercial aeroplanes has always been small, rarely numbering more than about half a dozen in the whole country. The Bolivian Development Corporation maintained a service of two—or at times three —planes between Reyes and La Paz and in 1951 an abortive beginning was made in connexion with a project to expand the meat trade between the Beni and the Altiplano.

There is no doubt that the air services have done much to mitigate the psychological as well as the physical isolation of the more remote populations. In towns such as Guayaramerin and Magdalena, which possess no cinema or any other form of amusement, the weekly arrival of the LAB plane is an event in which the whole community shares. Travel is now no longer a major feat of endurance. One can reach Trinidad or Santa Cruz from La Paz in under two hours by air. The journey to Cochabamba is scheduled to take fourteen hours by fast train. And from Cochabamba the only surface route to Santa Cruz was until recently by an old trade road, difficult and dangerous at best and possible at all only in the dry season. It was a road over which private cars did not venture and the uncomfortable journey by transport lorry often took between a week and a fortnight according to the time of year. Trinidad is still even more inaccessible. In Cochabamba the adventurous traveller must wait his opportunity to obtain passage in a cargo lorry over the quite perilous route to Todos Santos, a road which is cut by inundations for months on end. At Todos Santos he must remain for an indefinite time in primitive accommodation amid the humid and mosquito-infested heat of the Chapare until he can arrange transport on a launch carrying cargo up the Mamoré. This trip will take him about a fortnight and is more like a pioneering expedition than a pleasure jaunt. Finally, when he reaches La Loma, the port of Trinidad on the Ibare, if the country is not under water, he may obtain a horse and ride the twelve kilometres to Trinidad.

The increased movement produced by air transport has brought

D

benefits incalculably greater than can be measured by mere statistics and contacts now exist with many centres of population which were before virtually inaccessible. But it does little to solve the economic problems of Bolivia. For the cost of air freight is still prohibitive and everywhere to the east of Cochabamba the air-ports, which have no concrete runways, are rendered unserviceable for days or weeks at a time by rains.

Railways

La Paz is connected with the Pacific coast by three single-track lines, which total 1,490 miles of track and serve the Altiplano and high valleys exclusively.

The La Paz–Guaqui line (60 miles), a continuation of the Southern Railway of Peru, links La Paz with the Peruvian ports of Mollendo and Matarani by 511 miles of railway and 140 miles across the Lake. Its construction was begun by the Bolivian Government in 1900 and completed in 1902 as far as the Alto, on the lip of the bowl in which the city of La Paz is situated. The six miles of electric railway down the steep incline from the Alto to the city itself[1] were completed in 1905 with the aid of a loan from The Peruvian Corporation. The railway was purchased from the Bolivian Government in 1910 and is now operated under concession by the British firm The Peruvian Corporation Limited.

The shortest line to the Pacific is the Arica–La Paz railway, the Bolivian section of which is owned and operated by the State. It was constructed by the Chilean Government under the terms of the Treaty of Friendship of 1904, inaugurated in 1913 and delivered to the Bolivian Government in 1928. Its total length is 278 miles, of which 150 miles are in Bolivian territory. The ascent from the coast to Charaña, where it crosses the frontier at a height of 13,340 feet, is uncomfortably steep and rack rails have been constructed over a sector of twenty miles.

The La Paz–Antofagasta line runs through Oruro and Uyuni and crosses the frontier at Ollagüe. Its total length is 729 miles with 453 miles in Bolivian territory. It was operated under concession by two companies, the Bolivia Railway Company (owning the Viacha–Oruro section)[2] and the Antofagasta (Chili) and Bolivia Railway Company Limited, a British company which owned

[1] The ruling gradient of this section of the line is 7 per cent.
[2] This company is incorporated in the United States and is a subsidiary of the Antofagasta (Chili) and Bolivia Railway Company Ltd.

the sections between La Paz and Viacha and between Oruro and Ollagüe.[1] A branch line runs from Uyuni to Villazón, where it connects with the Argentine State Railways running to Buenos Aires. The Uyuni–Atocha sector of this branch (56 miles) was operated under concession by the Bolivia Railway Company and serves the former Aramayo mines at Quechisla. The Atocha–Villazón sector (122 miles) is owned and operated by the State. A second branch line runs from Oruro to Cochabamba (128 miles) and was operated under concession by the Bolivia Railway Company. This line runs through very broken and precipitous country and the descent to Cochabamba is so steep that at one point the line can be seen at five different levels below as it winds and circles in its downward course. Not only the roads, but some of the railways in Bolivia have to cope with the constant inconvenience of landslips during certain seasons of the year and on this line the writer has had to transfer to a train sent out from Cochabamba when the train on which he had travelled from La Paz was held up by a *derrumbe*. And from Río Mulatos, 252 miles south of La Paz, a third branch runs to Potosí, a distance of 108 miles, and is also operated under concession by the Bolivia Railway Company.[2] An extension of this branch from Potosí to Sucre (109 miles) is owned and operated by the State. From Machacamarca, 15 miles south of Oruro, a branch line runs to Uncia (67 miles) serving the Patiño tin mining district and owned and operated under private concession before nationalization by Patiño Mines and Enterprises Consolidated. Certain sections of these lines run through country which is liable to flooding during the rainy season of the year.

These three lines carry Bolivia's mineral exports to the Pacific coast and freight the very great majority of the country's imports.[3]

[1] In 1887 the Chilean section of the line was acquired from the Compañía de Salitres y Ferrocarriles de Antofagasta by the Compañía Huanchaca de Bolivia, which owned the important tin and silver mines at Pulacayo near Uyuni. In 1888 the Antofagasta (Chili) and Bolivia Railway Company Ltd was formed in London and purchased from the Compañía Huanchaca the railway and concessions from the Bolivian Government to extend the main line from the Chilean frontier to Uyuni and Oruro. Construction to Uyuni was completed by 1889 and to Oruro by 1892. The extension to La Paz was finished in 1917.

[2] This line and a branch running from Ollagüe to the Collahuasi mines in Chile are believed to be higher than any other lines of railway in the world, for they touch 15,705 and 15,809 feet above sea level, respectively.

[3] Between 1941 and 1945 an average of 18·7 per cent of Bolivian exports and 25·6 per cent of imports by value passed through Antofagasta, 13·6 per cent of exports and 19·7 per cent of imports through Arica, 2·4 per cent of exports and

They run passenger services once, or at most twice, a week, which were comfortable and well regulated. There is a deficiency of modern equipment, particularly locomotives, and maintenance has suffered from lack of funds. Rationalization is made difficult by the fact that the lines are operated by four different private companies and five state agencies. Their combined capacity is inadequate to the normal volume of Bolivia's traffic and heavy congestion particularly at the port of Arica is a usual occurrence. Bolivia has four 'free ports' on the Pacific, Arica and Antofagasta in Chile, Mollendo and Matarani in Peru. The one platform on which all Bolivians are politically united is their demand for an outlet on the sea and the lack of a sea-board is the country's most vociferous grievance. Yet without transport a port serves no purpose and an even more urgent requirement would seem to be the amplification of railway capacity to the existing ports.

Like much other Bolivian industry the railways went through a difficult time in the years following 1957. On 18 February 1959 the Antofagasta (Chili) and Bolivia Railway Company was obliged to suspend the operation of its railways in Bolivia and of those leased from its subsidiary the Bolivia Railway Company.[1] Therefore the Bolivian Government took over their operation from that

---

21·9 per cent of imports through Mollendo and 4 per cent of exports and 25·2 per cent of imports through La Quiaca by the Villazón–Atocha line.

[1] In order to give some idea of the labour conditions in Bolivian industry at this time (see pp. 133–8, 156) it may be of interest to quote part of the Company's statement: 'These railways have suffered great operational losses in Bolivia in the past two years. For 1958, the loss is estimated at £500,000 and for 1959 the indications are that the loss would be half as much again. Traffics have fallen by 40%, while inflation and depreciation of exchange have increased the cost of purchases of stores, etc. At the same time, the Company has been denied its right to introduce economies by the dismissal of superfluous employees and workmen. It has been maintaining an excess of 30% over the number of personnel which were necessary for the traffic carried. These men enjoy "fringe" benefits, including complete medical service, which more than double the wages bill. Although wages and costs have increased, railway tariffs have been frozen since December, 1956. The Government's Stabilization Law of 15 December, 1956, stated that increases of railway tariffs were to be authorised sufficient to cover operating expenses, depreciation and a just return on capital; and new tariffs were accordingly then authorised. That law also stated that those new tariffs were only provisional and that they should be readjusted definitely within the following six months. No such readjustments, however, were authorised. In fact, in 1957 railway tariffs were even reduced on some articles.' There was also considerable interference by the powerful Railway Labour Unions. All this made it impossible to run the railways as a commercial enterprise. (*Financial Times*, 14 Feb. 1959.)

date, but experienced similar economic and labour difficulties in running them. On 29 March 1962, however, an agreement was made with the companies that the Bolivian Government purchased the railways as from that date against adequate and effective compensation, the amount of which was to be decided by a Mixed Commission, on which the railway companies were represented, within a period of two years. As part of the agreement the Antofagasta Company undertook to manage these railways for a period of two years as Managing Agents of, and for the account of, the Bolivian Government, that is without any financial liability on the part of the company.[1] Following this arrangement loans were made by the British and American Governments to the Bolivian Government towards meeting, among other items, the cost of providing equipment, spares and stores for the rehabilitation of the by then badly run down lines.

As may be seen from a glance at the map, the foregoing railways serve the interests only of La Paz and the mining industry, with branches into the high valleys at Cochabamba and Sucre. The Department of Santa Cruz was without rail communications until the fifties, but has now been brought into contact with neighbouring countries by two lines.

Under the terms of treaties of 25 December 1928 and 25 February 1938, which are linked with a treaty on the export of Bolivian oil products, a line has been constructed with Brazilian capital by a mixed Brazilian-Bolivian body from Corumbá on the Brazilian frontier to the town of Santa Cruz, a distance of 422 miles. Except for the difficult bridging of the Río Grande it was almost complete and was already being used for desultory wood-burning locomotive traffic in 1950. The line was completed in 1955 and the bridging of the Río Grande in 1958.

A second line is being constructed with Argentine capital under the terms of a treaty of 10 February 1941 in return for an agreement concerning the export of Bolivian oil surplus to the needs of

---

[1] *Financial Times*, 3 Apr. 1962. In the Chairman's Statement accompanying the Company's accounts for the year ending 31 Dec. 1961 it was said: 'One of the basic conditions necessary for the efficient running of the railways in Bolivia is to have orderly and disciplined labour relations. A number of measures affecting labour and labour relations have been written into our Agreement. The Bolivian Government has undertaken to back us in these and in a correct application of the Bolivian Labour Code. I must, however, here state, quite categorically, that we shall not be able to accomplish our onerous Management Agency job unless we in turn get all necessary and proper support of Bolivia and its people.'

the country. It runs from Yacuiba northwards to Santa Cruz, a distance of 342 miles, and is an extension of the Argentine line from Buenos Aires to Yacuiba. It was largely completed by 1950 except for bridging and sections of the track have been in use since that time. But in 1960 some thirty bridges and fifty miles of track still remained unfinished.

Studies for a railway link between Cochabamba and Santa Cruz were pursued in a desultory fashion from about 1900. Part of the intervening country was explored by commissions under the German engineer Hans Grether and three alternative routes were considered. But the project was one of superlative difficulty and excessive cost, not only because of the forbidding nature of the mountainous country beyond Cochabamba but because much of the route lies across wholly unexplored and uninhabited forest country, much of which is liable to seasonal flooding. A section of line exists from Cochabamba to Vila-Vila, a distance of eighty miles, but the idea of linking Santa Cruz with the highlands by means of a permanent way to Cochabamba has been dropped in favour of the motor highway.

The Beni and Pando are to all intents and purposes without rail communication. A line is being built by the Bolivian Government to connect La Paz with the Beni at Rurrenabaque and Reyes through the Yungas, an estimated distance of 290 miles. A section is in very occasional operation from La Paz to Ingeniero Tejada, a distance of thirty-seven miles, and construction work is in progress as far as kilometre 105. Between La Paz and the Yungas the line runs over very uneven and often unstable ground, with excessive gradients. It will, when completed to Coroico, serve a useful purpose in linking La Paz with the most highly cultivated districts of the Yungas. But over the remaining sector to the river Beni the land, although less rugged, is subject to inundation and lacks stability. In the opinion of many engineering experts it is more than doubtful whether this extension to the Beni is a practical possibility and even were it achieved by some miracle of determination, it would still bring La Paz into touch only with the less important edge of the Beni, leaving the vast valley of the Mamoré hardly less isolated than before. The north-east corner of the Beni has also contact with the Madera–Mamoré railway, whose terminus is at the Brazilian town of Guajará-Mirim across the river from the Bolivian town and which was built on Brazilian territory at great cost in the heyday of the rubber trade. It follows the course of the Madera for 225 miles and covers the stretch where river navigation is made impossible by rapids. Its freight charges are extremely high and little traffic passes over it.

Bolivia has, therefore, well under 2,000 miles of track in effective operation. The British Railways operate over 52,000 miles of track within an area approximately one-eighth that of Bolivia.

Roads

According to the estimate of the Directorate of Highways Bolivia has 22,370 miles of roads, of which 6,210 miles are classified as main roads. But the second figure includes an unspecified mileage of roads still in the planning stage and the total includes sections which are no more than forest tracks or unregistered footpaths. (The total mileage of public roads in Great Britain is 183,658 miles.)

Bolivian roads are uniformly bad, usually incredibly bad and most often dangerous. The only surfaced roads are the Cochabamba–Santa Cruz motorway, roads connecting La Paz with the Yungas and a few miles of the Tarija section of the Pan-American highway. Outside the urban areas roads are rarely surfaced and little repair work is done on them. Many have been formed simply by the constant passage of lorries, as that from Santa Cruz to the Argentine frontier which is said to carry as heavy a traffic as any in the country. There is hardly a road in the country which is not put out of commission more or less regularly by flooding, landslides or subsidence and even those which run across the relatively flat stretches of the Altiplano are far from perfect. When a breach is made in them by the collapse of a culvert or a gaping crack which opens up in the soil, the lorries simply make a detour round the obstacle until they have beaten out a new track for themselves. Throughout the Oriente the roads are ploughed into furrows and ruts two feet deep or more by ox-carts in the season of the rain, baked hard and overlaid by a foot or so of dust in the dry season. Many roads cross river beds by natural fording places, the lorry drivers laying a base of leaves and boughs to give the wheels purchase in the shifting soil, and in the highlands the road is often simply a river bed used as such in the drier season. It is no uncommon thing for a road to be no more than an indication of direction and fording places by means of white stones laid across open country. Among the best roads in the country are those between La Paz and the Yungas, which are kept, if not in repair, at any rate passable by the revenues derived from the coca commerce. They are roads on which private cars can normally venture most of the year round. But even they are subject to the danger of landslides and it is no uncommon thing to see lines of a hundred or more lorries and cars on either side of a block which may take twenty-four hours or longer to clear. The inclines are steep, the blind bends frequent and the roads narrow; visibility is often limited by rain and mist and the rapid changes of altitude are a strain upon the driver. Wayside crosses mark the spots where unfortunate lorries have gone over the edge.

Traffic is necessarily slow, often averaging no more than ten miles or so an hour, wear and tear upon the vehicles is enormous, and breakdowns are frequent. Yet the great bulk of internal transport is by lorry. One can only admire the endurance and resource of the cholo lorrymen who drive under such conditions, where a momentary relaxation of attention often means certain death, for long hours day after day.

Inside the country and out Bolivian Governments are often accused of apathy and neglect for the appalling state of Bolivian road communications. Yet the task is stupendous. In the east and on the Altiplano the land is relatively flat. But on the Altiplano the surface consists largely of loose shale and sliding clay, which offers no solid foundations; and in the east it is practically impossible to maintain a permanent road against seasonal flooding and the encroachment of forest vegetation. In the intermediate zones the land is exceptionally broken and rugged, the gradients terrific, the danger of subsidence or of landslides from above is constant and the soil rarely offers a solid foundation. It is certain that the task of making and maintaining a good system of road communication throughout Bolivia is far beyond the country's own resources of finance and man-power. The importance of improving and extending Bolivia's road transport has been accorded a high priority in Technical Assistance studies.

Studies for a motor road between Cochabamba and Santa Cruz began in 1944 and construction was put in hand in 1945, partly financed by a United States loan to the Bolivian Development Corporation. Progress was impeded by various setbacks, but by 1950 about seventy miles had been completed at both ends of the road, at the Cochabamba end by an American and at the Santa Cruz end by a Bolivian construction firm. The writer was witness of the enthusiasm at Santa Cruz when this portion was opened by

President Hertzog in 1949. The highway was completed in 1954, though asphalting went on until 1958. The total length of the road is 317 miles, its paved width is six yards and the maximum gradient is 7 per cent. Motor coaches do the journey in twelve hours and cargo is carried by heavy lorries, though freight costs are high. The completion of this road has been the most important boon to Bolivian internal economy during the present century.

Since 1956 a highway has been made joining Santa Cruz with Montero and some progress has been made with access roads and roads of penetration into the Santa Cruz area.[1] Some investigation has been made into the possibility of running a branch road from the Santa Cruz–Cochabamba highway at Montepunco down to the river Ichilo with a view to opening up the Beni and Mojos. This could provide a viable river–road link between Cochabamba and Trinidad, by-passing the almost unusable Chapare route. Meanwhile the Bolivian Government are pushing ahead with a road from La Paz through the Yungas in the direction of Rurrenabaque and the river Beni. This may be expected to open up not only an important additional section of the Yungas valleys but should give direct communication via the river Beni between much of Mojos and the markets of the Altiplano.

ADMINISTRATIVE DIVISIONS AND LOCAL GOVERNMENT

For the purpose of administration Bolivia is divided into nine Departments and each Department is divided into provinces and cantons. The Departments are: La Paz (16 provinces), Cochabamba (14 provinces), Chuquisaca (9 provinces), Potosí (13 provinces), Oruro (6 provinces), Santa Cruz (11 provinces), Tarija (6 provinces), the Beni (8 provinces) and Pando (4 provinces).

There are in addition three *Delegaciones* lying outside the jurisdiction of the Departments. They are the Delegación Nacional del Chapare with its capital at Todos Santos, the Delegación Nacional de Guarayos with its capital at Ascensión and the Delegación del Gran Chaco with its capital at Villa Montes. They are each in charge of a Delegate appointed by the President and answerable to him through the Ministry of Agriculture and Colonization. His functions are to encourage colonization of his region and to be responsible for the welfare of the indigenous tribes of the area.

The superior political, economic and administrative govern-

[1] See below, p. 99.

45

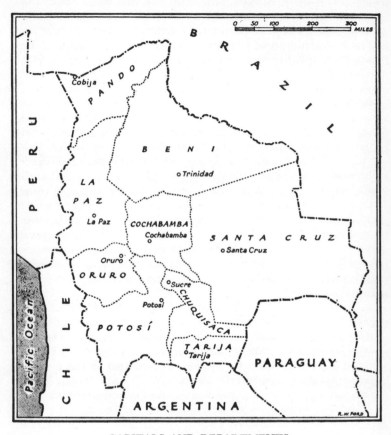

CAPITALS AND DEPARTMENTS

ment of the Departments is vested in the National Government, which acts through a Prefect appointed by the President of the Republic and responsible to him through the Ministers of State. As representative of the President and Government, the Prefect has very wide powers of control in his Department. His duties are financial, political and military and he is in authority over all local functionaries. The revised Constitution of 1931 created Departmental Assemblies, composed of elected *procuradores*, which brought some measure of local government to the Departments but these innovations did not persist. The autonomy of the Prefectures, even in the disposal of local funds, is very limited and prefectural budgets are subject to approval by Congress.

The provinces are supervised by Sub-Prefects, also appointed by the President of the Republic, and responsible through the Prefect of the Department to the central Government.

The cantons—which correspond to villages and very small market towns in Britain—are in charge of *corregidores* appointed by the Prefects of Departments. The office of *corregidor* has been carried over from the Colonial epoch with a very unsavoury reputation which republican practice has done little to modify. The remuneration of the *corregidor* is too small in relation to his duties to offer any temptation to honesty, supervision is very general in character, and corruption and abuse—largely at the expense of the Indians—are the rule. Professor Cleven remarks: 'To the critical observer of the political government of Bolivia, the *corregidor* seems the very opposite of what an official ought to be. In no vital part of the whole political government is there more urgent need of reform.'[1] This was written in 1940. The writer's own later observations show no reason to modify the verdict.

The more important towns have a municipal council of twelve, elected by vote and presided over by an Alcalde,[2] who occupies a position in relation to the affairs of the municipality analogous to that of a mayor in Great Britain. As the important towns are also capitals of Departments, the functions of the Alcalde and those of the Prefect to some extent overlap. Their respective influence is largely a matter of personality, with the scales weighted in favour of the Prefect.

The office of Prefect, Alcaldías and the more important Sub-Prefectures are exercised by whites or near-whites. The minor

[1] N. Andrew N. Cleven, *The Political Organization of Bolivia* (1940).
[2] Since 1952 all appointments have been made by the Government.

Sub-Prefects and the *corregidores* are often cholos.[1] The Indian communities are organized in traditional *ayllus* or clans, which are controlled by *jilakatas* (headmen) or *mallcus*. Although these enjoy no official recognition, their moral influence is often very strong.

[1] See p. 106 for an explanation of these racial divisions.

CHAPTER II

THE HISTORY AND THE PEOPLE

HISTORY AND FOREIGN RELATIONS

THERE exists a great deal of speculation and very little knowledge about man's earliest history on the Bolivian plateau.[1] The Altiplano is usually believed to have been the theatre for the first advances towards agricultural civilization in the sub-continent of South America, at a date which is very variously conjectured. And the founders of that civilization are usually thought to have been men who migrated, under what compulsion we can only guess, from the warm valleys and forests of the Yungas and succeeded in establishing themselves on the bleaker *sierra*, mainly through the discovery and cultivation of the potato—that lowly food-plant which has since had so important an influence upon the social and economic development of many nations—and possibly also through the domestication of maize. With somewhat less assurance it is believed by some archaeologists that about the middle of the first Christian millenium there arose on the Altiplano a powerful highland culture, sometimes referred to as the Megalithic Empire of the Andes, with its centre at Tiahuanaco on the southern shore of Lake Titicaca and its influence extending from Quito in the north down to Chile and Argentina in the south. The positive evidence for this culture is rather slight and little is known about the forms which it took. But in any case the existing remains of megalithic structures at Tiahuanaco and elsewhere, which in the technical perfection of their craftsmanship have nowhere been surpassed,[2] stand as irrefutable evidence that there must then have existed upon the Altiplano both a denser population than it now supports and a people who had achieved economic stability and political centralization adequate to sup-

[1] The early history is discussed more fully by the author in *Indians of the Andes*.
[2] Wendel C. Bennet says in the *Handbook of South American Indians* (1946), vol. 2: 'The Classic Tiahuanaco period places great emphasis on masonry. No other Peruvian period matches the exactness and precision of the stonework in its careful cutting, dressing, squaring and notching.' Sir Banister Fletcher in *A History of Architecture* (8th ed., 1928) describes the masonry of the cyclopean ruins at Tiahuanaco as 'a marvel of stone-cutting and fineness of fitting, similar to early Etruscan work.'

port the reserve of man-power necessary to carry out important works of construction over many generations. For the work represents generations of organized effort and the mere quarrying and haulage of the stones for Tiahuanaco, apart from the tradition of technical skill, would present a problem well beyond the resources of man-power available today.

Before the time of the Spanish invasion the Bolivian *sierra* had been incorporated into the empire of the Incas as the southern province of the Kollasuyu. The native peoples were Aymara and the extensive islands of Quechua-speaking Indians now existing around the lake in the north, in the eastern districts of Potosí, Cochabamba and Chuquisaca, and in the Department of Oruro —who are now more numerous than the Aymaras even in Bolivia itself—probably originated through the Inca policy of settling colonies in the outlying districts of their empire for the purpose of unification and cohesion.

Written history commences with the Spanish invasion. The Inca Atahuallpa was captured in 1532 and by 1537 the Spanish had consolidated their arms in Peru, had founded Lima and held Cuzco securely. Yet even before this Diego de Almagro, the associate of Pizarro in the conquest, had led an expedition into Chile and Spanish feet first trod what is now Bolivian soil. On this expedition the first Colonial foundation in Bolivia was established by Juan de Saavedra at Paria near the modern Oruro. Then after the return and death of Almagro from his disastrous Chilean venture, Francisco Pizarro despatched his brother Gonzalo at the head of an expedition to subdue the Collao, attracted no doubt by the fame of the silver mines of Porco which were already worked in Inca times and are still mined for tin. Gonzalo at any rate showed little interest in the main plateau but concentrated on the central sector of the eastern Cordillera, where he organized an administrative region under the name of Charcas. In 1538 Pedro de Anzures founded there in the valley of Chuki-chaca the famous City of Four Names—Charcas, La Plata, Chuquisaca, Sucre— which is still the legal capital of Bolivia. Chuquisaca was chosen as a centre because of its attractive climate and surroundings, situated as it is in a warm and sheltered valley, adequately watered and very fertile, amidst the barren grimness of the towering mountains which were to be exploited for their mineral treasure. In 1549 it became the seat of a bishopric and in 1559 Philip II created there by royal decree a second Audiencia within the Viceroyalty of Lima. In 1545 the famous silver deposit of Potosí was discovered and immediately leapt into prominence because of the abundance and high quality of its ores. The settlement which was built there grew rapidly in wealth and importance and in 1553 was granted the title of Villa Imperial de Potosí. In 1548, on the anniversary of the bloody battle of Huarina between Gonzalo Pizarro and Diego Centeno, La Paz was founded by Alonso de Mendoza, commissioned by Pedro de la Gasca, to commemorate the pacification of Peru..It was from the first a commercial city, lying on the main silver route to the coast, and it soon grew to be the most flourishing town of the Collao, though it could not rival the wealth of Potosí or the cultural importance of Chuquisaca. In 1570 the Villa de Oropeza, now Cochabamba, was founded on the orders of the Viceroy Toledo in a wide and fertile valley of the eastern Cordillera. By his orders too the town of Tarija was founded in the south by Luis de Fuentes y Vargas in 1574 to contain the fierce Chiriguani of the Chaco. The natives of the Tarija region are described as a tall, light race called Tomatas, 'the most noble, politic and valiant of all the Indians; and in truth their character was frank, civil and courteous.'[1] Both the people and their language are now extinct but the rural population of Tarija today, known as Chapacos, are considered one of the better products of the fusion of Spanish and Indian blood. In 1601 a fort was built at the site of the modern Oruro in the southern Altiplano near lake Poopó and became a city by royal order in 1606. Though a mining centre of considerable importance after Potosí, it was not to reach its apogee until tin attained commercial importance at the end of the last century and the famous Patiño deposit was discovered at Llallagua.

Thus by the end of the sixteenth century the pattern of the urban structure of Bolivia had been laid. These are the most important towns of western Bolivia today and were all founded by the Spanish during the first half-century of their occupation.

From 1563 to 1776 the Audiencia of Charcas covered, with minor modifications, most of the territory of modern Bolivia, together with the administrative districts of Tucumán, Paraguay

[1] Pedro Lozano, *Descripción chorográfica del terreno, ríos, árboles, y animales de las dilatadíssimas Provincias del Gran Chaco, Gualamba, y de los ritos y costumbres de las innumerables Naciones bárbaras è infieles, que la habitan.* (Córdova, 1733). Quoted by Bernardo Trigo, *Las tejas de mi techo* (1939). Many early writers bear enthusiastic witness to the fertility of the soil and the benignity of the climate of Tarija. It is, however, liable to some seasonal drought.

and Buenos Aires, the coastal region of Atacama and southern Peru as far as the district of Cuzco. Thus the three great provinces of south-eastern Spanish America—Buenos Aires, Tucumán and Paraguay—were under the jurisdiction of Chuquisaca. In 1776 Charles III was finally impelled by the active advances of the Portuguese to create the new Viceroyalty of Río de la Plata with an Audiencia at Buenos Aires. The Presidency of Charcas was transferred from Lima to the new Viceroyalty and its Audiencia lost jurisdiction over Buenos Aires, Paraguay, Tucumán and southern Peru, including the lacustrine districts of Chucuito and Puno. Charcas was now called Upper Peru (Alto Peru) and retained that name until the establishment of the Republic in 1825. Alto Peru itself was divided into four provinces: Charcas with its capital at Chuquisaca, La Paz, Potosí which included Tarija and Atacama, and Santa Cruz which covered Cochabamba and the governments of Chiquitos and Mojos. It embraced, therefore, practically all the territories of Bolivia, with the coastal region of Atacama in addition.

Throughout the eighteenth century Charcas enjoyed a large measure of independence both within the Viceroyalty of Lima and later under the new Viceroyalty of La Plata. It developed its own regional character, its own traditions and loyalties. The Audiencia maintained itself aloof from the innumerable disputes which distracted Lima, Paraguay and Buenos Aires, and exercised a powerful influence on the political life of the whole Colony. Its cities grew steadily in economic and cultural importance. The phenomenal yield of silver from the Cerro Rico had made Potosí the richest and most expensive city in the world, though its period of greatest prosperity had ended by the middle of the seventeenth century, and despite violent internecine disputes it had blossomed with an intensity of political, religious and artistic life such as can be paralleled only among the Italian republics of the Renaissance.[1] Chuquisaca established a firm and solid leadership in culture and learning, and its influence even outside Charcas earned it the title of 'the Athens of America', which it shared with Bogotá. Cochabamba increased powerfully in agricultural importance. The Vice-

[1] The history of Potosí in the sixteenth and seventeenth centuries has been portrayed with the art of the born raconteur by Nicolás de Martínez Arzanz y Vela, *Historia de la Villa Imperial de Potosí* (1943) and Bartolomé Martínez y Vela, *Anales de la Villa Imperial de Potosí* (1939). The historical novel *Cuando vibraba la entraña de plata* (Potosí, 1948) by José Enrique Viaña is set in seventeenth-century Potosí.

roy Manso de Velasco wrote of it in his *Memorias*: 'It is very densely populated with Indians and mestizos and abounds more in the latter than any other town in Peru; its territory is very fertile, produces wheat, maize and many minerals, and if the cost of transport were not so high, it could supply half the kingdom with wheat.' And later the Viceroy Armendáriz said: 'The town of Oropesa is the granary and deposit of abundance of the neighbouring towns in the province of La Plata.'[1] It was Simón Bolívar's preference for the capital of the Republic and is today second in importance to La Paz. La Paz itself surpassed the rest in commercial prosperity and in population. When the Audiencia of Charcas was established, its claims over Chuquisaca were strongly pressed and at the foundation of the Republic it made a strong bid to become the capital.

Thus as its cities matured in wealth and independence, with community of interests and common traditions, a robust sense of regional unity grew up in the Presidency. Politically and economically it felt itself to be a distinct province in dependence on the Spanish crown. The sentiment of nationality was born before the fact and in Charcas the ferment of new ideas and aspirations which inspired the struggle for independence found a most fruitful soil. Chuquisaca was one of the most fertile centres of liberal ideas on the continent and its University of San Xavier with the legal Academia Carolina were schools of theoretical and practical politics. From them the most advanced doctrines radiated throughout Spanish America and in them were trained many of the men who were later to become intellectual leaders in the Wars of American Independence. Then on 25 May 1809 Chuquisaca became the scene of the first overt action for independence and Bolivia claims in consequence to be the first country to have raised the standard of freedom, although it was the last to secure it.

After fifteen years of war the liberation of Peru from Spanish dominion was definitely secured by the battles of Junín and Ayacucho on 6 August and 9 December 1824. But in Alto Peru the royalist general Pedro Antonio de Olañeta still sustained opposition to the forces of liberation. When offers of negotiation failed, in 1825 the Liberator Simón Bolívar despatched an expeditionary force against him under the Colombian general Antonio José de Sucre, the victor of Ayacucho, and with his defeat of Olañeta at the battle of Tumusla on 2 April resistance was at an end. But the

[1] Quoted by Enrique Finot, *Nueva historia de Bolivia* (1946), p. 100.

destiny of Upper Peru, the old Presidency of Charcas, was by no means a foregone conclusion. Traditionally, both under the empire of the Incas and in the Spanish Colonial empire, it had formed a part of Peru. At the outbreak of the Wars of Independence it was subordinate to the Viceroyalty of Buenos Aires. Olañeta fought to establish there an independent kingdom loyal to Ferdinand VII of Spain. Sucre, supported by ardent local sentiment, rushed precipitately ahead with the creation of a free and independent republic. But it was the lifelong ambition of his second-in-command, the great Bolivian statesman and general Andrés de Santa Cruz y Calahumana, to bring about an equal coalition of Upper and Lower Peru and thus restore the ancient unity of the Inca regime. Simón Bolívar himself was reluctant to give immediate effect to the popular decision for independence and as Dictator of Peru may have felt some sympathy with the aspirations of Santa Cruz.

Immediately on entering La Paz, Sucre promulgated the famous Decree of Independence on 9 February 1825, convoking a deliberative assembly to determine the future political status of the country.[1] In its Preamble it stated that

the ancient Viceroyalty of Buenos Aires to which these provinces pertained at the time of the revolution of America lacks a general government which represents completely, legally and legitimately the authority of all the provinces . . . their political future must therefore result from the deliberation of the provinces themselves and from an agreement between the Congress of Peru and that which is formed in the Río de La Plata.

This decree was incontinently repudiated by Bolívar in a notorious letter of 21 February on the ground that the convocation of a national assembly was in itself an act of sovereignty and required the prior consent of the countries concerned. Sucre, however, stood firm to his views, maintaining the strength of separatist sentiment in Charcas and its extreme reluctance to accept amalgamation with either Río de La Plata or Peru. On 9 May the Congress of the United Provinces of Río de La Plata issued a decree in which the people of Charcas were invited to incorporate the province in Argentina but in which they were left 'full liberty to dis-

[1] After Ayacucho Sucre wrote twice to Bolívar in Lima asking for instructions what political course he was to pursue in Upper Peru. He received no reply and acted apparently upon a statement made by Bolívar in previous conversations that 'his intention for solving the difficulties of Upper Peru was to convoke an assembly of those provinces.' See Finot, *Nueva historia de Bolivia*.

pose of its destiny as they believe best accords with their interests and well-being.' Meanwhile Bolívar, now Dictator of Peru, was wavering in his opposition. On 16 May he issued a decree from Arequipa, in which he ordered: 'The provinces of Upper Peru, formerly Spanish, will unite in a general assembly according to the decree of the Marshal of Ayacucho, in which to express freely their will as to their interests and government, in conformity with the desire of the Executive Power of the United Provinces of the Río de La Plata and the said provinces.' But he added that the deliberations of the assembly would have no sanction until the installation of the new Congress of Peru the following year, and until that time 'the provinces of Upper Peru will recognize no other centre of authority than the supreme government of that Republic'. The assembly met early in July and found itself overwhelmingly in favour of independence. The 6th of August, the anniversary of the battle of Junín, was designated as the birthday of the new Republic and it was named *Bolivia* in honour of the Liberator. It was recognized officially by the Peruvian Government in the following year.

While it would be going too far to speak of the Colombian general Sucre as the architect of Bolivian independence, there is no doubt that the separatist aspirations of Charcas were effectively abetted by his energetic and determined championship and owing to it went ahead more rapidly than Bolívar had foreseen.

Bolívar's attitude was complicated by his obligations towards Peru and elsewhere. In inviting Upper Peru to decide its own political status Sucre's decree of 9 February recognized the right of self-determination alongside the principle of *uti possidetis* which had hitherto governed the formation of independent states from the old Spanish Colonial empire. Bolívar refused to recognize the validity of the Declaration of Independence until it had been ratified by Peru as well as Buenos Aires, and when he visited Bolivia made it clear that he went as head of the army of liberation and not as head of the government. For this reason in decrees issued from Bolivian territory he signed himself: 'Liberator and President of the Republic of Colombia, Liberator of Peru, etc.' without mention of Bolivia. He was undoubtedly flattered by the adulation with which he was greeted and in letters to the Vice-President Santander spoke of his great personal affection for the new Republic. But he remained never wholly convinced of the capacity of the Bolivians for self-government and he opposed the desire of Tarija and Arica for incorporation in the new Republic.[1]

The motives of Santa Cruz, the greatest of Bolivia's sons, are more obvious. Proud of his descent from the Inca nobility, he was influenced by a romantic attachment to the old Inca ideal and by his personal loyalties to both Upper and Lower Peru. He was born in 1792 at the little hamlet of Huarina on the Altiplano, of a Spanish father and an Indian mother, María Calahumana, who claimed royal descent from the Incas. From his father he learnt loyalty to the Spanish crown and by his mother he was taught to dream of restoring the ancient glories of the Inca empire. He adopted a military career in early youth, fought in the ranks of the Loyalists and was twice captured. From 1820 he changed his allegiance and fought in the Patriot cause, soon rising to prominence. During the formation of the Republic of Bolivia he was second in command to Sucre and by decree of Simón Bolívar was to act as President in case of the illness, absence or death of Sucre. In opposition to Sucre he worked stubbornly for the union of Charcas with Peru, an ideal which he was never to abandon. In 1826 he was appointed by Bolívar to the Presidency of the Council of Government in Lima and until his defeat in the presidential election of 1827 ruled Peru with integrity and success. He was Peruvian ambassador to Chile in 1828, when he was elected President of Bolivia, and in the ten years of his Presidency he left his mark indelibly on the formative years of the Republic. Yet his most cherished aim remained the amalgamation of the two Perus, both of which he felt to be his own, and in 1836 he was able to proclaim a Peruvian-Bolivian Confederation. He was defeated in 1839, and the Confederation annulled, owing to the combined opposition of Chile and Argentina. F. A. Kirkpatrick says of him that 'although intriguing and faithless in pursuit of his ambition, he was a resolute, able and laborious administrator of unimpeachable financial integrity and a born master of men.'[2] Santa Cruz is probably the greatest leader that Bolivia has produced.[3]

From the fall and exile of Santa Cruz there followed more than thirty years of anarchy and civil strife during which the land was

[1] Letters of 21 October 1825 from Potosí and of 11 November and 12 December from Chuquisaca. Vicente Lecuna, *Documentos relativos a la creación de Bolivia* (1924).

[2] F. A. Kirkpatrick, *Latin America* (1938), p. 201.

[3] *Santa Cruz, el condor indio* (Mexico, 1944) by Alfonso Crespo is a well written account of Santa Cruz in novel form, aided by the historical researches of Víctor Santa Cruz, a descendant of the subject.

never free from insurrection or threat of revolt and was ruled by a series of irresponsible military dictators who maintained themselves in office by brutal repressions and no less bloody reprisals. Sanguinary excesses were the order of the day and men's lives were lived in an atmosphere of terror and suspense. For the country it was a period of political disorder and economic prostration.

In 1841 Gamarra, President of Peru, believing himself to have been duped by Santa Cruz, invaded Bolivia purposing annexation. He was defeated and killed on the plains of Ingavi outside Viacha by General José Ballivián, who had earlier led the opposition in Bolivia against Santa Cruz's bid for amalgamation, and the battle of Ingavi has gone down in Bolivian history as the final seal set upon the Republic's undisputed independence.

Ballivián, a self-educated but comparatively enlightened autocrat, who was formally elected President in April 1846, retired into voluntary exile at the end of the following year, but continued to intrigue against subsequent usurpers of office.

Manuel Isidoro Belzu, a man of the people and a Brigadier-General of the army, came to power by a military revolution in 1848. A self-styled democrat, he courted the support of the ignorant and unlettered masses, whose lot he made no attempt to improve, against the more responsible elements of the community. He was a man without background or natural integrity but one who could instinctively adopt the methods most calculated to win to himself the transient sympathies of an uneducated and irresponsible populace. Under him political life reached the acme of vulgarity and the word 'belcismo' has become synonymous in Bolivia for blatant demagogy and venal opportunism. After a reign of terror lasting eight years Belzu resigned from office in 1855, declaring that Bolivia had become a country incapable of being governed, and went into voluntary exile.

An attempt at reform was made by José María Linares (1857–61), a capable and upright administrator who carried autocracy to the point of fanaticism and suppressed every stirring of opposition with no less ruthless ferocity than his predecessors, so that a Chilean historian has said of him: 'He believed that to kill the spirit of rebellion it was necessary to oppose to it the spirit of despotism.'[1] When on the point of laying down his office at the

[1] R. Sotomayor Valdés, *Estudio histórico de Bolivia bajo la administración del general D. José María de Achá* (1874). The Bolivian historiographer G. René Moreno also remarks: 'The most obstinate conspirators, Ballivián and Linares,

beginning of 1861 he was deposed by a conspiracy of his friends and followed Ballivián and Belzu into exile in Peru.

Mariano Melgarejo, who seized power from José María Achá in 1864, proved himself the most notorious and colourful of all the military tyrants who held the fortunes of the country at their mercy during these tragic years. A soldier who had come up from the ranks, he was a man of violent passions and a drunkard who owed his success to his physical prowess and his brute courage. He has been described as 'a rude soldier of great physical strength and intrepidity, but a grotesque tyrant, an habitual drunkard, who governed by brute force and terror, fleecing his subjects, killing a rival with his own hands and crushing in blood every disturbance, until at last armed revolt drove him in flight across the Peruvian frontier.'[1] He turned against Linares and was pardoned; he was the close friend of Achá whom he supplanted; on coming to power he mulcted and massacred the people of Cochabamba, to whose intercession he had owed his life when condemned to death under Belzu. Without loyalty or principles, his abysmal ignorance combined with his colossal conceit rendered him incapable of benefiting by the advice of those who might have guided him to moderation, and his intolerant stupidity did his unhappy country more damage than fifty years could rectify. He mortgaged the newly discovered wealth of the littoral for loans which were senselessly squandered and his incompetent intrusions into international affairs put Bolivia at a disadvantage in its relations with neighbouring countries for many years to come. Melgarejo was a typical product of an age of violence and abuse and only in such an age could such a man have risen to wield the reins of government. Sotomayor Valdés, who occupied a diplomatic post in La Paz during Melgarejo's administration, has left the following account of what he saw: 'The imprint of the sword is everywhere and the prostration of industry, the poverty of the Exchequer, charitable institutions suspended, educational establishments closed, public offices in chaos, justice neglected, public officials unpaid and abuse rampant, all combine to condemn the administration.'[2]

Melgarejo was defeated and driven out by Agustín Morales in

were veritable tigers against conspiracy when they came to power.' *El general Ballivián* (Santiago, 1894).

[1] Kirkpatrick, *Latin America*, pp. 202–3.

[2] Sotomayor Valdés, *La Legación de Chile en Bolivia* (Santiago, 1872).

January 1871 and was assassinated shortly afterwards by the brother of his mistress Juana Sánchez. Morales, who inaugurated his Presidency with the slogan: 'More liberty and less government', was another crude soldier given to paroxysms of ungovernable fury and was shot down in self-defence by a cousin. The last of the irresponsible military dictators was Hilarión Daza (1875–80), after whom, although military coups and insurrections did not entirely cease to disturb the country, the excesses of the last thirty years gave place to an era of more orderly and enlightened government.

During this period of internal anarchy Bolivia's international position was far from easy. Relations with Peru remained strained both owing to memories of previous quarrels and because Peru offered the most favoured haven from which political intrigues were directed against each successive dictator. Commercial difficulties between the two countries were temporarily settled by a Customs Agreement signed in 1864, the advantages of which were solidly on the side of Peru.[1]

With Chile suspicion and rivalry were turned into open war by a conflict of interests in the coastal region. For the discovery of rich deposits of guano and nitrates changed what had been an almost uninhabited desert, valuable only as providing theoretical access to the Pacific, into an area of booming economic importance. Bolivia was unable to populate the littoral and entered into contracts with private companies for the exploitation of the deposits. The Chilean Government suddenly awoke to the commercial possibilities of a stretch of country which had held no attractions when its original frontiers with Bolivia were fixed,[2] and in 1866 a treaty was signed which conceded to Chile half the profits on exports of guano and minerals from the southern portion of the disputed region, while fixing the 24th parallel as the line of demarcation between the territories of the two countries. Tension was brought to a head by the discovery in 1870 of the silver deposits of Caracoles, which for a space of ten years became one of the most prolific silver mines in the world.[3] Finally in 1879 Chile occupied the whole of the littoral and Bolivia, supported

[1] Luis Peñaloza, *Historia económica de Bolivia* (1946), ii. 82–83.
[2] The Chilean Constitution of 1833 described the territory of Chile as extending 'from the desert of Atacama to Cape Horn'. In the eighteenth century the frontier between Chile and the jurisdiction of the Audiencia of Charcas, which Bolivia claimed to inherit, was fixed at the river Salado (latitude south 26° 10′).
[3] Peñaloza, ii. 124–5.

by Peru, declared war. Military operations were conducted with none of the ferocity or enthusiasm devoted to civil warfare and a truce signed in 1884, followed by a Treaty of Peace in 1895, conceded the whole of the littoral to Chile, with the destiny of Arica to be decided by plebiscite. These agreements were not ratified and it was not until the Treaty of Peace and Friendship of 1904 that the differences between the two countries were settled. By this treaty the frontier was fixed along the line of the Cordillera, leaving Chile in possession of the coastal region, Antofagasta and Arica became 'free ports' for Bolivian commerce in perpetuity and Chile undertook to construct a railway between Arica and La Paz and to hand over to the Bolivian Government the Bolivian section of it within twenty-five years of completion. This undertaking was implemented.

The Bolivians have not acquiesced happily in their mediterranean status consequent on this treaty and have taken every opportunity of voicing their demand for an 'outlet on the sea'.[1] But despite a strong residue of popular bitterness against Chile, in the present century relations between the two countries have remained tranquil, if not cordial.[2]

Scarcely less damaging to Bolivia was a treaty signed with Brazil in 1867 by which some 100,000 square kilometres on the right bank of the rivers Paraguay and Mamoré were ceded to Brazil in return for illusory commercial advantages. Intrepid explorers had for some years been penetrating the Bolivian forests of the Amazon zone, following the tracks of the early Jesuit and Franciscan missionaries in the search for rubber, and in 1860 Palacios had reached Cachuela Esperanza on the river Beni, the future headquarters of Suárez Hermanos. There was, therefore, no ground for the Government to plead ignorance of the commercial potentialities of the ceded territory and popular indignation at the treaty was so violent that it became a contributory cause of the downfall of Melgarejo. At the end of the century a clash with Brazil resulted from a dispute over the territory of Acre, where an inopportune attempt on the part of the Bolivian Government to establish a customs post on the river Acre caused a local separatist rising, which degenerated in the course of a few years into open war. On the Bolivian side the war was maintained al-

---

[1] In 1920 the Bolivian case was put before the League of Nations at Geneva by a Commission of which the poet and reformer Franz Tamayo was a member.

[2] Diplomatic relations were severed in 1962.

most entirely by the rubber baron Nicolás Suárez and his col-
leagues with little practical support from the Government, and by
the Treaty of Petropolis in 1903 the region of the Acre, north of
the river Abuná and west of the Madera, was ceded to Brazil in
return for the construction of the Madera–Mamoré railway.

The third and most devastating of Bolivia's wars with neighbouring states was fought with Paraguay and was also caused by
a territorial dispute. From the time of the formal declaration of
Paraguayan independence in 1842 no settled line of demarcation
had been established between Paraguayan and Bolivian territory
through the undeveloped and largely unexplored region of the
Chaco. The northern fringe of the Chaco was undisputed Bolivian
territory. The Hayes Arbitration of 1878 assigned the southern
portion to Argentina, fixing the river Pilcomayo as the boundary
between that country and Paraguay. But there remained a large
intermediate section which continued to be the subject of rival
claims by Bolivia and Paraguay. Bolivia maintained its title to it
on the ground that the jurisdiction of the Audiencia of Charcas
had extended eastwards as far as the Pilcomayo and on the *uti
possidetis* of 1810. Paraguay based its claim on the fact that early
exploration had proceeded northwards from Asunción (an argument which could have been applied also to much of the Bolivian
Department of Santa Cruz) and on the doubtful grounds of effective and undisturbed occupation. In 1863 President Achá had
made an abortive attempt to agree a frontier by negotiation and
a Bolivian expedition had pushed along the right bank of the Pilcomayo as far as Piquirenda and set up a fort there. Then later,
when Bolivia's Pacific seaboard was lost to Chile in 1884, the de-
sirability of securing an outlet by navigable river to the Atlantic
became more pressing and the Chaco claims were pushed with
greater vigour. Nothing, however, was settled until by 1927 recurrent friction and frontier incidents had become acute to the
point where war seemed imminent. The Bolivian Presidents Siles
and later Salamanca showed a conciliatory temper and took every
means to avoid open conflict short of renouncing Bolivia's claim
to an outlet to the Atlantic, and had Paraguay been willing to
concede Bolivia a port on the navigable portion of the river Paraguay, war might have been averted. The attitude of both parties
may, however, have been hardened by the discovery of petroleum
in regions bordering on the Chaco, although in fact no petroleum
has been found in the territory which was in dispute.

Bolivia

In 1928 Paraguayan troops seized the Bolivian fort Vanguardia and the matter was brought before the Conference on Conciliation and Arbitration, which was assembled in Washington in 1929. The conference pronounced Paraguay the aggressor in the instance before it, but failed to achieve any permanent formula of agreement. A commission appointed by the Pan American Union in the same year met with no better success; Bolivia felt unable to forgo its claim to a port with navigation to the Atlantic and this Paraguay was unwilling to concede. Daniel Salamanca, who was constitutionally elected to the Presidency in 1931, proposed a pact of non-aggression to Paraguay, but an unfortunate incident led to a breach of diplomatic relations between the two countries and the quarrel was again referred to a commission of neutral nations. While conferences were proceeding in Washington, however, the occupation of a Paraguayan post by Bolivian troops, acting without orders from the Government, led to armed retaliation and regular war. Although Bolivia had the larger resources of manpower, conditions of fighting in the Chaco favoured the guerrilla tactics in which the Paraguayan soldiery excelled and the climate took heavy toll of the highland Indian troops of Bolivia. The Bolivian armies were gradually pushed back and in 1934 Ballivián, one of the two key-fortresses in inhabited Bolivia, had fallen, while Villa Montes was only saved by the heroic resistance organized by Bilbao Rioja. By 1935 a stalemate had been reached. Bolivia could no longer hope to enforce its hold on the Chaco, which had been the object of the war, while the Paraguayan troops, now far from their bases, had no prospects of inflicting a decisive defeat on the Bolivian armies. By the terms of the peace which was negotiated in 1938 the greater part of the disputed areas of the Chaco went to Paraguay—a decision which undoubtedly reflected the results of the fighting—and Bolivia lost the outlet to the Atlantic by way of the river Paraguay.

The strain of the Chaco war was severe. Casualties were very heavy for so small a population and disease was spread by the returning troops among the indigenous population. The drain on the economic resources of the country would have had more lasting effects but for the soaring prices of non-ferrous metals which followed the outbreak of the Second World War and rendered Bolivian recovery more rapid. Recovery from the moral effects of the war was slower and it left in its wake a lasting sense of exhaustion, bitterness and frustration.

In the First World War, from which Bolivia derived considerable economic benefits, the country was neutral until 1917 when diplomatic relations with Germany were severed after a Bolivian minister to Berlin was torpedoed at sea. Bolivia signed the Peace Treaty of 1919 and was an original member of the League of Nations. In contrast with the turmoil of its internal problems, Bolivia's international situation since the end of the Chaco War has been tranquil. It has taken neither a prominent nor a backward part in world affairs, has been represented without notoriety on international organizations and has exercised a relatively minor influence in South American politics. With its neighbours it has had no urgent causes of difference. Relations with Chile and Peru have given no cause for alarm, although Bolivia remains always acutely and resentfully conscious that these countries could, if they were disposed, subject it to slow strangulation by denying it that access to the Pacific upon which its economic life depends. Both Argentina and Brazil have displayed a discreet rivalry of interest in Bolivian reserves of oil and Argentina has shown also some interest in the mineral exports. Both countries have built railways of penetration whose effect must be to strengthen the economic link of Bolivia's eastern territories with them at the expense of the Altiplano. Argentina is also constructing a section of the Pan-American highway running up from within Argentine territory past Tarija.

On 1 October 1951 an agreement was signed between Bolivia and the United Nations implementing the recommendations of the Report of the United Nations Mission of Technical Assistance to Bolivia. After some preliminary hesitation the MNR Government decided to retain the services of a commission of experts which arrived in the country on 9 May 1952, the day on which revolution broke out, and a revised Agreement for Technical Assistance was made public in May 1953. The Report was very comprehensive in its scope and set out a scheme for the radical reorganization of Bolivian administration, finance, taxation, economic policy, production, transport, agriculture and labour legislation, a scheme whose successful implementation would render the country very largely self-sufficient in primary essentials and bring back to it a measure of prosperity which it has not known since the European conquest of South America. Although to one who knows the country well certain of its recommendations may seem to savour of a somewhat too complacent optimism, general-

Bolivia

izing out of regard for the exceptional severity of the physical difficulties to be overcome and the inadequacy and unadaptability of
the existing population, yet the energetic adoption of the Report,
backed by adequate funds, could not but produce results which
would revolutionize the life of a country which displays all the
signs of an unchecked decline.

Since 1952 Bolivia's foreign relations have been dominated by
the urgent need of financial aid in order to avert collapse.

The pattern of trade has been a curious one and is exemplified
by figures for 1960. In that year, out of a total export valued at
$68 million, 54·4 per cent, consisting mainly of tin ores, went to
Britain. Bolivian imports in 1960 came to $71·5 million, of which
Britain supplied only 5·1 per cent (consisting mainly of machinery,
vehicles and consumer goods), while the United States supplied
43 per cent. British imports from and exports to Bolivia in the
years 1958–61 were (in £ million):

	1958	1959	1960	1961
Imports from Bolivia	13·3	13·6	11·8	12·5
Exports to Bolivia	1·2	0·9	1·2	1·1

POLITICS AFTER THE CHACO WAR

As has been said, in 1880 Bolivia entered on an era of more
stable and more responsible government. The revised Constitution, promulgated in 1880, lasted until 1931, lawless dictatorship
came to seem like a nightmare from the past and by the twenties
of the present century comparative political tranquillity and evidences of increased material prosperity had won for Bolivia the
reputation of being one of the more stable and reliable of the Latin
American republics. It was a reputation which did not survive the
effects of the Chaco War. In 1930 Daniel Salamanca was elected
President on the fall of the republican regime of Hernando Siles.
Hampered by economic difficulties and saddled with the stigma
of the military reverses in the unfortunate Chaco campaign, he
was ousted by a coup d'état in 1934 and was succeeded by his
Vice-President Luis Tejada Sorzano. The latter proved no more
successful and was overthrown in 1936 by Colonel David Toro, a
military dictator who introduced a programme verging on state
socialism but was in turn driven from office by a bloodless revolution in 1937 and succeeded by another military leader, Lieutenant-

Colonel Germán Busch. Busch was elected constitutional President in 1938 and together with his advisers initiated a vigorous repressive policy and a social programme which was thought at the time to have been modelled on the contemporary regime in Germany. Their plans for the reconstruction of the country on socialist lines were brought to an abrupt conclusion by his death, officially by suicide, in 1939. But his associates, claiming that he had been assassinated[1] and unresigned to the loss of their own political influence, organized in exile the party of the Movimiento Nacionalista Revolucionario (MNR) through which they were to exercise a persistently disruptive role in Bolivian affairs until they came into power for the second time by the revolution of 1952.

At its first founding the programme of the MNR rested on three platforms: to avenge the death of Colonel Busch, to support the Axis powers in the Second World War, and to nationalize the mines and organize the native miners into politically self-conscious unions. With the course of time this policy matured and the more idealistic motives of social revolution became dominant in their professions. When out of power the leaders of the party succeeded by means of revolutionary threats from without and subversive action at home to undermine the stability of other political regimes and to prevent any Government between 1940 and 1950 from becoming securely enough established to pursue a strong or consistent policy of economic revival.

After the death of Colonel Busch General Bernardino Bilbao Rioja, an honest and capable man and a highly popular figure in the country as the hero of the critical defence of Villa Montes in the Chaco War, was nominated President but when he insisted on popular elections he was shanghaied and bundled out of the country by his political friends.[2] Under the short presidencies of Carlos Quintanilla, followed by General Enrique Peñaranda, there ensued a period of increasing political tension with unrest continually fostered among the native mine workers and revolutionary menace from the partisans of Busch, until in 1942 the MNR staged a well planned and successful revolt which brought them back to power with Major Gualberto Villaroel as President and Víctor

---

[1] The novelist Augusto Céspedes, a member of the Party, has since written a book, *El dictador suicida*, accepting the suicide theory.

[2] A life of this extraordinary Bolivian figure by the Chilean writer Aquiles Vergara Vicuña was published in 1948 at which time he was President of the Bolivian Development Corporation.

Paz Estenssoro as his Minister of Finance. The party were energetic in organizing a repressive regime with purges of their political opponents, declared war on the Axis powers and initiated social legislation calculated to win them the support of the mine-workers, at that time the only even partially organized element in the native population. Their social and economic aims, however, aroused the opposition of the powerful mining interests owned by the Patiño, Hochschild and Aramayo groups and alienated many of the smaller mine owners. In 1946 the regime was terminated by a brief but bloody revolt of the populace of La Paz, which had the appearance of being a spontaneous and unorganized uprising against an oppressive administration. Unlike most previous Presidents Villaroel did not escape to safety but was shot and his corpse hanged from a lamp-post outside the Presidential Palace in the Plaza Mayor by the angry mob. Attempts by his supporters in exile and their friends at home to represent him as a popular martyr made little headway until the party came back to power in 1952.

From 1947 the country was governed by a constitutional alliance of the centre, first under Dr Enrique Hertzog and then on his retirement under his Vice-President Mamerto Urriolagoitia. The intervening years were marked by continual changes of Cabinet and the Government was never able to achieve either a satisfactory majority or a stable coalition. The regime lived in constant dread of a coup from the exiled Villaroel party, which was actively intriguing from Buenos Aires under the leadership of Víctor Paz Estenssoro, and was determined to stage a come-back. It was harassed also by intrigues of the pseudo-communist party of the left, the Partido de Izquierda Revolucionario (PIR), and was always aware that a temporary alliance between the two oppositions would be sufficient to upset its precarious tenure. In addition the task of the administration was made more difficult by pressure from the Workers' Syndicates organized under the mine-workers' leader Juan Lechín Oquendo, whose political affiliations were not clearly defined.

That the Government fears were not unfounded was shown in August 1949 when the MNR made its first overt bid to oust the Hertzog regime by armed insurrection. In the past a political revolution in Bolivia had not been linked with social revolution as was the case with the French and Russian revolutions, but had usually been restricted to a limited, if sometimes bloodthirsty, conflict between rival aspirants to power. Since the bitterly fought Indian insurrection of Tupac Amaru in 1781 the terror of a native uprising had remained a powerful unconfessed deterrent in the minds of white Bolivians. Where the vast majority of the population was politically and socially apathetic, unmoved by the ambitions which actuated the dominant whites, civil fighting had not corresponded to a revolt of 'oppressed' classes against 'exploiting' classes and the idea of revolution had become dissociated from that of civil war, so that while to the European mind the two are closely linked this was no longer so in Bolivia. A revolution in Bolivia had come to mean a fairly gentlemanly and humane adjustment of power among the few *políticos* who happened to control or not to control the destinies of the country at the time, or at the most a short and limited conflict. But from the time of Colonel Busch the MNR had made it part of their policy to arouse the miners, and perhaps the rest of the Indian population, to political consciousness and to rule the country in reliance on their support and possibly in their interest. The emergence of such a policy at a time when Bolivia had been dependent as never before on the native population for fighting power in the war with Paraguay was psychologically understandable. And in accordance with it the insurrection of 1949, directed from Buenos Aires, was carefully planned on the idea of a civil war, the people of the country against the army, the provinces against the capital, and drew its main strength from organized risings in the mining centres.

The eastern provinces fell rapidly, including the oil centre of Camiri, and by a series of simultaneous and well planned coups the revolutionaries gained control in most of the mining centres, in several of which bitter fighting took place before peace was restored.[1] The attempt failed owing to psychological rather than strategic factors. The Bolivian mine-worker, little critical of political promises, is not difficult to rouse to opposition against whatever Government is in power. He enjoys the relaxation of dynamiting and looting in his home town. But a revolution must be short. If it is not successful in three days, he already begins to wonder what is wrong. If it is not successful in a week, he is convinced that it has failed—and he is no heroic supporter of lost causes. The rising was put down and peace restored within a fortnight to three weeks and its suppression established the regime

[1] The writer was caught by this revolution in the mining centre of Potosí where he was able to observe much of its progress and technique at close quarters.

more firmly, at least to superficial appearances, than at any other period in its career.

Dr Hertzog suffered a breakdown in August 1949 and Mamerto Urriolagoitia, who as Vice-President had shown firmness in quelling the revolution of the MNR, took over the Presidency formally in October. The Urriolagoitia like the Hertzog administration consisted of a loose alliance of splinter parties mostly deriving from groups of the centre representing the landed, professional and official classes. As had been the case with the Hertzog administration, its radical weakness lay in its lack of unity and in the continual jockeying for position among the component groups. During 1950 it weathered a succession of Cabinet crises arising partly from political rivalries and partly from economic causes which were rendered more acute by the fall in the price of tin which followed the devaluation of sterling in September 1949. Although this was somewhat relieved when the Korean War produced an upward trend in the price from June 1950, exports for the year showed a marked decline, while the cost of living in La Paz rose by 35·8 per cent between December 1949 and December 1950. Thus 1950 was a year of rising prices, political restiveness and growing disaffection among the labouring classes—a state of things by no means unusual in Bolivian history—and the Presidential elections of 1951 took place in an atmosphere of general unease.

The result of the elections came as a shock to the country. The more moderate parties of the centre upon whom the Government had relied for its support counted securely on the great majority of the electorate, which was limited to the 200,000 or so of the population who are literate. United under one candidate the moderates would have been unassailable. But their natural adherents were divided and confused by the appearance of a number of different candidates—in addition to the nomination of the Government party of the PURS (Republican Socialist Union Party) there were a liberal candidate, General Bilbao Rioja representing the socialist Falange and another representative of a new party. The opposition on the other hand was firmly united under the leadership of the MNR candidate, Dr Paz Estenssoro, who was permitted to contest the elections although he was in exile at the time. The Labour Movement put up no candidate of its own and the followers of Juan Lechín voted largely for Dr Paz, with the result that the latter led the polls by a substantial margin. His victory was not absolute, however, since his majority failed to achieve the 51 per cent plus one of all the votes cast which is required by Bolivian law in a direct election, and President Urriolagoitia announced that, as the Constitution required, he would submit the issue to Congress. What followed is not entirely clear. The intention of the President was, apparently, frustrated by the intransigence of the military, who were determined in no circumstances to allow the return of Dr Paz as President or to accept the MNR as governing party. On 16 May Mamerto Urriolagoitia resigned the Presidency and left the country by air, handing over the government to a Military Junta under General Ballivián, commander of the La Paz garrison. A purely military Cabinet was formed, which pledged itself to hold new elections later in the year but took no steps to implement its pledge.

The Junta Militar was handicapped both by its unconstitutional position and by difficulties arising from its failure to reach agreement on tin prices with the Reconstruction Finance Corporation or to sign a fresh contract for the sale of tin to the United States. Prices continued to rise and the accelerating inflation which had been endemic since the end of the Chaco War showed little tendency to abate, despite an ineffectual attempt to decree a freeze of wages.

THE REVOLUTION OF 1952

The end of the Junta came with unexpected swiftness and almost entirely without warning. Its overthrow was brought about by the long dreaded coalition between the MNR and the forces of organized labour. Revolution broke out in La Paz on the morning of 9 April 1952 and by the afternoon of the 11th the defending forces had been dispersed or forced to capitulate. The tide of fighting was turned by the victory of the armed mine-workers over the regular militia and as a result the mine-workers, controlled by Juan Lechín, became the most powerful armed force in the country.

The MNR leaders had now achieved the opportunity for which they had been planning since 1939, albeit at the cost of considerable commitments to the parties of the Left. A provisional Government was set up under the Presidency of Paz Estenssoro and a Cabinet was formed consisting of leading figures of the MNR movement together with three Labour Ministers, including Juan Lechín as Minister of Mines. Immediately after the revolution Lechín organized a Central Obrera Boliviana, or Workers' Union, on the Argentine model, and in the early stages at any rate the real power in the land certainly lay with the minority of the Left, if only because they had the armed and organized forces of labour with them. But the somewhat uneasy alliance between the interests of the Left and the Right which had made successful revolution possible was maintained. Final clashes of personalities were avoided and over the next ten years the MNR and their associates established themselves in the saddle at any rate more firmly than any of the preceding regimes. Paz Estenssoro was the first President since Bautista Saavedra in 1925 to complete his full term of office and in the elections of 1956 his Vice-President Hernán Siles Zuazo was returned with a large majority. After serving as Ambassador at the Court of St James Paz Estenssoro again went to the polls in 1960 and was returned to the Presidency for a second term.

Since the period of relative prosperity enjoyed by Bolivia in the first quarter of the present century, its record of government has. done little to inspire confidence but has created a feeling of instability at home and abroad, more particularly as changes of government were usually accompanied by a more or less radical change in personnel, policy and legislation, especially in the fields of labour, taxation and fiscal administration. Continuity of policy has been lacking and the uncertainty of fiscal and economic legislation has deterred the investment of foreign capital which in the three decades since 1880 had done so much to assist the material development of the country and the fruitful exploitation of its resources.

Moreover the purges in the higher ranks of the civil service which have ordinarily followed each change of government made for a constant fluctuation of personnel in a land inadequately supplied in any case with trained and competent administrative talent, encouraging prolonged inefficiency and corruption where a short expectation of official life put excessive strain upon mediocre standards of honesty. Over and above acute economic troubles which will be described in more detail later, the MNR came to power in a land lamentably short of competent and usable administrative personnel at all levels of the echelon from central government to the local administration of small cantons. Bolivia was also deficient in technicians and engineers, in medical and educational personnel. Even the mining industry, upon which the economy has always depended, had relied mainly on foreign technical and engineering staff.

The country itself was in a state of turmoil and confusion, industrial stagnation and political uncertainty for which the MNR themselves had been to some extent responsible. Inflation had got out of hand even for Bolivia. (The cost-of-living index rose by about 2 per cent a month through 1952 and by about 7 per cent a month in the first half of 1953. In May 1953 the currency was devalued from Bs. 60 to Bs. 190 to the dollar.) From the time when the Government took over the mining industry tin has been mined and exported at a loss to the Exchequer. Economic collapse was staved off and the new Government kept in being only by substantial economic aid from the United States and the International Monetary Fund. In July 1953 the State Department at Washington, describing the Bolivian situation as 'very serious', announced an offer of immediate and long-term economic aid, which has been continued over subsequent years.

The MNR were carried to power by the workers' leaders and came into office committed to the nationalization of the mining industry, the emancipation of the underprivileged native population, the parcelling of the land among the native agricultural workers and the introduction of advanced social and labour legislation. Representing their movement both externally and in their internal propaganda as a profound social revolution rather than one more swing of power from this political group to that, they have pursued these ends through financial emergency and continual threat of economic collapse with a mixture of genuine idealism, political opportunism and hard-headed realism.

The nationalization of some mining enterprises and the improved social legislation will be more appropriately discussed in a later context. Here it will be sufficient to say a little about the emancipation of the indigenes and the agrarian reforms.

THE CONSTITUTION

Bolivian constitutional history has been too complicated to be more than touched upon in a work of the present size. The famous first political Constitution of Bolivia was drafted by Simón Bolívar at the request of the General Constituent Assembly and was adopted on 8 November 1826. It was a document typical of an age of political idealism but was not adapted to the conditions of the country for which it was designed and would probably have proved unworkable even if a genuine effort had been made to put its spirit into execution. There is not and has never been on

Bolivian soil a large unprivileged class ready and anxious for emancipation to the rights and duties of full citizenship. The highland Indians, who form a large majority of the population, are eager for emancipation from the burdens of taxation and from the many undoubted injustices to which they have long been subjected; they do not want either the privileges or the responsibilities of citizenship in a modern economic state. This no less than the illegal and despotic character of most of the administrations which followed Santa Cruz was the reason why the Constitution remained little more than a dead letter for the first fifty years of the Republic's history. Much experimentation and adaptation were necessary before the modified Constitution of 1880, which maintained itself until 1931, was re-introduced in 1936, and after further revision in 1938 and 1945 persisted until 1951.

The executive power is vested in a President, who is elected by popular vote for a period of four years, and is exercised through the Ministers of State. The legislative power is vested in a bicameral National Congress consisting of a Chamber of Deputies and a Chamber of Senators, also elected by vote of the citizens, which meets theoretically in regular annual sessions. Until the electoral reform of August 1952 every male citizen over the age of twenty-one if single, or eighteen if married, who was literate in the Spanish language and had an income of not less than 200 Bolivianos a year,[1] had the right and the duty to vote. These are the main features in a Constitution of whose democratic character Bolivians have always been inordinately proud, as more recently they have pointed with pride to the advanced and enlightened spirit of their social legislation. But Bolivia is not the only South American country where one must make allowance for a wide gap between principle and practice. The Constitution breathed the spirit of enlightened democracy, yet two-thirds of the population have lived in a state of virtual serfdom and acute impoverishment, having no practical voice in the management of the country. Bolivia had universal suffrage and the condition of literacy was interpreted to demand no more than the ability to sign one's name in Spanish. Yet with a population of 3½ million the electoral roll in 1951 numbered only 200,000, of whom not more than 50 per cent exercised the right to vote which was legally obligatory on all competent citizens.

By a Decree of 2 August 1952 the new Government granted

[1] About £1 at the official rate of exchange in 1949.

universal suffrage without restrictions of literacy or income, thus giving legal effect to its programme of emancipation. The measure had considerable value for propaganda. Its theoretical effect was to shift the balance of power from the small 'white' minority which had traditionally ruled the country to the large Indian majority. But since the vast majority of the native population remain politically uneducated and apathetic, in practice it meant an increment of power in the hands of those leaders who from time to time control the small groups of organized native labour. Before it can have any profound social significance theoretical emancipation must be combined with a far-reaching campaign of political and social re-education. Nevertheless, looked at negatively, the abrogation of the restrictions of income and literacy with the consequent abrupt opening of the franchise to a large native majority, of whom only a relatively few who are industrially employed are interested to understand its uses, and they only as it affects their own immediate profit, introduced new and hitherto unprecedented problems of adjustment.

Other modifications of the Electoral Law were criticized in the country as being calculated to create a bias in favour of the party in power and at the beginning of 1963 two opposition parties, the Falange and PRA (Authentic Revolutionary Party), acting in conjunction, announced their intention to refrain from the 1964 elections in consequence.

AGRARIAN REFORM

On 2 August 1953 a comprehensive decree was promulgated in La Paz limiting the extent of individual holdings of land in private or collective ownership and granting powers for the redistribution of all lands held in excess of these limits. The intention of the decree was to abolish the large estates, break up *latifundia* and reduce holdings roughly to the amount of land which could be maintained in production by the owner and his family according to type and region. Excess holdings were to be redistributed, every Bolivian of either sex over the age of eighteen who was desirous of devoting himself to agriculture being made eligible for a grant of land. Indians settled on large estates on a wage or service basis were to become small proprietors and communal lands were to be restored to the Indian agricultural communities. Agricultural co-operatives were to be encouraged. Excess lands, waste lands, and lands in unpopulated territories were to revert to the state. Expropriated landowners were to be compensated at current prices by Agrarian Reform bonds carrying a 2 per cent non-capitalizable interest for a term of twenty-five years. The social and political importance of the decree was represented as a restoration to the Indian land-workers of their ancient title in the land they worked, and its object was held out in an intensive propaganda campaign to be to stimulate agricultural production, right the injustices suffered in the past by the indigenous population, encourage a return to the land and raise the status of the Indian to a full and responsible member of a modern state.

It is now very generally admitted that the conditions of land tenure have formed one of the darkest blots on Spanish-American history and were in some measure responsible for the progressive decline of agriculture on the Peruvian and Bolivian Altiplano. From the earliest days of the Conquest and throughout the Colonial period—and most particularly in Bolivia—agriculture was sacrificed to mining. The Indians were expropriated from the land which was once theirs, driven to subsist at starvation level on the most unfertile tracts of the unfertile plateau or forced to labour in conditions of serfdom on the estates of those who had despoiled them. The elaborate systems of irrigation and terracing, and the organization of collective labour for stone-clearing, sowing and harvesting, were disrupted and fell into decay, so that from being under the Incas one of the more advanced agricultural technologies which the world had known, Bolivian agriculture became, and has remained to this day, backward, primitive and hand-to-mouth. The system of planned surpluses which was fostered under the Inca empire has never again been realized and the native farmers have been defenceless against the periodic years of drought.

The MNR party came to office pledged to restore the land to those who work it and went ahead with the reform despite the critical need for a maximum of home production at a time when the country was already reliant on external aid in order to keep afloat. It is unnecessary to doubt that this reform was motivated by genuine idealism, by the desire to right the wrongs of the past and to integrate the Indian peasantry more closely into the fabric of the state. It was also a particularly astute political move. Every highland Indian is at heart and by long tradition a farmer, whether or not he takes on seasonal work at the mines, and one of his most cherished desires is for individual or collective ownership of the land which he works. Nothing could conduce better to secure the position of a Government which depends on Indian support than the popularity of this measure. It also fitted the 'image' of itself which the new Government was creating for external consumption as the protagonist of a social revolution based on the emancipation and integration of the hitherto exploited native population.

The economic aspects of the reform are more dubious. As will be seen from the table on p. 134, the years following the Agrarian Decree show a decline in production. The recovery in 1958 and onwards is thought to be due to the effect of new projects started in the Santa Cruz area rather than to a true revival of the traditional agriculture of the Altiplano—but even in 1958 agricultural imports were half the total imports. A temporary decline in production is usually expected to follow a redistribution of land. But in Bolivia conditions were exceptional. In pre-Colonial times, as has been said, when the Altiplano and the high valleys supported a flourishing agriculturally based population, they were cultivated by highly skilled, traditional techniques of terracing and irrigation involving complex social institutions of collective ownership and operation. These disappeared with the Spanish invasion and not even the most optimistic could regard their restoration as other than visionary. The Junta Nacional de Planeamiento, writing in 1961, recognized that the redistribution of the land had not been successful in its economic purpose of stemming the decline and stimulating a revival of production. They pointed out that owing to lack of financial resources the restoration of the Indian to ownership of his land had not been accompanied by provision of a minimum capital in stock and agricultural implements necessary to enable him to render his holding productive of surpluses. The ancient system of collective ownership and operation had survived only here and there, although the nature of Altiplano cultivation is such that collectivization of labour is essential to it. And finally, the parcelling into very small holdings militated against any increase of mechanization even if the finance for this were to become available.[1]

[1] There were also many technical defects and other shortcomings in the actual process of land distribution. The Junta sums up the matter in the following words (*Planeamiento*, Sept. 1961, p. 148): 'The process itself of Agrarian Reform appears to evidence an important weakness in that the distribution of lands has not been linked—or only to an insufficient extent—with other factors which would facilitate its consolidation from a technical and economic point of view. Too little attention has also been paid to the establishment of proper titles

There is, moreover, very real doubt whether intensive cultivation of the highlands by modern mechanized methods could ever become financially worth while. For the staples of the Altiplano are potatoes, *quinoa* and a little barley. It is not tolerant of most of the crops which are needed in greater abundance in order to reduce Bolivia's need of imports. For this, diversification is necessary with increased exploitation of the high valleys of Cochabamba, Chuquisaca and Tarija, and more especially Santa Cruz and the Oriente. Yet any large-scale projects of exploitation in the lowlands—besides being dependent on communications—require an influx of new population into the unpopulated development areas. And the only extensive reservoir of population upon which the Bolivian Government can hope to draw is that constituted by the Aymara, and to a less extent the Quechua, Indians of the highlands. But these are not merely essentially a highland race; they are rooted in the Altiplano itself by long tradition and strong bonds of sentiment. They are conservative by habit and temperament and desire. They are resistant to transplantation and, except for the Yungas, they will not spontaneously abandon the highlands to which they are physiologically adapted for more tempting and fertile lands at lower altitudes in the east. When they have been settled there under government colonization schemes they have generally proved less adaptable than Europeans or Japanese to the climatic conditions and the different agricultural demands and living con-

---

to the lands distributed and to the criteria for fixing the size of the new freeholds.

'The statements contained in the foregoing paragraph are particularly true of the regions of the Altiplano and the valleys.

'The acute problem of too small holdings which already existed in the so-called Indian communes was exacerbated by the Agrarian Reform in consequence of the parcelling up of many haciendas into insufficiently large lots. The problem became more serious because of the failure to make at the same time any effective effort to encourage co-operative labour or to regroup into a single holding the many small scattered morsels of land assigned to a single freeholder. Furthermore no vigorous action was taken to improve the systems of remuneration for agricultural labour employed on small holdings.

'This atomization of ownership could well prove a serious obstacle to the mechanization of agriculture. The lack of technical orientation among the owners of tiny holdings is a factor tending to lower output and may even lead to destruction of the soil itself by natural erosion and washing away. . .' It is now realized in Bolivia itself that this reform was put through hastily, inefficiently and with inadequate advance planning. Yet it must be admitted that had it not been so stampeded through on the crest of the wave, it might never have taken place at all.

ditions of the Oriente. Moreover the restoration to the Indians of their title to the land in the highlands has worked counter to the propaganda whose object was to induce them to migrate eastwards and take up land in the empty lowland development districts. Instead it has increased their reluctance to move and confirmed their attachment to the Altiplano.

Since 1953, but apparently unconnected with the government programme of agrarian reform and colonization schemes, two movements among the Indian population have taken place. There has been an increased influx among the younger age-groups into the towns, where they are available for factory labour. A new Indian settlement of some 25,000 has sprung up at the Alto above the valley of La Paz. And there has been a spontaneous extension of the Indian population of the Yungas in the direction of Rurrenabaque and the river Beni in advance of the road which is being slowly built from La Paz through the Yungas towards the Beni.[1]

Bolivian agriculture on the Altiplano is still in the rudimentary 'scratch and tickle' stage with techniques surviving essentially unchanged from a thousand years ago. Mechanization and scientific farming hardly exist. The only farm implements of the highland Indian are a home-made wooden plough with a metal blade for the fortunate, and a stick tipped with stone which he uses as a clodbreaker. Animals are rarely used for traction and wheeled vehicles still less frequently. Irrigation is lamentably inadequate and fertilizers an exception. The Indian has inherited a long tradition of collective labour, which is necessary to maintain even the minor works of irrigation that survive, for the maintenance of terracing and for the annual clearance of the soil from stones. Where this has broken down farming continues under difficulties, for single-handed farming on the Altiplano is not a practicable proposition. Everywhere one still sees the relics of ancient terracing up the sides of the hills, showing the ampler extension of cultivation in ancient times over areas which have now been abandoned. The Bolivian native agriculturalist is psychologically and by tradition a very different being from the peasant farmer of Europe; and he is faced with natural difficulties such as the European peasant would find it hard to imagine. Writing in 1947, Jorge Pando Gutiérrez said: 'distribution of the land to the natives, which would seem the most just, unless it were preceded by an adequate agricultural education, would be prejudicial even to the Indians themselves'. But no

[1] See above, p. 46.

less important than education is the supply of essential implements and stock when the former tenant-farmer becomes a smallholder and is no longer able to look to the *patrón* for the necessary tools of his trade.

The distribution of lands under the Agrarian Reform Decrees has proceeded irregularly and without uniformity or indeed impartiality, serving too often as an instrument with which to bludgeon those who failed to sympathize with the regime. And just as in the forties efforts to reform agricultural procedures were frustrated by lack of financial means, so the most serious handicap to increased production from 1953 onwards may have been the failure to equip the smallholder with the capital he requires.

EDUCATION

Neither the emancipation nor the agrarian reform could be expected to bear fruit without an extensive programme of re-education. Bolivia has a population between 70 and 80 per cent of which is Indian or near-Indian, a solid block living their own way of life by their own traditions, with little national consciousness (they think of themselves as Indians but not as Bolivians) and little amenable to the ordinary incentives of a modern economic state. Less than 40 per cent of the population speak Spanish, the official language of the country. Illiteracy stands at 70 per cent.

On the Altiplano the Indian farmer has for many generations acquired a reluctance for producing agricultural surpluses for the markets of the towns, and to a rather lesser degree a similar attitude (except for coca production) pertains in the Yungas. Having reduced his needs to a minimum, the Indian makes for himself practically everything he requires: his house, his clothes, his furniture and his implements. His only luxuries are drink and coca. Being thus virtually self-sufficient, he plans his operations within the limits of his own needs and those of his immediate family. He has little sense of social responsibility outside the Indian commune (and in the days before the Reform, to the *patrón*) and is not readily susceptible to the usual incentives which operate through the monetary economy of a modern state. He makes little demand on factory industry and still less on imported goods. The MNR Government has realized that a long and intensive educational effort is necessary in order to weld the native population into a unified and integrated society and it has given high priority in its programme to rural as well as urban education.

The Government has taken this task seriously. After allowing for the increase in State Obligations, the vote for Education was proportionably even higher by 1960 than it had been in the Budgets for the years 1945–51. But the task is a colossal one and a vast force of apathy and resistance remains to be overcome. A high proportion of the rural Indian communities are so scattered and so small that it is impracticable to provide teachers and schools for more than a small percentage of centres, while the presumed advantages of learning Spanish are seldom sufficient inducement to encourage school attendance from children who according to Indian tradition are already of an age to be gainfully employed on the land. The Inca and Pre-Inca cultures had no written language and possibly for this reason the Indians do not take easily to reading or writing. The elementary hygiene and domestic science offered to the girl pupils in rural establishments have no great appeal for Indian children brought up, and expecting, to live according to conflicting beliefs in an incompatible environment, and the rudimentary ideas of modern agriculture and craftsmanship mean little to boys whose main need is capital and equipment. The extreme shortage of trained teachers fluent in the Indian languages, of educational establishments and of equipment of all kinds is beyond the resources of the country quickly to remedy.

In view of all this it seems doubtful whether the educational achievements are doing more than keep pace with the growth of population. The Junta Nacional de Planeamiento speaks of the impossibility of obtaining accurate statistics of school attendance, but accepts the estimate of UNESCO that in 1960 facilities for primary education in urban centres fell short by 12,000 children. In the five years 1956–60 the very high and increasing proportion of those who register for primary education and fail to complete the course (24 per cent in 1956 and 72 per cent in 1960) reveal, in the words of the Junta, 'the social ineffectiveness of the primary education, showing that neither by society nor by the family is its value sufficiently esteemed, since no effort is made either by the parents or the pupils themselves to keep them at school for a longer time and that they apparently do not find in it adequate incentive to complete the primary grade' (*Planeamiento*, Sept. 1961, p. 255). The figures for failure to complete the course of secondary education are even higher, reaching in 1960 94 per cent of those who registered for it. The following figures (which are not entirely consistent with themselves or with those accepted by the Junta de Planeamiento in 1961) are taken from the *Boletín Estadístico* of 1962 published by the Ministry of Finance and Statistics and give some indication of the range of absolute increases in the years from 1950 to 1960.

Teachers

	Total	Basic	Primary	Secondary
1951	9,498	3,687	4,486	1,325
1956	14,642	5,751	6,827	2,064
1960	19,904	6,605	7,637	2,662

Educational Establishments

	Total	Controlled by	
		Min. Education	Min. Rural Affairs
1951	3,418	728	2,690
1956	5,438	1,176	4,262
1960	6,306	1,444	4,862

Schools, Teaching Staff, and Pupils

	Schools	Teachers	Pupils (registered)
1951	3,418	10,433	246,530
1956	5,438	16,083	391,073
1960	6,306	18,430	503,736

By and large even the most optimistic assessment could hardly claim that the education programme since 1952 has wrought any absolute improvement in an increasing population. This is borne out by the estimates of illiteracy which in the census of 1950 were put at 68·9 per cent of persons over six years of age and in 1961 were assessed at 66·8 per cent (on the assumption that all those who had registered for primary education had in fact overcome illiteracy). The Ten Year Plan is based on the same assumption. It is, moreover, a factor of which account must be taken that the mere conquest of illiteracy and the dissemination of a knowledge of Spanish may not of themselves automatically solve the difficulties of integrating the Indian population fully into the new planned society.

THE TEN YEAR PLAN

Despite intensive propaganda and advanced social legislation the MNR regime has not been enthusiastically acclaimed in neighbouring countries as a spontaneous manifestation of national spirit or a popular social revolution. It is difficult to escape the impression that there was a tinge of the doctrinaire about the movement. It was not entirely a response to popular demand in so far as part of the programme of reform—and indeed a fundamental and essential part from the first—has consisted in the need to create the popular demand which, in the opinion at any rate of the leaders, ought to have been there. The Aymara and Quechuan Indian knows himself to be an Indian but does not feel himself to be a Bolivian or even want to feel that. His yearnings and aspirations need still to be guided in that direction. The principles which inspired the Government in 1952 were largely those which had been worked out by men who had spent the greater part of the last ten years in exile from their country. Many of their measures were received with enthusiasm in the early years but over the longer period they have not met with a lasting readiness to put up with material sacrifices in the present for the sake of social reconstruction or ideals realizable only in a distant future. Rather they have been compelled by persistent and clamorous demand to pander to the organized workers far beyond the limits which the financial position of the economy could justify. The difficulties of economic depression and galloping inflation from 1953 onwards were exacerbated by continuous industrial and political unrest. Strikes, agitation, absenteeism and riot became the order of the day and a very widespread feeling of apathetic despondency has supervened over the buoyant optimism of the early years. However admirable one may judge their aspirations to be, it is for their own convictions—their own blueprint of a new Bolivia—not through a spontaneous upsurge of popular enthusiasm that the MNR leaders have been content to turn their country into an economic dependency of the United States.

By a decree of 11 October 1960 President Víctor Paz Estenssoro brought into being the Junta Nacional de Planeamiento which, with Juan Lechín as its President, was to study the utilization of the country's economic resources and draw up a plan for social and economic development. The Junta was able to avail itself of work previously done in the same sphere by the Comisión Nacional de Coordinación y Planeamiento, whose place it took, and its findings were to some extent a summation or culmination of the many technical studies which had been undertaken by foreign and Bolivian organizations. Working in co-operation with the United Nations Advisory Group, combining members of the Economic Committee for Latin America (ECLA or CEPAL), the Technical Assistance Organization of the United States and FAO, the Junta produced in 1961 a Ten Year Plan which was sponsored by the Government. The verdict of history on the MNR movement must depend upon the measure of success with which this Plan, which relies heavily on foreign assistance both financial and technical,[1] is realized over the next decade.

THE BENI[2]

It was in the early stages of the conquest of the New World that Spanish militant explorers first heard from the native tribes on the fringes of Central America whispered stories of a mysterious people in the south whose cities were paved and palaced in solid gold and of a kingdom ruled over by a mighty priest-king called El Dorado —the Gilded Man—because his body was covered in powdered gold. There is no reasonable doubt that these rumours were garbled accounts of the Incas, the fame of whose empire in the Andes had reverberated far beyond the limits of the ordered civilization they had built up and was celebrated among the barbarous peoples of the fringe in exaggerated stories of marvel and wonder. It was these stories which lured the Conquistadores to push south from Panama in their restless endeavour to penetrate ever deeper into the blind wastes of an unknown world, adding to the ruthless rape of a continent the accolade of great adventure. Having set themselves in the seat of the Inca and seized the Inca gold, they had attained their goal. But they did not recognize it for the goal they sought and, with the reality already within their grasp, they still sought the illusion. For the legend of El Dorado persisted—and has persisted to this day—luring countless intrepid romantics to

[1] The total foreign aid needed is estimated at $370 million.
[2] The history of the Beni stands somewhat apart from the main course of Bolivian history. The earlier history is not readily accessible elsewhere and has for that reason been treated somewhat more fully.

their death in the pathless jungles and fevered swamps of the Amazon valley, searching for the rumoured land of gold. One of the most persistent rumours has centred about the mysterious lake Guatavita, high in the mountains behind Santa Fé de Bogotá, into whose waters offerings of gold were cast to the god. From Gonzalo Ximenes de Quesada who sought to recover the secret in 1569, roasting the local Chibcha chieftain over a slow fire, to the British company which in 1913 sank £15,000 in a vain attempt to drain the lake, Guatavita has proved a will-o'-the-wisp to many sanguine hopes and there is a long list of those who perished in the forests beyond, seeking the country where the legendary gold of Guatavita had its origin. No less tempting proved the fabulous country of Manoa or Omoa, located in the unexplored hinterland of the river Orinoco near the mythical lake Parima, which was marked in maps of South America on the borders of Venezuela and Guiana until its existence was disproved by von Humboldt. Among the most famous expeditions in search of El Dorado of the Omaguas, as it was called, was that of Diego de Ortaz in 1537. One of his men, a certain Juan Martínez, who became separated from his companions, re-appeared many years later from the jungle, exhausted and emaciated, and swore on his deathbed that he had been entertained by El Dorado himself. In 1541–5 the expedition of Philip von Hutten followed the trail of the old German knight Georg von Speier into the country beyond the Putumayo, a river later to become infamous as the scene of some of the worst atrocities of the rubber boom. In 1595 Sir Walter Raleigh declared his faith in the legend of Omoa and hoped to renew the search. All the expeditions into the Amazonian jungle—and they were many—came upon rumours of El Dorado among the native tribes, rumours which directed them always a little farther on. What they did not realize was that these rumours were tribal lore handed down from generation to generation which had their origin in the fame of the great empire of the Incas at Cuzco—whence the expeditions of discovery had come. Though they did not know it, they were being directed back to their point of departure.

In a class of their own belong the rumours of El Dorado of Paititi, an immensely wealthy country situated east of the Cordillera of Charcas near the source of the river Paraguay and ruled over by a great and powerful monarch, El Gran Moxo—the *Musu* of the Inca Quechuas. Stories of El Gran Paititi—the Great Tiger Lord—came to Spanish ears also in Paraguay and La Plata and between 1539 and 1630 many expeditions set out both eastwards from the Andes and to the north-west from Paraguay to discover and annex it. The goal they sought was the present Department of the Beni in eastern Bolivia, part of which is still known as Mojos. But the conception of this region as a land of gold, the illusory El Dorado, was again but a reflection of the traditions of Inca splendour which survived among the people of the region and from the Beni filtered through to the tribes of Chiquitos and the Chaco and thence to the Spanish in Paraguay. Not unnaturally the latter located the marvellous El Dorado of their dreams at the source of the rumour, in Mojos, although in fact the El Dorado of which the peoples of Mojos told was the El Dorado of Cuzco. In 1553 Núñez Cabeza de Vaca despatched a certain Hernando de Ribera up the Paraguay and in the marshes of Xaragues at the entrance to Chiquitos the latter came across Inca trade goods among the village headmen and brought back the usual stories of great and powerful peoples to the north-west, a land of gold, a country of Amazons, a race of white Indians, and all the customary paraphernalia of the El Dorado legend. In 1580 Lorenzo de Figueroa reached the country of Mojos from Chuquisaca and his lieutenant Juan Torres de Palomina sailed the river Guapay. In 1617 and 1624 Gonzalo de Solis de Holguín fitted out military expeditions from Chuquisaca into the plains of Mojos but abandoned the enterprise under the conviction that the country was not worth the effort required in its conquest. In fact the Beni was never conquered by arms, either by the Incas or by the Spanish. Its ultimate incorporation into the Spanish Colony of Peru was due to the more peaceful penetration of the Jesuit missionaries.

In the early years of the seventeenth century the peoples of Mojos began to establish contacts with the Chiriguani tribes of the Santa Cruz region, ascending the river Guapay in their canoes to trade cotton cloth and handicrafts for the iron tools which filtered through to the Chiriguani from the Spanish. On their side the Jesuit missionaries of Santa Cruz, which had been founded in 1651 by Nuflo de Chávez, took advantage of these trading contacts to penetrate northwards into the closed region which had hitherto proved inaccessible to the military arm and about which such strange and exaggerated reports were current. They too went first as traders, taking advantage of the keen desire of the Beni peoples for iron tools to obtain for themselves the immunity and welcome which all the world over is accorded to merchants who bring new and desirable products with them. Not that penetration was easy, for the proudly independent *Mojo* opposed a fierce resistance to premature attempts at acculturization or conversion. In 1626 Father Diego Martínez was expelled and the Fathers Miguel de Urrea and Bernardo Rheus lost their lives. The first to succeed in settling on a more or less permanent basis in the Beni were the three Jesuit Fathers Pedro Marbán, Cipriano Barrace and José del Castillo in 1675. These three men established missions and planted the seeds of Christianity. According to an inscription discovered there in 1859 the earliest mission was at Loreto, founded in 1675. Trinidad, now the capital of the Beni, followed in 1687, and at the death of Father Marbán in 1718 there existed sixteen missions and the Jesuit influence in Mojos was secure.

Materially the pre-Spanish culture of the peoples who occupied the broad region between the river Guaporé and the foothills of the Cordillera belonged to what ethnologists call the 'Tropical Forest' type. They had made considerable strides along the road to civilization and were looked up to with admiration and respect by the border peoples on their fringe. They were proficient farmers in the 'slash and burn' tradition—which is to this day prevalent in a region where land is abundant and nature prolific—and cultivated yucca, groundnuts, sweet potatoes, gourds and pumpkins, bananas, papaws, sugar-cane, tobacco and cotton, besides maize which they had acquired from the highlands. And if one adds coffee and cacao, this still represents a pretty fair list of the main agricultural products of the Beni today. Their villages were characteristically large for peoples of the tropical forest area and were connected by wide causeways raised above the level of the floods, while the ditches from which they dug the soil for the embankments served as canals connecting the natural waterways. The Spaniards who first saw the country in the expedition of Solís de Holguín expressed amazement at the size of their plantations and at the broad roads which connected their settlements. In all kinds of handicraft the peoples of Mojos especially excelled. Through the Sub-Andean tribes of the Mosetenes and the Chunchos they maintained a trade with the Incas, exchanging cotton piece goods, beautiful mosaics of coloured feathers and basketry for metal implements. This natural aptitude was fostered by the Jesuits[1] and

[1] Alfred Metraux says of them: 'In their well organized missions the natives rapidly assimilated European culture and were free from exploitation and want.

G   85

for a short period the products of the Beni were famous in the courts of Europe. Even in the middle of the nineteenth century Alcides d'Orbigny said of them: 'Today the people of Mojo are, without manner of doubt, the most industrious and the cleverest of all the indigenes of Upper Peru, both for their woven textiles and for the countless handicrafts which they produce.'[1] And now nothing of this survives. There are now no roads in the Beni; the canals and the causeways have disappeared. The native peoples themselves are reduced to a few sorry communities on the fringes of the white settlements or to tribes who have resisted acculturization and reverted to barbarism. Their handicrafts are gone, the old Jesuit missions disrupted, and the whole Beni languishes of inanition.

From the time of the expulsion of the Jesuits in 1767 began a period, which is not yet ended, of wasteful and senseless despoliation—senseless because no effort was made to protect or conserve the natural and human resources which have made the region so rich for exploitation for so long. It is a sad record of maladministration, irresponsibility and corruption which it would be profitless to recount in detail. Bolivian Governments have treated the Beni as a source of revenue to be squeezed for the benefit of the Altiplano—an attitude which is not yet obsolete—and a private Siberia to which political 'criminals' were relegated. It was abandoned to the wasteful and destructive depredations of merchants and underpaid minor officials and not even ordinary precautions were effectively taken to keep alive the goose which laid so many golden eggs. The human resources, which as has been shown were of no mean material, were ravaged with the same thoughtless disregard for the future with which the material resources were plundered. It is significant that, although the natives of all Bolivia obtained theoretical independence at the foundation of the Republic, in 1842 President Ballivián promulgated a decree granting

---

These missions may well serve as examples of reasonable and humane colonization, for in spirit they were far ahead of their time.' (*Handbook of South American Indians*, v. 645.) Under the Jesuits were developed flourishing local industries of bronze casting, gold and silver work, tanning and leather work, wood-carving, hats which in their day were as famous as those of Guayaquil today, cotton textiles, basketry and feather embroideries. They even introduced printing presses for the dissemination of their literature. We are told that the products of the Province were 'cotton, cacao, beeswax, tamarind, vanilla, coffee, tobacco, sugar, fats and vegetable oils'.

[1] *Voyage dans l'Amérique méridionale* (1844).

citizenship for the first time to the natives of Mojos: 'Because', as he says in the Preamble, 'the missions of the Province of Mojos are reduced to a deplorable condition of slavery, oppression and misery, while labour and services beyond their powers of endurance are exacted of them, even from the women.'[1] This was the beginning of a long line of similar pronouncements, none of which had the slightest influence on practice. Under the lash of the whip the unfortunate Mojenos were herded into servitude outside—the '*camba*' slave traffic has been but a short time dead—or were compelled to work under slave conditions at home. Their skill at weaving and their ability as carriers and rowers were exploited with utter disregard for the preservation of the race. In general the Beni peoples have proved submissive and easily manageable, patient under suffering and abuse, indolent but capable of immense physical endurance under pressure. In 1881 they were at last driven to hopeless rebellion under a messiah, Andrés Guayacho, but for the most part they preferred to suffer in silence to the point of extinction or to flee far from their oppressors into the wildernesses of the jungle. They have lacked the element of shrewdness and prudential self-interest which a 'lower' race must possess in order to survive within a civilization created by the white man. And added to the results of human abuse their numbers have been depleted by the ravages of smallpox and influenza. In the last hundred years, when flashes of great prosperity were brought to the Beni by the quinine and the rubber trades and a new white immigration penetrated far into the untrod forests, the natives suffered only an intensification of abuse, a more frenzied ruthlessness of exploitation. Forced to work as peons on the rubber posts, to act as carriers and galley slaves in the movement of the produce which was enriching the land, their numbers were depleted with a frightening rapidity which had not been equalled before. One of the most arduous tasks to which they were subjected was rowing the heavy boats which carried the merchandise enormous distances by river. Despite the appalling conditions of the work, which even their physical powers of endurance rarely resisted for more than a few years, they yet preferred this life which brought them into contact with the forest and river and was adapted to their nomadic instincts. The frenzied search for quinine and rubber also brought under the yoke and exterminated numbers of tribes which had hitherto remained secluded in the forests and successfully

[1] Manuel Limpias Saucedo, *Los gobernadores de Mojos* (1942).

87

escaped the benefits of civilization. Even today one comes across instances of Indians engaged in heavy work on the *chacras*, cattle stations or *siringueros* for no more than a shirt, a pair of pants and a few metres of cloth for their families once a year from the *patrón*. The final blow to the native peoples of Mojos was the recruiting for the Chaco War in the nineteen-thirties, to which many went and from which few returned. The once prosperous Indian peoples survive only in small pockets, usually attached to the outskirts of the towns, and the whole region is utterly devoid of adequate supplies of common labour. For the whites have not flowed in in sufficient numbers to make up for the native peoples whom they have destroyed. Far more than the Altiplano the whole Beni is suffering from the problem of inadequate man-power.

This description is not written as a commentary upon the elementary human rights or upon the morality of cruelty in oppression, but rather as a reflection upon the results of a long continued policy of irresponsible wastage and short-sighted exploitation and to show that the serious difficulties of underpopulation from which the Beni suffers today are not a consequence of any irreparable defect in the country itself but a direct outcome of its unfortunate historical past during the last two hundred years.

The livestock of the Beni, still the main and almost the only negotiable wealth of the region, is by no means the least of the many debts it owes to the Jesuits. Horses and cattle were, of course, unknown in South America before the arrival of the Spanish. Cattle were first introduced into Mojos by the Father Cipriano Barrace who was one of the three Jesuit missionaries first to establish themselves there in 1675. Horses followed soon afterwards. The native peoples soon became expert horsemen, riding bareback without bridle or bit and using the lasso with the skill of the *gaucho*. The cattle found an ideal habitat in the wide pasturelands of Mojos and rapidly increased to immense herds which have ever since roamed wild and untamed over the broad plains and forests. Even today the master bulls of the wild herds are a danger to solitary travellers on horseback, especially in the Province of Yacuma between Santa Ana and Lake Rogoaguado, where alone some half-million head of cattle are estimated. But with the expulsion of the Jesuits in 1767 the cattle and horses of the Beni were regarded as an unlimited reservoir of natural wealth, without private rights of ownership, to be exploited for the enrichment of the Government, the official and the merchant. For close on two centuries a veritable war of extermination has been conducted against them. Government officials descended like vultures upon the Beni with every encouragement to make a rapid, if not an honest, fortune at the expense of the livestock there. The Government itself discovered the convenient and pernicious recourse of paying its debts in 'letters of credit' entitling the beneficiary to so many thousand head of cattle from Mojos. The cattle were hunted and slaughtered wantonly for the hides, or the fat, and the carcasses were left to rot upon the plains. They were herded and driven on the hoof to Santa Cruz and farther south. The breeding ranches instituted by the Jesuits did not long survive their departure and for a century and a half no serious attempt has been made to preserve or improve the stock. Horses and mules were commandeered for the army and taken out by way of Todos Santos and Cochabamba or exported through Santa Cruz. In his privately printed book *Los gobernadores de Mojos* the historian Manuel Limpias Saucedo describes this short-sighted policy of abuse as follows:

The cattle which grazed in their thousands on the immense plains were decimated, driven in herds to Santa Cruz or slaughtered in the open country for the sake of the fat. The carcasses were abandoned in the pampa and they did not even trouble to select the beasts for slaughter. The land was depleted of cattle and horses to cover the letters of credit which the Government issued against the wealth of the Beni and to meet the demand for horses for the Army. In September 1842 Captain Luis Cecilio Moreno, bearer of a Supreme Order of 18 March, drove off through Chiquitos 1,436 horses in a single raid as remounts for the Army. In July 1840 6,000 head of cattle were levied in Loreto to found the new estate of Yotaú in Guarayos. In July 1841 the Prefect of Santa Cruz said to a subordinate: 'The Government is confident that somehow or another you will manage to relieve the embarrassment of the National Treasury by the prompt dispatch of fat cattle for consumption.'

And so it went on decade after decade, and a swarm of private merchants aped for their own account the example of wanton plunder set by the Government.

Added to the evil of these destructive depredations the twin scourges of inundation and disease have made themselves felt increasingly in the last hundred years. So severe was the combined effect of disease and military levies upon the stocks of mules and horses that about a century ago the Indians were forced to use the ox as a riding animal and, although horses are still reasonably plentiful throughout the Beni, there is no surplus now for exportation and the riding ox—*buey caballo*—is a common feature of the country. The cattle have resisted better, but their survival is still a constant struggle against the combined forces of natural and human despoliation. Although all the Beni, and all the livestock it contains, is now claimed for private ownership, many of the old practices remain and a great deal of the cattle-stealing of which the owners complain is simply a survival of the old tradition when the livestock of the Beni was considered a common reserve for the exploitation of all comers. And most of the estates are so large, often embracing vast tracts of practically virgin jungle and pampa, that few owners have any reliable knowledge of what cattle they own.[1] Until a few years ago a regular traffic of cattle-on-the-hoof maintained through Santa Cruz to Argentina. There, within the Argentine border, the cattle from Mojos were fattened up after their long trek and often re-exported by train as Argentine cattle to La Paz. The losses on the journey were terrific. For in the season of drought as much as 80 per cent of the cattle which started out from the Beni might perish of thirst or exhaustion and during the time of inundation as high a proportion might drown or die of hunger in the midst of the floods. But the profits were adequate, for the cattle cost nothing in the first place and the extent of the losses did not matter. This traffic has now virtually stopped, but the writer has had pointed out to him the fords and *barracas* by the banks of the rivers which marked the old cattle routes to the south. There is still a small illicit trade across the Brazilian frontier, both of cattle-on-the-hoof and of dried meat or *charqui*. It is estimated that about 15,000 or 20,000 head of cattle a year are exported in this way to Brazil and when the writer was in Guayaramerin in 1949 he was able to verify fairly exactly that Puerto Velho alone took about 500 head a month, most of which entered as contraband. There is also a small regular export of carcases from Trinidad and from Reyes to the Altiplano. Large projects are continually being mooted to set up cold-storage plants in the Beni in order to make Bolivia independent of imported meat from Argentina, but so long as the only means of transport is by air nothing important is likely to come of them. And perhaps this is as well, for without attention to breeding and the preservation of stock even the prolific herds of Mojos must eventually be exhausted by a regular exploitation to satisfy the consumption of a whole coun-

[1] The Land Reform decree of August 1953 demands the abolition of these large estates.

try. It is in a sense a vicious circle. To those who blame the *rancheros* of the Beni for their careless indifference to the preservation of stock and their continuance of the old policy of wanton depletion, there is the obvious answer that, as long as he has not an adequate outlet for his products, no owner can be reasonably expected to invest capital in breeding and maintenance.

Fundamentally the cattle of the Beni are of good sound stock upon which to build. They are seldom used for milch purposes but are large and well built, good meat animals, though unable to fatten on the sour pasturage. Some of the more progressive owners, such as Suárez and Solares, have experimented with good results in crossing them with the Cebu of Brazil, but this has been only on a small and amateurish scale. There is excellent material for large and scientific experiments in breeding which might turn the Beni into one of the important cattle producing areas of the world; but the economic conditions for it are so far lacking. And there are disquieting signs that the zenith of the Mojos herds is in the past and that in the last fifty years the character of the land has been changing to their detriment. The rank pasture of the areas subject to constant inundation can no longer fatten the beasts and what disease, inundation and human depredation were unable to do the gradual influence of inundation in souring the soil bids fair to achieve. Whole tracts of country which even ten or twenty years ago were thick with wild or half-wild herds are now bare, and the few production centres of the cattle trade have to go farther afield year by year for their stock. Although there are still immense areas rich with cattle, the process of decline may well have started and once started it will require heroic measures to arrest.

Benianos of Spanish descent are people capable of great exertion, with latent reserves of intrepidity and courage and unexpected powers of endurance to face the exacting demands of forest enterprise or the cattle pampas, yet little apt for a humdrum life of routine application. But there is now no incentive left, nothing upon which to harness the energy which curdles within them. The Beni is a land where Nature's unstinted prodigality offers the bare essentials of life cheaply, where it is not difficult for a man to exist without toil. But for the enormous surpluses of natural wealth there is no market outside and hence there lacks any inducement to exploit them or to produce more than enough to keep body and soul in distant touch. True, the barren austerity of the life could be made more amenable by a more active cultivation of local resources—green vegetables and fish, for example, could be made to supplement the monotonous diet of steak and rice and yucca and banana. But this does not appeal to the soul of the Spanish pioneer adventurer which still lives in the heart of every white, or near-white, *Beniano*. What they need is some high and dangerous enterprise, some stirring and grandiose project which will promise unlimited prosperity to the fortunate and a lonely and forgotten death in the depths of the jungle to the rest. But for this the opportunity is past and so their frustrated energies are sapped with futility, their mental fibres eaten through with slow necrosis. The whole people suffer from a pathological lethargy, the indolence of the tropics and something more. A black weight of frustration oppresses them and the curse of commercial stagnation rests upon the region like a mantle of doom.

The foregoing account of the Beni was written in 1952 and it needs no modification in 1962.[1] In contrast with Santa Cruz the long tradition of neglect by the central Government continued during the decade 1952–62, economic stagnation grew even more inveterate and complete, the vast areas of countryside became even more empty of population. Owing to the devaluation of the cruzeiro the small and irregular trade with Brazil in cattle, rubber and Brazil nuts was no longer profitable (since Brazil has identical products, the trade had in any case depended on exploitation of advantages in the exchange) and the small labour force still employed in these industries was thrown on the market. Disastrous floods in 1959 further depleted the countryside, destroying plant and stock irremediably, and led to an inflow of casual labour into the towns, where since there was no work available they created—perhaps for the first time in this region where it is not difficult to live off the land—a problem of idle unemployed. The price of labour fell and the cost of living rose. The cost-of-living index in Trinidad (1931 = 100) rose from 3,081 in 1950 to 416,502 at the end of 1961.[2] In 1962 a day labourer earned Bs. 10,000 while a kilo of meat cost between Bs. 3,000 and 3,500 and a kilo of rice Bs. 2,000. The cattle population is believed to have fallen to less than a million as against the 4 million (or even 8 million accord-

[1] The section as it stood in the first and second editions of this book derived from personal observation and research. What follows is necessarily based upon the reports of others—the best that is available to me.

[2] The figures as given in the *Boletín Estadístico* for 1962 are: 1950: 3,081; 1951: 4,508; 1952: 6,140; 1953: 10,572; 1954: 20,618; 1955: 37,133; 1956: 152,400; 1957: 291,455; 1958: 267,931; 1959: 339,602; 1960: 385,687; 1961: 416,502.

ing to some guesses) in the days when the Casa Suárez dominated the Beni. Experiments in colonization in the Beni (including La Loma, the former river-port of the Casa Suárez outside Trinidad) have been even less successful than in Santa Cruz and are certainly premature until a commercial outlet has been created. A number of agricultural research stations set up under the auspices of the Servicio Agrícola Interamericano justly complain of isolation and neglect from the headquarters staff of United States experts. Foreign funds made available for Bolivian economic recovery have not been utilized for setting up new enterprises in the Beni or Pando.

In contrast to this neglect a preliminary United Kingdom Agricultural Mission of Technical Assistance, reporting in 1962, was believed to have concluded that primitive and disorganized as the agricultural economy of the Oriente is at present, the Beni could make Bolivia independent in the whole range of tropical field crops and could become a beef-exporting area comparable with Argentina, Venezuela and Brazil. Yet the indifference which the Government has shown to the Beni is not entirely wanton or inexplicable. For economic and agricultural recovery, in the Beni as in Santa Cruz, must come second to communications. Projects for stepping up production are fruitless unless output can be placed in markets of consumption at economic rates. This is not possible so long as the only access to markets at home and abroad is by air freight. Road communications linking the riverine network with the Altiplano must precede purely economic measures for recovery in the Beni. As happened with Santa Cruz, only the provision of surface communications with the markets can create the conditions for the injection of new life into the Beni and Pando.

The two feasible surface links between the Oriente and the highlands would be (1) by way of the Mamoré from Trinidad, if a road were constructed from the Ichilo through the mountain tangle at Montepunco to cut the motor highway between Santa Cruz and Cochabamba; and (2) a direct link with the upper Beni if the road from La Paz through the Yungas were brought to the river Beni at a point below Rurrenabaque. Both these links are necessary. The former was investigated by the writer in the course of a river voyage from La Loma outside Trinidad up the Mamoré and the Ichilo to the Sacta and thence on to Puerto Grether, followed by an air survey of the section of mountain and forest between the Ichilo and the Cochabamba–Santa Cruz highway, across which a road of access must be constructed. (This sector has been further studied subsequently under the auspices of foreign technical missions.) He studied the latter more casually, but sufficiently to satisfy himself of its practicability, in the course of a visit to Reyes and thence by mule to Rurrenabaque on the river Beni. The construction of these roads of penetration is assigned top priority, in theory at any rate, by the Bolivian Ministry of National Economy; and in collaboration with the United States Agency for International Development (AID) a firm of consulting engineers was employed in 1962 to make preliminary studies for six roads of penetration in the Beni and Pando. How the construction is to be financed remains a problem for the future, and quick results can hardly be expected. There is, too, a danger that money and energy could be frittered away in building roads within this vast region. Throughout these wide lowlands, where areas which are not subject to seasonal flooding are covered by quick-growing tropical forest and all contours are unstable, the rivers offer the natural and most feasible means of communication. Roads are hard to construct and impossible to maintain in service. The essential is to complete the two links with the outside world which have been described. As with Santa Cruz, these would provide the necessary conditions for economic and agricultural revival. Without them even the construction of cold-storage plant for the cattle industry will continue to be abortive.

SANTA CRUZ[1]

Santa Cruz de la Sierra, one of the oldest of the Spanish colonial cities, was founded by Nuflo de Chávez from Paraguay in 1561, some thirty years after the discovery of Peru, at a site about 150 miles to the east of its present position. As it proved to be there too vulnerable to attack from the forest Indian tribes, it was trans-

[1] This note on the Santa Cruz area has been included in this revision owing to the outstanding importance of this region for the agricultural revival which has taken place there since 1954. The author has not himself visited Santa Cruz since 1948 when he went there from Puerto Grether after travelling up the Ichilo from Trinidad. In writing this note he has been particularly indebted to the following sources:

J. Colin Crossley, 'Santa Cruz at the Cross-Roads. A Study of Development in Eastern Bolivia', *Tijdschrift voor Economische en Sociale Geografie*, Aug.–Sept. 1961.

D. B. Heath, 'Commercial Agriculture and Land Reform in the Bolivian Oriente', *Inter-American Economic Affairs*, vol. 13, no. 2, 1959/60, pp. 35–45.

J. P. Cole, 'The Cochabamba–Santa Cruz Highway, Bolivia', *Geography*, vol. 43, no. 202, Nov. 1958, pp. 273–5.

ferred to its present location on the river Piray about twenty miles from the foothills of the Cordillera Real towards the end of the century or in the early years of the seventeenth century. Economically and culturally Santa Cruz was an outpost of the Province of

Machicado H. Vásquez, 'Los Caminos de Santa Cruz de la Sierra', *Revista de Historia de America,* no. 40. 1955. pp. 487–551.

O. E. Leonard, 'Santa Cruz: a Socio-economic Study of an Area in Bolivia.' U.S. Dept. of Agriculture, *Foreign Agriculture Report,* no. 31. 1948.

Ovidio Urioste, *Impresiones de viaje* (Cochabamba). An account of a Commission which left Cochabamba in 1922 to explore the Ichilo to Santa Cruz in connexion with plans for building a railway between Cochabamba and Santa Cruz.

Readers who wish to obtain a less serious background impression of the region and its people are advised to read J. Duguid, *Green Hell* (1935), an account of an exploration of the forest of Chiquitos by the author together with Señor Mamerto Urriolagoitia, later President of Bolivia; and Enrique Kempff Mercado, *Gente de Santa Cruz* (La Paz, 1946), a collection of short stories.

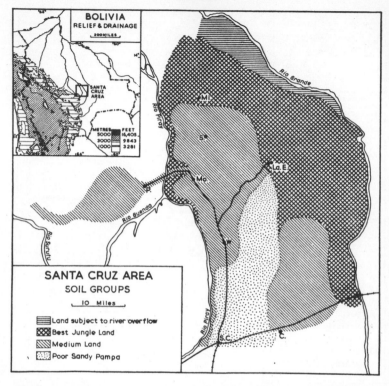

BOLIVIA
RELIEF & DRAINAGE
200 MILES

SANTA
CRUZ
AREA

METRES   FEET
5000   16,405
3000   9843
1000   3281

SANTA CRUZ AREA
SOIL GROUPS
10 Miles

Land subject to river overflow
Best Jungle Land
Medium Land
Poor Sandy Pampa

Charcas or Alto Peru, supplying the silver producing city of Potosí and Sucre, the capital of the Province, with sugar, cotton, rice and tropical fruits in return for European products imported from Spain.

Until the latter years of the nineteenth century Bolivia was more or less self-sufficient in foodstuffs and Santa Cruz supplied the internal consumption of sugar and rice with some surplus for export to Argentina and Peru, and did a flourishing trade in cotton and tropical fruits. For more than three centuries the colony prospered and its industries flourished. The decline—and it was rapid—set in when the highlands of Bolivia were connected with the outside world by railways in the latter years of the last century. For, as a result of this, everything which had been supplied by Santa Cruz could be imported more cheaply from outside the country. The only communication from Santa Cruz to the Altiplano was by

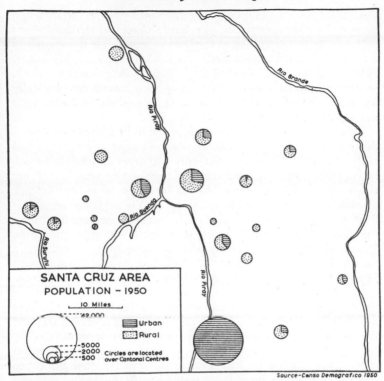

SANTA CRUZ AREA
POPULATION – 1950

10 Miles

42,000

Urban
Rural

5000
2000   Circles are located
500   over Cantonal Centres

Source–Censo Demografico 1950

way of a mule-track through the mountain tangle of the Cordilleras to Cochabamba, a route which took three to five weeks even
when conditions were favourable. The road was made passable
for lorries in the thirties. But even when I knew it during the
forties and early fifties one was lucky to get through in ten days or
a fortnight by lorry in the dry season. In the wet season no one in
his senses made the attempt. So long as all transport had been by
llama or mule Santa Cruz was the most economic supply centre
for the Altiplano. But it was unable to compete with the cheaper
railway freights when imports of consumer goods were carried to
balance the outgoings of mineral ores. Olen E. Leonard has estimated—I think reasonably—that in 1947 the freight rate for a
metric ton of goods by the road from Santa Cruz to Cochabamba
(from where they would still have to be carried on to La Paz) was
Bs. 2,860 or some 50 per cent more in the wet season. In contrast

97

the freight of a ton of sugar by rail from Mollendo on the Peruvian coast to La Paz was only Bs. 332. Santa Cruz was virtually as cut off from the rest of Bolivia as the Beni except for air transport and a trickle of native surface trade. As J. Colin Crossley has put it: 'There seems little doubt that the coming of the railway to Bolivia was for Santa Cruz the equivalent of its being transferred physically to the far side of the earth in so far as its position in the nation's markets was concerned.'[1]

From about the turn of the century the industries of Santa Cruz declined into stagnation. Cotton was no longer grown. Rice was cultivated for local consumption only and sugar only for the manufacture of alcohol. The abundance of fruits which were brought to the market in Santa Cruz could not be offered elsewhere for lack of sufficiently rapid and cheap transport. Yucca, bananas, grapefruit, oranges were consumed locally but were not exported from the Santa Cruz area in more than inconsiderable quantities. During the twenties much consideration was given to building a railway between Santa Cruz and Cochabamba and a Commission headed by the German engineer Hans Grether reported favourably on the project. Nothing came of the project since finances were lacking; but it is doubtful whether it was feasible or feasible at less than prohibitive cost. The terrain is not of the easiest and the choice between three alternative routes was never decided by the experts. At least money was not dissipated in abortive attempts as with the ill-fated La Paz–Yungas railway. Another project to link Santa Cruz by permanent way with the Argentine railhead at Embarcación was not supported by the Bolivian Government which feared lest the odium felt by the Cruceño for the *kolla*, whom he blamed for his precidament, might lead to secessionist aspirations if Santa Cruz were linked by railway with the outside before internal communications with the Altiplano existed. Thus, 'no longer an outpost of the west, Santa Cruz was left suspended in the heart of the continent.'[2] Ovidio Urioste, who visited Santa Cruz in the early twenties after having explored the Ichilo in connexion with the project for a railway between that town and Cochabamba, wrote in *Impresiones de Viaje*:

There is no greater aspiration in that town than to be linked by railway to anywhere at all. It is already feeling the suffocation which is the pre-

[1] *Tijdschrift voor Economische en Sociale Geografie*, Aug.–Sept. 1961, p. 4.
[2] Crossley, ibid.

cursor of death in spite of having before its eyes the infinite resources which Nature so abundantly bestows on it. On the whole of our journey, from Las Piedras to Santa Cruz and from there towards Cochabamba, we were impressed by the ubiquitous signs of industrial and commercial decline. There are sugar producers, for example, whose establishments are capable of producing twice or three times their actual output but who are forced to restrict work for lack of markets. The same thing can be observed in all other materials. The endless succession of plains where cattle breed untended makes one think of the enormous unutilized potential for the dairy industry alone. But as things are today whatever is produced in excess of local needs goes to waste. . . . Santa Cruz is certainly passing through a most difficult period economically. Commerce is reduced by about 80 per cent. Life is cheap, yet the market is poorly furnished even with local produce since there is little money about. . . .

He speaks of a separatist party, who maintained that 'the state of neglect in which the Oriente finds itself is due to the hatred of the kolla for the Cruceño, since the former unlike the latter has Aymara or Quechua blood. People are saying that Santa Cruz has already made too many sacrifices for Bolivia and is not disposed to make more.'

The isolation and stagnation which beset Santa Cruz in consesequence of the railway links between the Altiplano and the outside world were aggravated in the period following the Chaco War by the policy of successive Governments to subsidize the import of essentials by means of preferential rates of exchange. Santa Cruz was unable to compete even in Cochabamba with sugar and other produce imported through Peru at these preferential rates and during the forties and early fifties, even in the Santa Cruz region itself, imported goods took the place of some products upon which the prosperity of Santa Cruz had formerly rested.

Finally, in the forties the construction of a motor highway through the mountains from Santa Cruz to Cochabamba was begun by the Bolivian Development Corporation with the aid of United States financial credits. After ten years of difficulties and frustration the highway was at last completed in 1954. It has been described as 'the most important road ever built in South America'; its importance for the economic unification of Bolivia at any rate can hardly be exaggerated. Providing as it does the much needed link with the main internal markets of consumption it has made possible, together with the policy of the National Government to foster home production by restricting importation, the first steps towards a revival of the Santa Cruz region. Because of it, practical measures have become possible to rescue the Santa Cruz region from the long lethargy into which it had sunk.[1]

The Santa Cruz area is defined by Olen E. Leonard as 'that territory lying as far west of the city of Santa Cruz as the foot of the Andean mountains, as far south and east as the Rio Grande River, and some 100 miles north of Santa Cruz city or to the beginning of the old Spanish mission area.'[2] J. Colin Crossley says that it comprises 'a zone about 30 to 40 miles wide which runs north from Santa Cruz City for a distance of 50 to 60 miles.'[3] The climate is subtropical to tropical, with adequate or heavy rainfall most years but a marked dry season which may be sometimes prolonged. The vegetation is marginal between the tropical rain-forest of the Amazonian region and the drier forest of the Chaco. As has been said, its main crops are sugar, rice, cotton, yucca and fruits.

The first practical steps towards renewed exploitation of the agricultural resources of Santa Cruz were taken during the Second World War in the context of a programme of self-sufficiency launched by the Bolivian Development Corporation under the direction of General Bilbao Rioja with the object of rendering the country less reliant on agricultural imports when its purchasing power diminished after the end of the war. The first modern sugar mill began operation at La Esperanza in 1944 and some progress was made in the use of modern agricultural machinery on the larger fincas for the cultivation of rice and maize. But these advances were not followed up and were indeed stultified by the Government's import policy, since sugar from Santa Cruz was unable to compete in Bolivian markets with the artificially cheapened imported sugar, while rice, maize, cattle and fruit crops could be produced only for subsistence uses.

None the less the more far-sighted Bolivian, and foreign, planners realized that if ever the time should come when Bolivia seriously set about exploiting its own potentialities for the production of foodstuffs and other agricultural products instead of following the facile path of importation, Santa Cruz would be a key area. That time seemed to have come in 1953 when the MNR Govern-

---

[1] The railway links with Brazil and Argentina which also came into operation during the fifties (see pp. 41–42) have had much less significance for the economic revival of the region.

[2] *Bolivia* (1952), p. 129.

[3] *Tijdschrift voor Economische en Sociale Geografie*, Aug.–Sept. 1961, p. 1.

ment, faced with imminent economic collapse and the necessity
for a drastic curtailment of imports, put forward its plan for Economic Diversification, the two chief planks of which were development of the petrol industry for home consumption and export and
development of agriculture to reduce the need for importation.
The eyes of both foreign technical advisers and Bolivian planning
agencies were focused on the Santa Cruz area. The Keenleyside
Report of the United Nations Mission of Technical Assistance to
Bolivia (1951) had already drawn attention to the potentialities of
Santa Cruz. In 1954 the United States Santa Cruz Area Development Mission reported that the uncultivated lands in the area were
suitable and sufficient to produce most of the foods then being
imported. Santa Cruz is not really well adapted to provide dairy
produce and there are more suitable areas for growing wheat and
grapes and tobacco, while the Mojos and Beni are more important
cattle and timber regions. But Santa Cruz was clearly the most
promising district for reintroducing the commercial cultivation of
cotton, sugar and rice; and since 1952 the main efforts of the Inter-
american Agricultural Service, a division of the United States
Operations Mission in Bolivia, have been concentrated on this
area. An Experimental Station at Saavedra was responsible for
the introduction of higher-yielding strains of sugar-cane, rice and
maize and has investigated the use of fertilizers and insect control.
Seeds, fertilizers, insecticides and implements have been made
available at or below cost and pools of agricultural machinery for
hiring were set up at Santa Cruz and Montero.

As a result of this stimulation production increased, the larger
estates began once again to cultivate sugar and rice commercially,
oil-seeds were introduced and the output of maize, yucca and
bananas expanded to take the place of imported wheat flour. The
sugar mill at La Esperanza was enlarged, two private mills were
built and the Bolivian Development Corporation's mills with a
capacity of 18,000 tons a year went into production in 1956. Although the general picture is clear, statistics both reliable and
exact are difficult to come by.

Sugar

Relying on a statement by Siles Zuazo, Crossley gives the area
under sugar-cane in 1958 as 6,200 hectares with a production of
253,300 metric tons; total consumption of sugar was 54,300 metric
tons, of which 39,000 tons were imported and 15,300 tons home

produced. The Junta Nacional de Planeamiento says that in 1958 there were 12,000 hectares under sugar-cane, that imports of sugar were 33,500 tons and home production 15,460 tons. The figure for imports agrees with the *Boletín Estadístico* (and probably comes from the same source).

Rice

Crossley, following statements by the Bolivian Agronomists' Society, says that in 1958–9 the Santa Cruz area accounted for 13,000 out of a national total of 15,700 hectares under rice and that in 1957, when the areas were similar, Bolivia produced 15,000 tons out of a total consumption of 26,000 tons. The Junta states that in 1958 there were 19,300 hectares under rice and that local production was 13,500 tons and imports 10,425 tons. The *Boletín* gives the imports of rice for that year as 11,216 tons.

Cotton

Bolivia's cotton textile factory was opened in La Paz by Said in 1928 and has remained one of the most successful of the country's manufactories. Until the opening of the Santa Cruz–Cochabamba highway, freightage on Santa Cruz cotton would have been prohibitive, and the industry worked with imported raw materials. Cotton grows wild in Santa Cruz and was cultivated in Colonial times by the Jesuits. In 1952 a subsidiary company of Said, the Compañía Algodonera Boliviana, was formed to develop cotton cultivation in Santa Cruz on the basis of experiments and research which had been taking place for some years with a view to creating a national source of supply. By 1958 1,000 hectares were under cultivation for cotton and a ginning mill had been built. Production in that year was 300 tons, which rose to 700 tons in 1960. The output of cotton cloth had risen from 7 million metres in 1950 to 9 million metres in 1960. But imports were still running at 845 tons of raw cotton and 157 tons of cotton yarn.

Cotton is particularly exhausting to the soil and this leads on to a general problem which faces the modernization of agriculture in the lowlands of Bolivia. The traditional slash-and-burn style of cultivation is based on a system of land rotation, a four- to eight-year period of cultivation being followed by eight to ten years of reversion to brushwood. The period of reversion allows soil recovery and (the writer has been assured) the periodic burning counteracts the souring of the soil which results from stagnation after flooding. Forest lands have traditionally been preferred because the humus is deeper and richer than that of the pampa. But there is a danger that when the land is cleared by bulldozers and cultivated by mechanized methods, the humus will be destroyed and soil erosion become a serious menace. As new farming population is drafted in and the old methods and know-how die out, unless scientifically calculated techniques of crop rotation and fallow periods are introduced in their place rapid and permanent exhaustion might seriously diminish the productivity of the region.

Santa Cruz has, not surprisingly, been a favoured area for trying out projects of colonization, and there have been many experimental colonies in recent years both by internal immigration and from abroad. Colonization by highland Indians has been tried under the auspices of the Colonial Division of the Bolivian Army, the United Nations and the Directorate of Colonization of the Ministry of Agriculture. Foreign colonies that have been tried have consisted of two Mennonite groups, two colonies of Japanese settlers and a small group of Italian families. These experiments have all been on a very small scale and have not been outstandingly successful. There have been problems of capitalization and a high rate of return in the case of highland Indians who have been settled there. The question of populating the region, if more intensive development takes place, still remains to be solved.

The people of Santa Cruz pride themselves on the purity of their Spanish descent. They are capable of energy and endurance in bursts on hunting expeditions or journeys of penetration into the forest, but they do not take kindly to energetic living as a routine. They value leisure and ease above riches for their own sake. Subsistence farming with a little over and above seems natural to them and their horizon ends with a life of comfort. A half-day holiday stretches to a week and the Santa Cruz carnival is famous through the length and breadth of the land. Many of these people would be equally flattered and surprised to hear Colin Crossley's summary: 'As never before perhaps, the Santa Cruz Area is a laboratory of human experiment and the scene of pioneer endeavour.'

THE PEOPLE

Reliable demographic data are impossible to come by in Bolivia. The Civil Register came into effective operation only in 1940 and is still partial and imperfect in its scope, the native population of

Bolivia

the country districts being recalcitrant to registration. Precise statistical information is lacking in all branches and the generalizations that follow must be taken with the utmost reserve.

In 1948 the total population was estimated at 3·8 million by the Directorate of Statistics in the Ministry of Finance. The estimate was reached by calculating with an assumed percentage of increase from the last census of 1900. But the rate of increase is unconfirmed, the census of 1900 is admitted to have been unscientific and almost certainly erroneous (it gave a figure of 1,675,451 as compared with 2,326,126 in the census of 1854 and 2,133,896 in that of 1846), and exact figures are not available for the losses suffered in the wars of Acre and the Chaco, in epidemics and by depletion of territory. The census taken in 1950 surprised Bolivian experts by yielding a figure of only 3,019,031 inhabitants. But the indigenous population of the Altiplano fear and resent the census, doing all in their power to elude registration, while of the native peoples of the Oriente many are semi-nomadic and some tribes are still entirely outside the law.

The official estimates during the fifties, as shown in the *Boletín Estadístico* published by the Dirección General de Estadística y Censos of the Ministry of Finance and Statistics, are as follows (in thousands of population):

1952	1953	1954	1955	1956	1957	1958	1959	1960	1961
3,104	3,146	3,190	3,234	3,279	3,324	3,369	3,415	3,462	3,509

The average density of population is, therefore, about 9 to the square mile. But it is very unevenly distributed over the whole country, as the table opposite shows.

Although the Department of La Paz comes second to Cochabamba in density of population, it includes the large and very lightly populated Province of Caupolicán (area: 5,792 square miles; estimated population 18,307) and the not very heavily populated districts of the Yungas. By far the greatest density of population, both agricultural and industrial, is collected in the northern half of the Altiplano. According to a 1959 estimate the largest cities were La Paz (409,305), Cochabamba (99,099), Oruro (77,874), Potosí (52,278), Santa Cruz (49,305) and Sucre (44,913). Santa Cruz, however, has grown rapidly, and in 1962 its population was estimated at about 80,000. That of Trinidad, capital of the Beni, in the same year was estimated only to be of the order of 14,000, despite an influx from the depleted countryside.

Department	Area (sq. m.)	Population				
		1961 official estimate ('000)	1950 census ('000)	Density (per sq. m. estimate)	Estimated annual increase (%)	Departmental capital 1950 ('000)
La Paz	51,605	1,140·0	948·4	22·1	2·13	302
Potosí	41,298	609·2	534·4	14·1	1·88	40
Oruro	20,387	260·7	210·3	12·7	1·85	50
Cochabamba	23,030	545·9	490·5	23·7	1·38	76·5
Chuquisaca	18,140	315·4	283·9	17·4	1·48	30
Tarija	9,570	141·5	126·0	14·7	1	17
Santa Cruz	147,046	314·3	286·1	2·1	1·41	33
Beni	80,302	157·7	119·8	1·9	1·67	9·1
Pando	23,877	24·0	19·8	1·0	1·54	5
Total	415,255	3,508·7	3,019·0	8·5	1·75	562·6

Source: Official statistics.

The 1961 official estimates divide the population into 1,707,000 males and 1,802,000 females, and give the following figures for age-groups, which indicate a young and growing population with a comparatively short expectation of life.

Age	1–9	10–19	20–29	30–39	40–49	50 and over
Number	987,000	748,200	556,200	397,400	274,500	351,400

In *Planeamiento* (Sept. 1961), the official organ of the Junta Nacional de Planeamiento, the total population for 1960 is estimated at 3,824,500, of whom 2,066,600 were of working age between 15 and 64. The increase of working population since 1950 is said to have been 400,000 or roughly 25 per cent. The same source gives the expectation of life at birth as 48 for men and 50 for women.

Statistically Bolivia is predominantly a coloured state, but historically and effectively it has been ruled by a white minority in that minority's own interests. The breakdown of population is given as 52·9 per cent Indian, 32 per cent cholo (mixed blood), 14·8 per cent white, and 0·3 per cent other races. In fact, however, the ethnic distinction has become blurred at the edges, while the differentiation into indigene, cholo and white functions rather as a social stratification. There are few if any white families in highland Bolivia now without some admixture of native blood (there has been less miscegenation in the east) and the more energetic cholo families, whose members have attained wealth and standing, tend to intermarry with the whites and in the course of a few generations are absorbed into the ruling class. At the lower end of the scale the people themselves think of the distinction between Indian and cholo as social rather than racial. The Indian is a 'poor native' who lives in agricultural communities, as a depressed serf on the land or as a hanger-on and common labourer in towns or mines; a creature to be bullied and exploited by cholos and whites alike. The cholo is a near-native who has acquired an economic competence which enables him to dress in factory-made clothes, to engage in minor commerce or to occupy a minor administrative post. Dr Juan Manuel Balcazar, attempting a classification of population on a sociological basis, estimates 70 per cent Indians on the land or employed in the mines, 25 per cent cholos or urban workers, and 5 per cent literates (preferring this distinction to 'whites'). From his own observations the writer would judge that this gives a fair picture of conditions, although any such classifications obviously depend upon where one decides to draw the line between the several groups.

The rigid social distinction between these three classes plays an important part in the life and economy of the country. The Indian is effectively barred from rising to anything higher than a manual labourer. The cholo can in general expect to attain a position of authority or influence only by becoming accepted into the class of the whites. The white is by right of birth a superior. There is now, apart from irregular unions, very little admixture of classes except at the vaguely defined fringes where one merges into another. A regular marriage between an accepted white and an Indian has been a rare exception since Colonial days.

The native population of Bolivia consists mainly of the Aymara-speaking and Quechua-speaking groups descended from the peoples of the old Inca empire. The many native races of the lowlands and the Yungas are now sadly depleted and are tending to disappear without the emergence of a numerous mestizo class like the cholos of the highlands. The highland Indians are the depressed and pauperized descendants of a great civilization of the past—the only civilization which has succeeded in making the Andes genuinely habitable to man. They still look upon themselves as the true heirs to the land and regard the whites as usurpers in it. They have practical intelligence, mechanical aptitude and organizing ability of at least normal standard. The Report of the United Nations Mission of Technical Assistance finds that 'the indigenous population of Bolivia has inherited traditions of discipline, toil and endurance, as well as of skill and patience in various handicrafts.' And the following statement by William A. Neiswanger and James R. Nelson reveals balanced judgement, although many Bolivians would find difficulty in accepting it.

The human resource offers Bolivia great promise and a difficult problem. The labour force is predominantly Indian. The Indians of Bolivia possess the usual share of native intelligence, mechanical aptitude, and managerial ability found in any cross section of mankind, as has been shown where education and other opportunities for advancement have been available. The physical remains of pre-conquest Indian civilizations found in Peru and Bolivia reveal a high degree of mechanical and engineering skill. Writings of the early Spanish historians indicate a well-integrated social organization featuring an agricultural system complete with 'ever normal granaries' which provided a high degree of economic security for the Indian. This skill, specialized knowledge, and social organization passed with the coming of the Spanish, as did other less admirable aspects of the Indian culture. . . . Establishment of the Indian as an educated, responsible member of the economic community is a prerequisite for any permanent economic progress.[1]

The Andean Indian is of predominantly mongoloid type, of medium to short stature and his colouring ranges from xanthous brown in the warmer valleys to deep chocolate on the *puna*. The hair is coarse, lank and black, little subject to baldness. The men are in general without facial hair. The teeth are strong and normally free from decay. The eyesight is keen. Longevity is normal. The epicanthic fold is more or less pronounced, giving to the face its well-known mongolian appearance. The lower lip is fleshy and prominent, sagging in the middle. The Aymara is dour, taciturn and resentful; the Quechua in general more urbane and adaptable. Both groups belong to a human type capable of exceptional physical endurance and, although their strength is not extraordi-

[1] *Economic Problems of Latin America*, ed. Seymour E. Harris (1944).

nary, they are able to sustain prolonged periods of exacting labour under the severest conditions. They have a high degree of insensibility to hunger, cold, fatigue and pain. There is no other race capable of such sustained toil on so little sustenance. The women, who toil alongside the men, are strong and fertile, but infant mortality is high.[1]

It is fashionable to regard the Indian in Bolivia as backward, stupid, depraved with coca and alcoholism, inherently incapable of education and advancement, incurably wedded to his outmoded traditional ways of life and an economic deadweight in the life of the country. Such a view is not entirely without excuse. The majority of the Indians are still living entirely outside the monetary economy on a self-sufficing agricultural basis. They have been accustomed for generations to an extremely low standard of material living and cannot easily be induced to produce more than is necessary to satisfy their own basic requirements. They are not consumers of most of the products of modern mechanized industry. They have little or no ambition to better the basic pattern of their existence or to share in the amenities of modern urban civilization.[2] When they acquire a monetary surplus—as for example from coca growing in the Yungas—they squander it upon their traditional *fiestas* but do not seek to improve the general level of material comfort. They are fanatically traditional and highly resistant to acculturization—which in the past has always meant for them exploitation. Any attempt therefore to integrate the Indian population into the economic life of the community must reckon with obstinate resistance from the Indian himself.[3]

[1] The life of the Bolivian miner has been made the theme of the following novels: Roberto Leitón, *Los eternos vagabundos* (Potosí, 1939); Fernando Ramírez Velarde, *Socavones de angustia* (Cochabamba, 1947); Augusto Céspedes, *Metal del diablo* (La Paz, 1946). The last is based on the life of Simón I. Patiño, founder of the firm.

[2] The only two products of industrial civilization which have penetrated to any extent to the Indian communities are sewing machines and tin chamber pots.

[3] 'Three hundred years of severe exploitation under the Spanish colonial government, followed by slightly more than a hundred under a republican regime that has been perhaps less lenient in its protection of the rights of its indigenous population, has fostered in the Indian a deep and lasting fear and distrust of other than his own immediate fellows. Out of this fear and distrust has sprung the general belief that his only chance for any remnant of social, political and economic security lies in his ability to remain apart and among his own kind.' Olen E. Leonard, *Bolivia* (1952), p. 97. While this is certainly true, it is true also that the security the Indian looks for is security in the life that is traditional for him

The Indian is, also, fixedly attached to the land—niggardly as
it is—of the Altiplano and to his traditional agricultural communes. The ethnologist George M. McBride, who spent several
years studying the Aymaras of Bolivia, has written of them:

> The Indians not only love their land; they cling to it generation after
> generation. Most of the families have lived on their present holdings from
> time immemorial. Nothing will induce them to move. There is far more
> fertile soil in the valleys east of the Cordillera. A milder climate may be
> found in the valleys which the Indian traders visit from time to time. But
> these facts do not entice them to abandon the lands upon which their
> fathers lived. Even the inducement of good wages in the cities, at the
> mines, or upon the railways can seldom uproot these devoted farmers
> from their little plots of ground. Even if, as often happens, the land be
> absorbed by an adjoining hacienda, and passed repeatedly from one
> owner to another, the Indian remains on it, being transferred with the
> soil. Only by the use of violence and by the demolition of his humble
> cottage, the destruction of his sheep corral, and the appropriation of his
> fields, can he be driven from the place. Centuries of occupation have
> fixed him to the soil.[1]

Moreover, while the Indian in his agricultural setting lives in
accordance with a very high tradition of morality and hard work,
he rapidly degenerates, as experience has shown, when removed
from the restraining environment of his own ways and laws of life.
There is not only lack of understanding but a fundamental clash
of interests between the native agriculturalist and the economic
planner. The native desires chiefly to perpetuate the pattern of life
which he has lived for generations, to be free from interference
and taxation, and to be allowed to build up surpluses sufficient to
tide him over years of drought with security. The advantages of a
planned economy supporting an enlightened modern state have no
appeal for him and he feels no inducement to produce agricultural
surpluses in order to sustain the life of the towns and obtain for
himself the conveniences and amenities of factory-produced consumer goods. He is conservative, ignorant and unambitious.[2]

and not a security in the modern state which would involve radical changes in
his traditional way of life.

[1] *The Agrarian Indian Communities of Highland Bolivia* (1921). Today there is
also in some regions a problem of the migration of redundant Indians to the
towns for easier living and employment.

[2] The agricultural Indian of Bolivia is portrayed in the following novels among
others: Alcides Arguedas, *Raza de bronce* (La Paz, 1919); José Felipe Costas
Arguedas, *El sol se iba* (Sucre, 1944); Raul Botelho Gosálvez, *Altiplano* (Buenos

The many experts who have freely offered the Bolivians the benefit of their advice on how to develop the rich resources of their country have too often forgotten that the total population of Bolivia is equal only to the population of Buenos Aires, while the larger part lacks flexibility and cannot be deployed in new occupations. Colonization[1] in Bolivia is not a matter of planning only but a matter of compulsion, training and hope. Most of the prospects of development which might bring to Bolivia a more balanced economy lie away from the Altiplano in the east, and with the best of will and energy it must take a generation or more before the Altiplano Indians can be productively settled elsewhere or occupied successfully in other fields than their traditional modes of agriculture and mining. The cholos are intelligent, volatile and alert; far more versatile than the pure Indians; good material still to be fashioned.[2] As a class they are increasing. But they are as yet too few to provide the solution to the country's problems of man-power. In particular Bolivia is now feeling the effects of the short-sighted decimation of the native populations which once flourished in the eastern territories. Immigration is a recourse which has been often mooted and the country offers obvious scope for immigration an no inconsiderable scale. But to this there are both financial and psychological drawbacks. Bolivia is without the resources to finance immigration on a scale which might effectively increase the general productivity. Moreover, the Bolivian is not unnaturally averse from increasing the already large preponderance of the native element by encouraging an immigration of coloured people, while an immigration of white workers is foreign to his ideas. By temperament and tradition the Bolivian of Spanish descent is an employer of labour, not a labourer; and this seems to him the natural function of the white. When the writer has dis-

---

Aires, 1940); Max Mendoza L., *Sol de justitia* (La Paz, 1947); Josermo Murillo Vacareza, *Aguafuertes del Altiplano* (La Paz, 1946); Alfredo Guillén Pinto and Natty Peñaranda de Guillén Pinto, *Utama* (La Paz, 1945). *Trópico del norte* (La Paz, 1949) by Nazario Pardo Valle pictures the life of the forested province of Caupolicán.

[1] This word in Bolivia means the resettlement of natives for the exploitation of unoccupied territories within the Republic.

[2] Among the interesting novels which have been written of the cholo and his way of life are: Carlos Medinaceli, *La Chaskañawi* (La Paz, 1947), Antonio Díaz Villamil, *La niña de sus ojos* (La Paz, 1947), Víctor Hugo Villegas, *Chuño Palma* (La Paz, 1948), and Frederico Avila, *Montañas adentro* (Roma, 1953). The study by Alcides Arguedas, *Pueblo enfermo* (1917) is still of interest.

cussed immigration with intelligent Bolivians of every class and
avocation, it has always been explained to him that what the
country needs is an increase of working potential and not an increment of employers of labour.[1]

An absolute shortage of man-power and the stubborn inflexi-
bility of the native element which forms the bulk of the existing
population are likely to prove serious impediments to any large-
scale projects for overall development of natural resources. And
no ready or rapid solution seems likely to present itself for either.

The urban population may be estimated at about 20 per cent
of the whole. (The 1950 census gave 1,013,350 urban to 2,005,681
rural, but this result certainly reflected the greater difficulty of
registering the rural than the urban population.) The Junta Nacional de Planeamiento (*Planeamiento*, Sept. 1961) quotes figures
of 1,096,500 urban and 2,728,000 rural population in 1960. But
the figure for 'urban' population includes the inhabitants of all
centres of more than 2,000 inhabitants. It therefore includes very
many as urban whose occupations and way of life are rural. The
towns of Bolivia are few and with the exception of one or two
capitals of Departments are no more than large hamlets or small
market towns: their inhabitants are still predominantly rural in
character, whether officially classified as rural or not.

According to the 1950 census Bolivia had in that year a population of 1,443,000 persons between the ages of 15 and 64 and of
these about 88 per cent were actually employed. It was estimated
that something over a million persons were engaged in agriculture,
115,000 were employed in industry including workshop industry
(but excluding mining) and 228,000 in services (transport, commerce, public administration, the professions, &c.). The figure of
45,000 given for mining was almost certainly underestimated and
it is probable that between 50,000 and 60,000 were so employed
when the mines were in full production. Part of the labour em-

---

[1] Reviewing the *Report of the U.N. Mission of Technical Assistance to Bolivia*, T.
Ifor Rees, formerly H.M. Ambassador in La Paz, has said: 'In view of the scanti-
ness of Bolivia's population, it is rather surprising that the Mission should not
have devoted more attention to the question of immigration. In a paragraph on
colonization the Mission gives its opinion that for a number of reasons (which
are mentioned) efficient colonization by large numbers of European colonists
would not be possible in a short time. This is probably true enough, but taking
the long view in this case, a fresh strong infusion of European blood, such as has
stimulated the development of the Argentine, Brazil and Chile, would be an in-
estimable boon to Bolivia' *Atlante*, Jan. 1953.

ployed in the mines is seasonal, the men putting in several months of the year at the mines and devoting the rest to cultivating their agricultural holdings. According to the Junta Nacional de Planeamiento (*Planeamiento*, Mar. 1961) it is difficult to evaluate labour tendencies since 1950 partly because statistics are 'either lacking or contradictory' and partly because there appears to have been no uniform tendency of development since then. It judges, for example, that there was a significant expansion of non-agricultural labour up to 1956 but that since then it has contracted in various sectors. The labour force employed by the nationalized mining industry also increased significantly up to 1956 and was somewhat reduced after that year. As a tentative analysis of the labour population in 1959 the Junta suggested: agriculture 1,320,000 persons, mining and petroleum 75,000, manufacturing industry 55,000, workshop industry and artisans 65,000, services 245,000. Total 1,760,000.

Thus more than two-thirds of the active population are engaged in agricultural pursuits, and of these certainly more than 90 per cent are Indians or near-Indians.

The qualities of toughness, frugality and physical endurance which characterize the native element in the population are offset by a very low level of education, which reduces their value as industrial workers. The Indians and the rural cholos are completely or almost completely illiterate. The Indians speak their own languages. Aymara or Quechua, and some of them, especially those who have contacts with the towns, possess a modicum of Spanish. The cholos are bilingual and most of the highland whites speak at least one of the native languages. Spanish is the official language of the country and literacy in Spanish was until 1952 a technical qualification for the vote.[1] Roman Catholicism is the religion of the country and the natives combine a superstitious reverence for the rituals of the Christian faith with traditional survivals of their pre-Colonial cults. Religious freedom is guaranteed by law.

The standard of life of the greater part of the Bolivian people is

[1] Pando Gutiérrez (*Bolivia y el mundo*, I. 41) gives the following percentage estimates:

Spanish-speaking	43·2
Quechua-speaking	35·9 (about 1,300,000)
Aymara-speaking	25·1 (about 900,000)
Speaking native languages of the Oriente	1·5
Speaking foreign languages	0·5

low. Housing, nutrition, clothing, sanitation and hygiene among
the native classes are admittedly appalling. Bolivian labour legislation is recent and in general is more advanced than accords with
the conditions of the country; but its application in practice extends little beyond the mining centres and a few of the larger industrial undertakings. The organization of social welfare is in
principle good; but it is limited in practice to the mining and
urban populations and is rudimentary in all towns outside La
Paz. To enter into detail of either of these branches of legislation
would be to give a false picture of the conditions of the country
at large, for the gap between legislation and practice is unusually
wide. (Owing to the danger of accidents on the roads there exists
a regulation that not more than two passengers besides the driver
may travel in the cabin of a lorry, and therefore whenever a lorry
comes into sight of a control-post the third passenger clambers up
on top. And this is an analogue of Bolivian legislation as a whole:
the law is considered to be sufficiently obeyed so long as it is not
ostentatiously defied—and neglect is not defiance.)

There are no reliable data on nutrition, but it is generally and
probably correctly assumed that the native population is chronic-
ally under-nourished. In a country where some two-thirds of the
people live on the land, figures of rural consumption are necessarily difficult to secure. And even in the towns a large proportion
—and in the smaller towns a majority of the food consumed is
purchased in the native markets where records are not kept. A
survey of the consumption of average wage-earners' families in
La Paz conducted in 1949 by the Ministry of Labour gave a consumption index per adult male equivalent of about 2,000 calories
a day, which is approximately two-thirds of the generally recommended allowance. But there are very great differences between
the consumption of various classes of society and in the various
parts of the country. There is no doubt that the native worker
habitually consumes less than the wage-earner in La Paz. Balcazar
estimated the daily consumption of the Indian heavy worker at
between 1,500 and 2,000 calories with the addition of possibly
500 to 800 calories from *chicha*, a fermented drink from *quinoa* or
maize.[1] The Indian who earns good wages in the mines, and whose

[1] Balcazar, *Epidemiología boliviana.* Leonard, *Bolivia*, p. 238, quotes the following estimate of the average annual food consumption of a family of five among
Indians living near the north-east corner of Lake Titicaca (from an unpublished
study *Hacienda Belen* conducted in 1946 by the sociologist Eduardo Arze under the

work is unusually heavy, does not normally increase his consumption but spends the excess on *fiestas*, religion and drink. The diet of most sectors of the population is qualitatively deficient, particularly in animal fats and proteins. Milk and milk products are to all intents and purposes confined to the well-to-do minority. Fruit and vegetables are deficient on the Altiplano, owing mainly not to lack of supply but to lack of means and habit; the native agriculturalist is unaccustomed to spend money on food (with the exception of coca) but consumes what he produces or satisfies his needs by barter. The diet of the highland Indian consists mainly of dehydrated potatoes, *quinoa* and some maize. He rarely eats wheat bread, his consumption of sugar is small and he is in general intolerant of unaccustomed foods. Throughout the eastern provinces the diet of the generality is hardly more varied than that of the Altiplano, being limited to meat, rice, yucca, bananas, coffee and imported sugar in accordance with each man's means. Fruit is eaten in season; vegetables and dairy produce are almost unknown. Yet the only excuse for such deficiencies in the east is the apathy and inertia which grips the tropical populations, for there is little that is necessary to a complete and well-balanced diet that the country could not readily produce.

Remarkable differences exist between various estimates of Bolivian consumption of meat. The Report of the United Nations Mission of Technical Assistance calculated that in 1949 meat consumed by low-income workers in La Paz was about 67 kilograms per consumption unit (adult male equivalent). Balcazar estimated 21·02 kilograms per unit of consumption in working-class families. The former estimate would put Bolivia among the higher meat consumers of the world and the latter among the lowest. In fact there is a fairly large importation of meat into the Altiplano from

auspices of the Bolivian Ministry of Education). It must be remembered that the Lake Titicaca region is one of the most fertile parts of the Altiplano.

Potatoes	1,700 lb.	Sugar	100 lb.
Barley	100 lb.	Rice	100 lb.
Quinoa	350 lb.	Mutton	132 lb.
Horsebeans	400 lb.	Pork	110 lb.
Maize	150 lb.	Bread	44 lb.

An estimate made in 1958 from the total availability of foodstuffs and the estimated population—a method which leaves out of account the very great differences of consumption among various classes of the population and from region to region—gave the average consumption as 1,800 calories and 52·3 grams of proteins per person. The Ten Year Plan aims at a minimum of 2,475 calories and 62 grams of proteins per person.

Argentina and smaller quantities from the Beni; Cochabamba is kept fairly well supplied from Trinidad in the Beni. But this meat is very unevenly distributed. The average working-class families in La Paz and Cochabamba are relatively high consumers of meat. The mining establishments were in general well supplied, the mining companies being compelled by law to provide meat for the workers from their own resources. But the agricultural Indian population rarely eats meat and the agricultural cholo consumes only a little dried meat or *charqui*. No averaging out of consumption per head of population can give a realistic picture of the facts, but for what it is worth the figures given in the *Boletín Estadístico* for the consumption of meat in the capitals of the Departments during 1960 and 1961 are as follows (in kilograms):

City	1960	1961
La Paz	6,409,537	4,334,749*
Potosí	1,365,722	1,491,607
Oruro	1,200,285	1,188,890
Cochabamba	6,000,623	6,422,087
Sucre	1,073,120	682,610
Tarija	1,082,180	974,820
Santa Cruz	1,029,600	1,423,620
Trinidad	808,540	763,400
Cobija	121,440	118,320

* Incomplete.

The relatively high figure for Cochabamba and the low figure for Santa Cruz, where meat is more plentiful, remain unexplained.

A few words must here be said about the ancient and widespread addiction to coca among the highland Indians. There is some evidence that under the Incas an attempt was made to restrict its use to the aristocratic and privileged classes; but the habit was evidently very general among the indigenous commonalty within a few years of the Spanish Conquest and it has remained general ever since. The cultivation, processing and sale of coca has been one of the most important internal industries of Bolivia since Colonial times. Today every Indian, male and female, chews coca leaves from childhood onwards as a daily routine. Coca is a ritual and an indulgence which for the Indian population of the highlands has become a necessity of life. There is no doubt at all that its effect is to produce some lessening of sensitivity to hunger, cold, pain and fatigue—this is universally claimed by all who have acquired a toleration for it and has been experienced by the writer in his own person. In the addict it can induce a general feeling of well-being and indifference to hardship and anxiety. Almost from the beginning of the Colonial period protests have been raised against its use, which have nevertheless always been powerless in face of the stubborn demand of the Indian, who will refuse to work when he is deprived of it. The most usual verdict of modern research, both lay and medical, is that the cumulative toxic effect of the alkaloids of cocaine ingested from the leaves is to stupefy the faculties, dull the senses, undermine will-power, cloud the intelligence and generally weaken the system, producing an attitude of stoic fatalism which in extreme cases may simulate complete aboulia and mental deficiency. There have been many in Bolivia who have held coca primarily responsible for the alleged degeneracy and irresponsiveness of the Indian. Their case has not been made out. In an earlier study of the subject the present writer said:

I have indeed upon occasion seen an Indian who appeared to be in a state approaching stupor from coca or from cold or from the combined effects of the two. But from my own observation I am convinced that those Indians—and they are the vast majority—who take coca as an adjunct to the rigorous toil of the mines or of agriculture, or to sustain them in their long treks across the Altiplano, do not visibly display these symptoms of addiction.[1]

And Olen E. Leonard, who moved and worked for some years among coca-consuming Indians, was led to wonder 'if a few coca leaves do not have about the same significance for the Indian as the afternoon tea has for the Englishman or the morning and afternoon cup of coffee or coca cola to a sizeable portion of the population of the United States.'[2] Be that as it may, the Indian values coca for its analgesic and euphoric qualities and is unlikely easily to acquiesce in any proposals that would deprive him of it.

As might be expected from the general living conditions, the health of the population is not good. Although the Indian is constitutionally robust, his resistance to disease is lowered by his manner of life and possibly also by his addiction to coca. He still has more faith in ancient shamanistic remedies than in the devices of modern medicine; dried llama foetuses and similar curative

[1] *Indians of the Andes*, p. 249.   [2] *Bolivia*, p. 246.

phantasmagoria are sold openly in the native street-markets of La Paz and traditional witch-doctors are in demand. In the highlands the prevalent diseases are whooping-cough, measles, exanthematic typhus, typhoid, pneumonia, and respiratory complications deriving from malnutrition; in the valleys potential health problems are leprosy, rabies, and malaria. Malaria has been virtually eradicated by the *Servicio Nacional de Malaria*; only small trouble spots remain in the tropical region, where intestinal parasitosis and yellow fever are also encountered. Tuberculosis has begun to decline, following a period of extremely widespread infection. A programme for the eradication of this disease has been brought into operation in the *altiplano*, assisted by the WHO and UNICEF. During the ten years 1955–65 attention paid to public health throughout the country improved considerably, though budgetary limitations on public health services were still severe. By the mid 1960s the Ministry of Public Health had 6,200 hospital beds available. Throughout the country 977 doctors were working for the Ministry, the National Social Security Service, or for other autonomous Social Security organizations. Doctors still tend to be concentrated in urban areas, but, thanks to new organization of work and the national health programmes, more attention is being given to rural regions. These had 79 doctors, 40 nurses, and 157 nursing assistants (of their own). The Nationalist Government has made efforts to remedy this state of affairs and it may be seen from the 1962 budget that the vote for Health has somewhat improved. But the task is a formidable one, particularly for an impoverished country, and no sudden or revolutionary improvement may be looked for.

Estimates of birth rate and death rate have the authority only of individual impressions. Sporadic statistics for a few urban centres have been officially guaranteed, but it is universally recognized that in the native quarters even of the towns no machinery exists for accurate registration of births and deaths. For the rural areas one can but guess in the dark; even the ecclesiastical registers are wildly inadequate owing to the inability or reluctance of the Indian to pay the ecclesiastical fees for baptism and burial. The figures that follow must, therefore, be regarded as no more than provi-

<hr>

[1] It has not been possible to obtain more recent figures, but certainly any change in the last ten years has been insignificant in relation to the country's needs and to the growth of population.

sional generalizations from very imperfect data which may be very wide of the mark.[1]

Reckoning from official statistics of selected urban areas, Balcazar gives the general birth rate as 33·9 per thousand. He estimates that about 57 per cent of births are Indian, 28 per cent cholo and 15 per cent white. The official birth rate in 1945 was estimated at 31·5 per thousand. The United Nations Mission of Technical Assistance found that tested samples from mining centres gave an actual birth rate of over 50 per thousand and assumed a general birth rate for the whole country of 45. There seems to be some evidence, however, that in the mining camps, where the native element preponderates, the birth rate is unusually high even for Indian communities and 45 may well be an exaggerated figure for the country as a whole. On the other hand any figure based upon actual registrations must certainly be too low. There is equal uncertainty about the death rate. It is known that infant mortality is very high among the Indians and it is commonly said, possibly with truth, that only one child in three born in Indian communities on the Altiplano is expected to reach the age of five. Figures for infant mortality in Oruro and Potosí are given as 301 and 300 per thousand respectively and Balcazar estimates infant mortality over the whole country at 289·4 per thousand. The United Nations Mission regarded a figure between 200 and 300 as a conservative estimate for urban areas and stated that for the country as a whole 'the rate is not likely to be much below 400'. Balcazar quotes statistics of the general death rate accredited to several towns, which vary from 15 per thousand in La Paz to 55 in Trinidad, but ventures no estimate for the whole country. The United Nations Mission reports that the general death rate for the country at large can hardly be below 30 per thousand of population and may be 35 or more.[2]

[1] The *Boletín Estadístico* publishes figures for births, deaths and marriages by Department, distinguishing between the capital city and the rest of the Department in each case, but with a footnote to the effect that from 1952 onwards the statistics are incomplete. Since the figure of births in the Department of Chuquisaca, for example, is given as 4,985 in 1960 compared with 10,360 in 1950, and the figure for deaths as 1,533 in 1960 compared with 3,474 in 1950, one suspects that they may be very incomplete indeed.

[2] Leonard, *Bolivia*, pp. 65–66, says: 'Data that exist regarding mortality in the population of Bolivia serve for little more than to indicate the inadequacy and incompleteness of death registration.' He shares the popular belief that the high altitude of La Paz is not conducive to longevity, but admits that the evidence in support of it is 'far from conclusive'.

If one assumed a general crude birth rate of 45 per thousand and a death rate of 30, the annual crude rate of natural increase would be about 1·5 per cent. If this rate were maintained, the population would double in about fifty years. The Junta de Planeamiento, however, estimated that in the decade 1950 to 1960 the working population (i.e. those between the ages of 15 and 64) had increased by about 400,000 or 25 per cent (from 1,627,000 in 1950 to 2,066,600 in 1960). From the decrease in overall figures of production per person[1] it was estimated that in 1960 the shortfall in productive opportunities of employment was equivalent to a 'concealed unemployment' figure of 200,000, of whom about 150,000 were unproductive in agriculture. The Ten Year Plan was based on an estimated working population of 2,366,800 in 1965, 2,709,600 in 1970 and 3,536,600 in 1980. The estimated increase of some 300,000 persons of working age between 1960 and 1965 meant that, in order to absorb the backlog of 1960, it would be necessary for the Plan to provide productive employment for about 60,000 additional persons a year in the five years 1961–5. And it should be noted that if this were achieved, it would do no more than break level with the productivity rate per person which prevailed in 1950 —and from personal knowledge the writer can affirm that by outside standards that rate was very far indeed from what would be regarded elsewhere as a maximal exploitation of man-power potential. The possibilities of boosting production, given the means, are massively in excess of the goals which the planners have set themselves within the limits of practicability.

---

[1] This was calculated at $120 per person annually for the years 1950–2 and barely exceeded $90 in 1957–9.

CHAPTER III

THE ECONOMY

THE FECKLESS FORTIES

In common with several other countries of South America Bolivia has the disadvantage of being an exporter of raw materials in order to finance the import of manufactured goods. Bolivia is also a classic example of the vulnerability of a monoproductive and unbalanced economy. The following export and import figures for the years 1948 and 1949[1] are symptomatic of the situation which the country had reached by the mid-century and reveal the main source of its economic problems and difficulties.

Exports and Imports 1948 and 1949

($'000)

Exports			Imports		
	1948	*1949*		*1948*	*1949*
Tin	80,183	72,865	Foodstuffs	21,280	20,526
All minerals	111,156	99,036	Raw materials	9,147	10,890
			Manufactures	38,308	46,944
Total exports	112,826	101,158	Total imports	68,736	78,359

These tables tell a curious story indeed, but they tell it with exemplary clarity. On the side of exports, by the middle of the century mineral exports accounted for some 98 per cent of the total. (In the ten years 1938–48 they averaged 95 per cent.) And tin concentrates accounted for some 75 per cent of all mineral exports. This meant that a labour force of some 60,000 Indian

[1] The statistics of Bolivian commerce are taken from Banco Central de Bolivia, *Suplementos Estadísticos* and from Dirección General de Estadística, *Anuarios de comercio exterior*. Bolivian import figures until 1955 represent f.o.b. values and should be raised by approximately 20 per cent to obtain real cost. Export figures represent c.i.f. values and figures for mineral exports take no account of charges for freight, smelting, insurance, etc., which are paid by the exporters and decrease the real value of such exports by some 10 or 15 per cent.

miners, less than 3 per cent of the whole population, was responsible for earning the foreign currency needed to purchase imports for the whole country. It meant also that the financial position of Bolivia had become peculiarly sensitive to—indeed dangerously dependent upon—the fluctuations in price which follow changes of demand in the world markets for non-ferrous metals. Moreover, owing to the inaccessibility of the mines, the long distances over which the concentrates have to be freighted and various other factors which have been mentioned, Bolivia is a high-cost producer and the margins of profit are small. Many of the smaller mines operate at so small a margin that when prices drop they go out of production. Therefore a decline in world prices reacts to produce a lowering of output and has the double effect of reducing earnings on a reduced volume of exports.

Although the excessive emphasis on mining has been traditional with Bolivia since the time of the Spanish Conquest when Alto Peru was exploited for the greater glorification of Spain, the economy has not always been quite so completely one-sided but the scourge of monoproduction has descended on the land almost by a series of accidents. The rubber of the Beni is recognized to have greater elasticity than any other known product. But apart from temporary booms in the two World Wars the flourishing rubber industry which brought wealth and prosperity to the land at the turn of the century declined before the greater accessibility of plantation rubber; and when the writer visited Cachuela Esperanza, the once important river port of the great rubber firm of Suárez Hermanos, in 1950, there was little movement to be seen there but the last pathetic death throes of that once great enterprise. The subsidiary exportation of Brazil nuts declined before the competition of more accessible sources of supply. Even two small extraction plants at Riberalta manufacturing oil for local Bolivian markets were unable to stand the competition of cheaper imported products and went out of business. Owing to costs of transport the Beni timber industry never progressed beyond the experimental stage. The small but once useful cinchona industry was killed when synthetic quinine destroyed the markets for the natural products. And attempts to develop a market for coca were frustrated when synthetic anaesthetics took the place of natural cocaine. Thus deprived of one alternative after another Bolivia was left with only the traditional mineral industry and—with the decline of silver—principally with tin. The Report of the United

Nations Mission of Technical Assistance published in 1951 was doing no more than underline the obvious when it pointed out that 'the periodic dislocation of Bolivian economy, resulting from such variations in the world price of tin, constitutes one of the major problems faced by the country that depends so directly upon a single export commodity' (p. 45).

The economic history of Bolivia in the last half-century is exemplary of the principle that a monoproductive system can be justified, if at all, only in a country which is basically self-sufficient in most primary necessities and which relies upon imports to supplement rather than to supply the essentials of national life. At the turn of the century Bolivia was to a large extent self-sufficing in most primary foodstuffs and in many agricultural raw materials. Since the First World War it has ceased to be so. It has already been explained how the advent of the railways—by no means an unmixed blessing—was allowed to stifle the productivity of Santa Cruz, since the foodstuffs produced there were no longer able to compete in the markets of the Altiplano with cheaper goods imported by rail. The cattle industry of Mojos suffered in the same way. It was even cheaper to take cattle on the hoof from the Beni to the Argentine, losing a high proportion by starvation on the way, to fatten the remainder inside the Argentine border and then to import them as Argentine produce by rail for the slaughterhouses of La Paz than to slaughter them in Trinidad and freight the carcasses by air to the Altiplano. Bolivia became an importer of meat. And throughout the length and breadth of the country the same process went on. Commercial cultivation declined and subsistence agriculture became the rule. Almost the only foodstuffs in which the country remained self-sufficient were potatoes and *quinoa* on the highlands, yucca and bananas in the lowland plains. Even rice began to be imported in increasing quantities. Writing in 1947 Jorge Pando Gutiérrez, who had made a very thorough study of Bolivian agricultural problems, said:

as things are now the 2 million natives who are occupied in agriculture are unable to satisfy the requirements of the million and a half remaining consumers and large quantities of foodstuffs which Bolivia could produce have to be imported every year. This is due to inefficient methods of cultivation. The Indian works from sunrise to sunset and is barely able to produce sufficient for his own sustenance.[1]

---

[1] *Bolivia y el mundo*, i. 39.

Since the period of the Chaco War the process of deterioration which we have described was accelerated by the practice of importing foodstuffs and raw materials at preferential rates of exchange while the prices of home-produced products were controlled at unrealistically low prices. The purpose was to benefit the Bolivian consumer during periods of hardship and inflation, but the effect was to subsidize foreign imports by a concealed tax on the mineral industry at the expense of home agriculture. Colin Crossley quotes two examples on the authority of a 1951 report of the Economic Commission for Latin America: 'in 1950 sugar costing U.S. $5·90 per 100 lbs. c.i.f. Mollendo was retailed in La Paz for $4.60 at the real rate of exchange; similarly rice, c.i.f. Antofagasta at $6·20 per 100 lbs., was retailed for $4·56'. It has sometimes been claimed that support for this policy and opposition to a sound economics of self-sufficiency came from the large mining companies since development towards self-sufficiency would decrease the country's dependence on the earnings of mineral exports and would make native labour less readily available for the mines. In fact the mine labourers were the most highly paid in the country and enjoyed large concessions in the way of cheap consumer goods at the *pulperías* which the companies stocked with special imports. The truth is that there was no Government since the thirties strong enough to put into practice a firm economic policy. Ninety-five per cent of the country's foreign exchange derived from mineral exports and some 50 per cent of the ordinary Government revenues from direct and indirect taxation of the mining industry. National finance in Bolivia has therefore been peculiarly sensitive, as has been said, to fluctuations in the world market for non-ferrous metals. Bolivia is apt to benefit by an outside war which drives up these prices, and suffers correspondingly if they—and particularly the price of tin—during periods of normalcy drop more rapidly than the prices of the commodities which it imports. During the Second World War high demand for non-ferrous metals at good prices gave rise to balance-of-payments surpluses which necessarily-reduced imports of consumer goods were unable to absorb, so that at the end of the war fairly large reserves of purchasing power remained. These reserves were frittered away by heavy importation of consumer goods which brought with them no permanent benefit to the country and within a few years of the end of the war Bolivia entered upon a period of chronic shortage of foreign exchange for fundamental development needs.[1] The foreign-exchange policy of successive Governments during the forties swung wildly between excessive liberality and sporadic restrictiveness, while perpetuating certain common tendencies. The large mining companies were obliged to sell a high (though varying) proportion of their foreign-exchange earnings to the Government at an artificially low rate of exchange (Bs. 42 to the dollar until April 1950 and Bs. 60 after that date), while retaining the remainder for their own purposes of reinvestment, legally compulsory imports, payments of dues, freight, shipping, insurance, smelting charges, etc. The Government made exchange available at the same artificially low rate for the importation of foodstuffs and raw materials, which thus obtained a concealed subsidy by what was virtually an impost on the mining industry. Less essential but approved imports were allowed exchange purchased by the merchants at a differential and variable rate of about Bs. 100 to the dollar, the difference between the rates at which the Government bought and sold this exchange going to swell the budgetary revenues. Finally, luxury imports were spasmodically but on the whole fairly liberally admitted with free market exchange obtainable at a very variable rate which rose to Bs. 210 to the dollar at the end of 1951 and stood around 220 in the spring of 1952. The issue of foreign exchange for importation or other purposes has notoriously offered a fertile field for corruption and partiality and those merchants who were well in with the Government of the time, or who

[1] Balance-of-payments figures over a period of years show a swing to the debit side.

	Revenue ($'000)	Expenditure ($'000)	Balance ($'000)
1940	53,768·4	50,292·4	3,476·0
1941	66,531·1	65,034·4	1,496·2
1942	78,790·1	80,523·7	−1,742·6
1943	96,636·6	96,308·5	238·1
1944	84,675·0	82,107·0	2,567·9
1945	90,336·8	77,871·7	12,465·1
1946	81,930·5	89,697·2	−7,766·7
1947	82,248·6	104,972·6	−16,724·0
1948	119,218·7	126,188·7	−6,970·0
1949	107,634·1	124,911·4	−17,277·3
1950	102,840·8	106,968·7	−4,127·9
1951	140,896·1	114,550·0	26,346·1

knew where and when to bestow largesse, were able to build up considerable fortunes for themselves.

The general effect of this policy of subsidizing essential imports, living upon the mining industry, was to perpetuate the stagnation of home production, benefiting only some few small factory industries (such as textiles, glass, cement) which obtained their raw materials cheaply. But even these suffered from recurrent changes in the economic situation and political outlook. Periodic shortages of foreign exchange withheld from them the supply of raw materials, no longer available from domestic sources, limiting production and reducing output. Occasional restrictions on the importation of luxury and semi-luxury goods encouraged the growth of a number of small factories producing them for home consumption. But their stability was always uncertain since the home market was very small—the large native population not being consumers—and was inclined to give preference to imported goods whenever a relaxation of the control put them on the market again. Breweries at La Paz and Cochabamba, jam factories in Cochabamba, a button factory, soap factories, a small wine industry from the valleys of Sucre and Tarija, cigarettes, soft drinks—these and a few others managed to struggle on in a small way. But for the most part the local manufacture was reduced to workshop industries. Almost as much damage was done by the variability and uncertainty of government policy in the manipulation of foreign exchange and the control of imports as by the policy of subsidization itself.

In considering Bolivian imports it must be borne in mind that large sectors of the native and rural population are practically self-supporting on the land and depend only marginally on monetary purchases. To all intents and purposes they are non-consumers of imported goods. This is the case not only with the Indian population of the Altiplano, who grow most of their own food (supplementing by smuggled imports), build their own houses, make their own clothes and purchase few factory-made goods. In most of the smaller and more isolated *pueblecitos* of the Yungas valleys and the eastern lowlands a majority of the inhabitants live to a very large extent outside the monetary economy, are self-supporting in basic foodstuffs such as rice, maize, yucca, sweet potatoes, bananas, fish and game, and barter their surpluses of these with the local trader in exchange for their few outside needs such as kerosene and cigarette papers. Nevertheless the scale of imports has grown and the pattern which developed fairly consistently during the forties showed about 50 per cent foodstuffs and raw materials, 50 per cent industrial consumer goods. If the former category is examined in detail it will be found that a large number of the commodities regularly imported were those which the country is capable of producing in adequate quantities. That this is so is revealed by the following percentages which prevailed at this time:

Percentage of Total Imports

Meat & dairy products	8	Rice	2½
Cereals & flour	10	Timber	1½
Sugar	8	Wool	1½
Petroleum & products	8	Cotton	1½

Sources: Based on official statistics for the 1940's.

These are commodities which could be produced in the country even in excess of the needs of the population and they together account for more than 40 per cent of annual imports. If one includes a host of smaller items and articles which are manufactured locally from them, the percentage will be appreciably higher. In discussing Bolivian economy it is, therefore, almost inevitable to consider what might be, alongside the lamentable reality of what is. Having given a short survey of the situation at the mid-century and the tendencies which brought it about, we shall then look at what happened in the decade following the revolution of 1952 and then say a few words about the Ten Year Plan in the light of the possibilities which the past has revealed.

COLLAPSE

By the middle of the century the Bolivian economy had already sunk dangerously into decline and the social structure added to the economic difficulties. Two-thirds of the population were engaged in primitive methods of scratch-and-tickle or slash-and-burn agriculture at no more than subsistence level. Overall production was less than $120 a head annually. The level of exports stood at about $33 a head. Less than 40 per cent of the rural population spoke Spanish, illiteracy was prevalent and health conditions were poor. The greater part of the native population were apathetic and not easily amenable to new ways of life and technological methods or transferable into other and more productive sectors of industry. Geophysical conditions still isolated large sections of the country from their natural markets and the lack of internal communications impeded the full exploitation of the country's resources.

Since the Chaco War inflation has been endemic to Bolivian monetary economy. The cost-of-living index in La Paz (1931 = 100) had risen to 390 in 1937, stood at 733 in 1939, 2,044 in December 1949, 3,972 in December 1950 and reached 5,043 by the end of 1951.[1] In 1951 the cost of living rose by 33·2 per cent and in 1952 by 24·1 per cent, or 2 per cent a month. The incidence of rising prices falls with very different effect upon different sections of the population. It impinges least strongly upon the rural population who are engaged in subsistence agriculture. The figures give a more or less accurate indication of the incidence upon the working-class and cholo-population, who during this period relied little upon imported goods other than those which were subsidized as has been explained. The classes which consume the country's non-subsidized imports experienced a much greater increase in the cost of living than the figures indicate. Meanwhile, as the cost of living was rising and the level of reserves rapidly declining, expansion of the money supply reached unprecedented proportions. The total currency in circulation rose from Bs. 863 million in December 1940 to over Bs. 4,000 million by the end of 1949, Bs. 5,525 million in December 1950 and Bs. 6,893 million in December 1951.[2] The most important factor influencing this expansion was the recurrent financing of annual budgetary deficits by the Central Bank.[3] As

[1] These figures were prepared by the Directorate of Statistics on the basis of the estimated consumption of an average middle-class family in La Paz, which was assumed to consume practically no imported goods (with the curious exception of sardines) apart from such basic foodstuffs as wheat, rice, etc., which owing to the concealed government subsidy were available at artificially low prices.

Taking December 1948 as base *International Financial Statistics* (Apr. 1953) gives cost-of-living figures for La Paz as follows: 1937=15; 1938=19; 1939=29; 1940=32; 1945=71; 1946=82; 1947=95; 1948=100; 1950=149; 1951=189; Nov. 1952=221. Comparable figures for wage increases are not available except for a limited number of industries, but they by no means kept pace with the rise in prices for analogous sections of the population.

[2] The native population have always been great hoarders of currency. On the other hand in 1950 alone the value of notes in circulation rose from Bs. 2,546·8 million to Bs. 3,431·6 million, an increase of 34·74 per cent, and that in an economy already inflationary.

[3] Budgetary deficits for 1945, 1946 and 1947 are given by *International Financial Statistics* (Apr. 1953), in millions of Bolivianos, as 7, 254 and 299, respectively. According to the *Publicación del Banco Central de Bolivia* No. 6, 1952 (*Bolivia en la Conferencia Financiera de Mexico D.F.*) heavy budgetary deficits began in 1946, a

Bolivia

will be seen from the table given below, government indebtedness increased more steeply during the decade.[1] In 1951 decrees were passed authorizing the issue of currency up to 50 per cent of the Bank's cash reserves for the purpose of loans to public corporations, excluding from the limits of fiscal credits the debentures of Departments, municipalities and bodies of a public or semi-public character in general and consolidating the budgetary advances granted by the Monetary Department for the years 1948, 1949 and 1950 in a bond of Bs. 1,134 million not to be computed within the fiscal credits. In October the Monetary Department was authorized to acquire part of the loans of the Banking Department up

surplus of Bs. 50 m. being claimed for 1945. The deficits in subsequent years are given as follows:

	(Bs. million)		(Bs. million)
1946	108	1949	372
1947	193	1950	533
1948	276	1951	332

In a speech delivered in La Paz in June 1953 W. W. Morton, United Nations technical expert attached to the Bolivian Ministry of Finance, stated that the budgetary deficits in 1950 and 1951 were Bs. 539 and 350 million respectively, while the deficit for 1952, although final figures were not yet available, might be expected to reach Bs. 1,500 million (*La Nación* (La Paz) 19 June 1953).

Published budgetary surpluses and deficits in any year ignore outstanding commercial obligations of the Government for that year. Income and expenditure between 1 Jan. and 31 Mar. referring to items in the previous year's budget are incorporated into the income and expenditure figures of the previous year.

The President is required by law to submit his budget for the ensuing year to Congress for approval before 31 Dec., to take effect in the new financial year beginning 1 Jan. In practice the Government promulgates the budget at any time between April and August of the year in which it is current, by Supreme Decree. In the last twenty years a budget has rarely if ever been regularly approved by Congress, nor has Congress legally approved funds for the Government. The Banco Central has advanced loans to successive Governments beyond the legal limits of borrowing and on the authority of decrees which were promulgated as money was needed, while authorization of Congress has been waived.

[1] *Fiscal Obligations*
(Bs. '000)

1941	514,805	1947	1,346,854
1942	634,807	1948	2,034,967
1943	739,235	1949	2,443,630
1944	734,293	1950	3,515,597
1945	748,440	1951	4,197,738
1946	981,038	1952 (Mar.)	4,321,472

to Bs. 500 million on the ground that the greater part of the resources of the Banking Department had been employed in operations of a fiscal nature. This legislation was of obvious inflationary tendency, producing an increase in money by some Bs. 800 million in the second half of the year with a further Bs. 500 million to come, and with no corresponding augmentation of consumer goods. There were thus clear signs of a pending financial crisis before the political crisis which occurred early in 1952. The value of the Boliviano in the free market sank from 130 in December 1950 to 210 at the end of 1951, 275 at the end of 1952 and 950 at the end of 1953.

Thus it is apparent that the economy had already reached a dangerously critical state of imbalance when the MNR party assumed the reins of government in April 1952. They came into office committed to an extensive programme of nationalization and social improvement which aggravated the short-term requirements of foreign exchange and the dependence on imported products, while their plans for economic diversification (by which was meant a renewed development of the national resources which had been left unexploited or allowed to sink into decline) and national recovery could be expected to bear fruit only in the long term, and could indeed hardly be set on foot without very substantial foreign aid. The nationalization of the mines occurred at an unfavourable period in the industry and was followed by massive and disastrous decline in production. The Agrarian Reform had as its immediate consequence a diminution in agricultural production and therefore a greater requirement of agricultural imports. During the year which followed the revolution industrial wages rocketed owing to the wage policy of the Government and commodity prices soared. Ceiling prices were raised by 100 per cent on most commodities and many disappeared from the open market. In May 1953 a series of economic and social decrees were passed in an attempt to stave off disaster.[1] The Boliviano was devalued from 60 to 190 to the

---

[1] The following block of economic decrees was promulgated on 14 May.

1. Establishing the parity of the Bolivian peso at Bs. 190 to the dollar.
2. Abolishing differential rates of exchange and placing the Banco Central in control of imports, exports and foreign-exchange transactions in general. This decree recognized a free-market rate in addition to the official rate of exchange and made provision for the authorization of certain classes of business to operate in the free-exchange market.
3. Enjoining the issue of a gold coinage, which should be freely exportable by private persons.

dollar. But even so the quotation for the Boliviano on the free market, which had been fluctuating between Bs. 530 and 750 to the dollar, found a temporary level at 600 but had reached 1,000 by the end of the year. To offset the increased cost of consumer goods a flat cost-of-living benefice of Bs. 4,000 a month was decreed for all employees. This, together with previously legalized wage increases, and family and housing subsidies to be met by the employer, meant that an average urban worker's pay in La Paz, which six months before had stood in the region of Bs. 3,500 a month, rose to approximately Bs. 11,000. Many of the smaller businesses, already hard hit by inflation, were unable to assimilate this additional burden and had either to dismiss their workers or enter into a compact with them to pay less than the legal requirement.[1] The mining industry was particularly hard hit. Following on the devaluation the Asociación de Industriales Mineros Pequeños (representing the smaller mining enterprises) addressed a petition to the President representing that as their obligations (in the case of lead) had been increased by 126 per cent by the new social legislation and their returns would go up only by 36 per cent on prices calculated at an exchange rate of Bs. 190 to the dollar, they would be operating at a loss and would be compelled to close

4. Establishing a tax of Bs. 35 to the dollar on the proceeds of mineral exports and duties of 50 or 100 per cent on imports not regarded as essentials.

5. Abolishing subsidies on articles of consumption, fixing ceiling retail prices for essential foodstuffs and maximum import prices, obliging employers to pay a tax-free compensation of Bs. 4,000 a month to workers, maintaining house-rents at the current figure and forbidding any reduction of wages for a period of six months.

6. Limiting Bank credits to the figure pertaining on 30 April 1953.

7. Creating a Stabilization Office with duties to advise the President on measures necessary to ensure the stability of prices and wages.

8. Entitling government employees to a compensation of Bs. 4,000 a month to offset the increased cost of living due to depreciation of the currency, and readjusting government expenditure to the new parity (Subsecretaría de Prensa, Informaciones y Cultura, *Los Decretos del 14 Mayo de 1953*).

These decrees represented a curious combination of doctrinaire reformation of abuses with panic salvage measures but failed to provide a coherent structure on which sound economic revival could be built. The Government was still shirking its problem of the reorganization of labour.

[1] On 13 June 1953, a decree was passed rendering illegal the collective or individual dismissal of employees and reinstating those who had been sacked since 18 April. Any firm desiring not to continue its business under these conditions was required to report to the Ministry of Economy and Labour, which would decide either to take over the business or to hand it over to the appropriate ᶜyndicate or to close it down.

down.[1] The Asociación Nacional de Mineros Medianos (representing the medium-sized enterprises) submitted a similar memorandum alleging that with current obligations they were unable to operate at prices lower than those calculated at an exchange rate of Bs. 250 to the dollar.[2] On 3 June an Extraordinary Congress of the Minería Nacional addressed a Note to the Banco Minero on behalf of the small and medium mining concerns rejecting the 'derisory' prices which had been fixed.[3] The Government was itself now the largest mine operators in the country and in ensuing years was hit by the slump which followed.

In a broadcast speech on 15 May the President claimed that the abolition of concealed subsidies on essential imports would encourage home production and that the issue of a gold coinage would stimulate the flagging gold-mining industry.[4] Neither prognostication was fulfilled. The subsidization of imports in fact continued until 1958. It even had the curious transitional effect of stimulating certain minor industries—though not to the advantage of the economy—for by obtaining their raw materials at lower than market prices they were able to offer their processed goods in outside markets at favourable prices and there began a veritable flow of illegal exports to neighbouring countries through the smuggling organizations. In its Report of 1961 the Junta Nacional de Planeamiento refers to this as follows: 'In effect it was in the years 1954 to 1956 that the peak production was reached (in the manufacturing industries), in large measure as a consequence of the prevailing exchange arrangements which stimulated a flow of exports (a high proportion of which were clandestine) based upon the importation of raw materials at preferential rates of exchange.'[5] This import policy (together with the inflow of surplus foodstuffs from the United States) continued to exercise a depressive influence on agriculture, since commercial outlets for home produce were found chiefly in illegal export. According to C. H. Zondag[6] (quoted by Colin Crossley) 95 per cent of the freight on the Santa Cruz–Corumbá railway in 1956 consisted of products of prime necessity

[1] *El Diario*, 21 May 1953.   [2] Ibid. 1 June 1953.
[3] Ibid. 7 June 1953.
[4] Bolivia. Subsecretaría de Prensa, Informaciones y Cultura, *Los decretos del 14 Mayo de 1953*.
[5] *Planeamiento*, Sept. 1961, p. 41. See also p. 42, where it is said that the temporary boom encouraged the importation of manufacturing machinery which later lay idle or in some cases was not even installed.
[6] *Tijdschrift voor Economische en Sociale Geografie*, Aug.–Sept. 1953, p. 7.

destined for contraband export to Brazil. Even counterpart agricultural products and foodstuffs imported as emergency aid from the United States were being surreptitiously diverted into the export markets.

By the end of the forties informed observers from outside were confidently predicting an inevitable collapse. The policy of the MNR did nothing to temporize but rather accelerated the inevitable. Collapse came in 1953. Complete disaster with internal anarchy and possible communist infiltration, or even the partition of Bolivia among neighbouring states, was staved off by timely emergency aid from the United States. Early in 1953 a ninety-day loan was negotiated with the New York Federal Reserve Bank against gold deposited to the amount of $9,500,000 in order to maintain the flow of essential imports and this was followed by a withdrawal of $2,500,000 from the International Monetary Fund. In July the State Department announced a three-part programme of United States assistance for Bolivia which comprised: (1) A one-year contract to buy Bolivian tin concentrates at the world-market price at the time of delivery. (2) An offer to discuss with the Bolivian Government 'what further steps the two Governments might take together to bring about a long-term solution to Bolivia's economic problems'. The offer included a proposal to send a United States economic commission to Bolivia to study the problems on the spot. (3) A recommendation by the Mutual Security Agency that the United States financial contribution to the technical-assistance programme in Bolivia, which at that time stood at about $1,500,000 a year, should be more than doubled.[1] The announcement was timed to coincide with the arrival in La Paz of Dr Milton Eisenhower for a three-days' conference with Bolivian government leaders. At this time a Programme of Economic Diversification was drawn up at the instigation of the President, Dr Paz Estenssoro, and was handed to Dr Eisenhower. An amplified version of it was put out by the Ministry of Foreign Affairs in December 1954. This was the precursor of the Ten Year Plan which was drawn up in 1961. The object of the plan was simple: it consisted in the revival of home production and the recovery of a degree of self-sufficiency which would reduce the country's import requirements within the scope of the foreign exchange which it can earn by its exports of minerals. But the difficulties are colossal and no one expected that

[1] *New York Times*, 7 July 1953.

results could be anything but gradual. Meanwhile the country's needs were crying and urgent. In October 1953 President Eisenhower ordered that agricultural products to the value of $5 million, free of freight charges, from the reserves of the Commodity Credit Corporation should be made available to meet Bolivia's urgent requirements. A further $4 million from the Mutual Security Fund was granted for the purchase of articles of first necessity, the greater part of the proceeds of the sale of these articles in Bolivia being utilizable by the Bolivian Government for financing projects of economic development. An increase of $2 million was made in the United States contribution to the programme of technical assistance, the additional funds, together with an equivalent contribution from the Bolivian Government, to be devoted to an emergency programme for increasing the production of foodstuffs.[1]

Although this aid was projected in 1953 as an emergency salvage operation, it was continued from year to year on a scale of $20–25 million a year and came to represent some 30 per cent of the national Budget, besides help in kind. By 1956 it had become apparent that Bolivia was settling into the position of a permanent dependent unless drastic steps were taken to put the economy on its feet again. The Junta de Planeamiento sums up the position in the following words:

The American aid was decisive to enable the Government to cope successfully with urgent problems; but without belittling it, it is important to recognize that its amount was restricted to what was strictly necessary to enable the country to cope with its most immediate problems as they arose but insufficient to stimulate the national economy to the point where it could by its own force initiate a continuing process of development. Rather than an impulse to improvement the aid has represented a means only of preventing worse deterioration in the situation as it existed.

In other words, Bolivia was rescued from the most disastrous results of economic collapse but by 1961 had not effectively begun to remedy the conditions which were responsible for collapse.

THE FRUSTRATING FIFTIES

As one examines the records of the years which have elapsed since the revolution—just over the decade at the time of writing—it is impossible to feel confidence that the new regime, despite its

[1] Exchange of Letters between President Paz Estenssoro and President Eisenhower. *La Nación* (La Paz), 16 Oct. 1953.

change of vision and despite the material and technical support it has obtained from outside, has yet gone far effectively to stem the tendencies which caused the economic collapse of 1953.

The net turnover per capita fell from an estimated $118 in 1951 to $99 in 1959. By the same year the per capita value of exports had dropped to $19. Agricultural production showed a steep decline until 1958 and the subsequent revival still failed to keep pace with the growth of population. Mineral production underwent a steep and serious decline. Manufacturing industry jumped up owing to the abnormal foreign-exchange policy which prevailed between 1953 and 1956 but figures for output have dropped since 1957. No advance has been made in closing the trading gap between imports and exports: as the value of exports has fallen, the value of imports has risen. Foodstuffs and raw materials continue to account for more than half the total of imports. These economic troubles resulted in large part from labour unrest and redundancy in the mines, the railways and other industries and this in turn was a consequence of giving too much power too suddenly to an irresponsible and undisciplined labour force, or to their leaders. Bolivia's inevitable economic difficulties were exacerbated by social sickness, since the revolution had put in the saddle those who had not yet learnt to have the general good of the country at heart. Social recovery must precede economic. The following tables, though the figures must in some cases be regarded as estimates rather than exact, nevertheless give a sufficiently clear picture of the situation as described.

Estimates of Net Product 1950–9 (in $ million, 1958 rate)

	1950	1951	1952	1953	1954	1955	1956	1957	1958	1959
Agriculture	118·1	118·1	113·1	105·8	101·7	107·6	104·2	110·7	121·5	132·6
Minerals	52·1	57·4	58·3	59·1	48·3	51·0	46·1	47·4	32·7	37·7
Petroleum	2·5	2·1	2·1	2·5	6·9	11·1	13·1	14·7	14·2	13·1
Manufactures	48·0	50·0	49·0	49·0	54·9	55·7	51·4	36·0	39·5	42·0
Total: all branches	355·9	378·6	387·8	343·7	346·2	371·3	354·8	342·9	351·2	370·6
Total per capita ($)	118·0	122·0	122·0	106·0	104·0	110·0	102·0	96·0	96·0	99·0

Source: From *Planeamiento*, Sept. 1961.

Exports 1951–61

	Total		Minerals		Tin	
	'000 tons	$'000	'000 tons	$'000	'000 tons	$'000
1951	267·2	150,590	241·7	145,680	90·7	93,225
1952	268·5	141,303	245·4	137,800	87·6	84,133
1953	218·2	112,700	202·0	110,000	91·4	71,986
1954	181·5	99,453	163·8	96,200	72·9	54,516
1955	251·0	102,374	171·8	97,770	74·9	57,067
1956	273·4	107,437	169·9	100,012	71·4	58,247
1957	351·4	97,667	183·8	89,271	77·3	56,893
1958	307·5	64,737	131·9	56,560	46·0	34,777
1959	273·3	77,634	130·4	69,246	65·9	50,675
1960	275·0	67,828	119·4	59,873	52·3	40,553
1961	239·2	76,136	128·6	68,996	56·0	45,965

Imports 1953–60

	Totals		Foodstuffs		Raw materials		Manufactures	
	'000 tons	$'000	'000 tons	$'000	'000 tons	$'000	'000 tons	$'000
1953	333·5	68,006	162·9	25,732	127·3	9,970	43·0	31,649
1954	292·0	65,483	158·6	23,066	81·1	9,810	52·3	32,607
1955	265·8	82,394	139·0	24,664	59·1	9,281	67·6	47,491
1956	213·1	84,158	110·1	21,549	38·5	7,198	64·4	55,311
1957	354·3	90,288	232·0	27,438	52·9	5,724	69·4	57,081
1958	242·9	79,592	135·6	15,446	31·8	4,742	75·5	59,404
1959	125,510	33,723	63,406	6,731	32,877	3,164	29,213	23,818
1960	150,450	71,476	123,684	13,925	65,173	5,892	61,647	51,655

Foodstuffs for which the country has sufficient production capacity continued to be imported in quantity, as is illustrated by the graphs on page 136, and from the following tables.[1] In each case the percentage is related to the volume of imports in 1950 (1950 = 100). Imports of sugar and rice were in excess of the 1950 level until 1960, imports of wheat until 1958 and imports of wheat flour rose to more than four times the 1950 level by 1960.

[1] From *Boletín Estadístico* for 1962

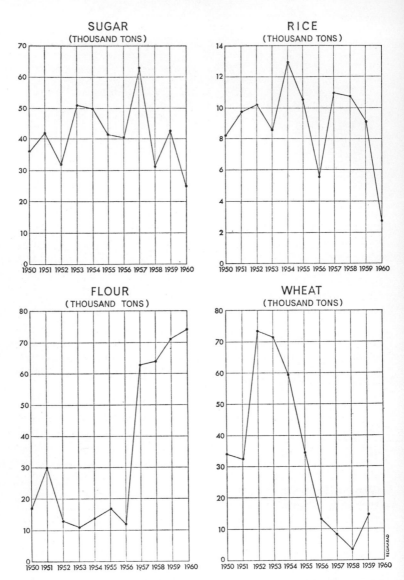

IMPORTS OF SUGAR, RICE, FLOUR, AND WHEAT

	Rice '000 kg.	%	White sugar '000 kg.	%	Wheat '000 kg.	%	Wheat flour '000 kg.	%
1950	8,211	100	36,824	100	33,881	100	17,399	100
1951	9,737	119	43,474	118	32,487	96	32,927	189
1952	10,672	130	33,084	90	73,725	218	16,414	94
1953	8,507	104	51,586	140	71,570	211	11,210	64
1954	13,221	161	50,087	136	58,792	174	19,357	111
1955	10,739	131	42,766	116	34,387	101	21,913	126
1956	5,559	68	41,190	112	13,192	39	14,781	85
1957	11,384	139	66,733	181	54,722	162	63,047	362
1958	11,216	137	33,519	91	3,351	10	64,913	373
1959	8,565	104	46,082	125	14,336	42	71,902	413
1960	2,340	29	25,687	87			77,584	445

The Junta de Planeamiento can have surprised nobody when it summed up the situation by saying in 1961 that:

An overall evaluation of the position allows it to be said that the relation of production to capital continues to be very unfavourable and that a more intensive utilization of capacities for production and basic plant already available would permit one confidently to rely on an increase in national production within the next few years greater in volume than the investments being made.

In 1953, when the Boliviano was devalued, attempts were made to check inflation by limiting bank loans and pegging wages and prices. But no effective progress was made in this direction until the measures for stabilization taken in 1957. The value of the Boliviano in the free market, which was down to 1,000 by the end of 1953, continued to fall and descended to 1,820 by the end of 1954, 4,018 by the end of 1955, 7,760 by December 1956, 8,565 in December 1957 and 11,935 in December 1958. Through 1959 and 1960, as a result of stabilization measures, it stayed firmish at 11,885. The cost-of-living index showed a similar rhythm of increase. With 1950 as a base the Banco Central published the following estimates of the cost-of-living index in La Paz and percent-

	Index	% increase 1950 = 100		Index	% increase 1950 = 100
1950	100		1956	3,751·3	178·8
1951	133·2	33·2	1957	8,070·1	115·1
1952	165·3	24·1	1958	8,320·4	3·1
1953	333·1	101·5	1959	10,009·7	20·3
1954	747·6	124·4	1960	11,080·7	10·7
1955	1,345·7	80·0			

age annual increases between 1950 and 1960. In the years 1950–2 the annual rate of increase was of the order of 30 per cent. Between 1952 and 1958 there are all the signs of runaway inflation with rates of increase in the cost of living between 100 and 150 per cent, rising to 178 per cent in 1956. After 1957 the process was checked and increases dropped to the order of 12 per cent. It is clear that 1957 was a turning-point and that an effective check was put on the rate, if no more, of deterioration in that year.

Under pressure from the United States, whose experts began to realize in 1956 that their emergency aid was effecting no radical cure and that the import of counterpart goods was even exerting the deleterious effect of inhibiting attempts to rescue home production from its stagnation, drastic measures were taken at the end of 1956 for the stabilization of the currency and to check the rhythm of inflation. Preferential and arbitrary rates of exchange were finally abolished, in fact as well as theory, and the Boliviano was allowed to find its own level, being made freely convertible for all purposes at an initial rate of 7,500 which later settled at about 11,885 to the dollar. Restrictions on imports were removed along with subsidies and price controls. In 1957 active social measures were taken in support of the budgetary decrees with the object of restricting the demand for consumer goods within the limits of availability. Wages, including the salaries of public employees, were frozen for a year—a period which was later extended—and every effort was made to cut administrative and governmental expenditure. A propaganda campaign warned the public that any further increase in the cost of living would have to be countered by austerity. Despite an unfriendly reception manifested in almost continuous disturbances, riots, and strikes, the Government did not give way and managed to hold to its point until the vicious spiral of rising prices and increased wages was broken and the economy settled down on a sounder, if not a flourishing, basis. Things were helped by a loan of $25 million which was subscribed by the United States, together with the International Monetary Fund, to cushion a possible weakening of the Boliviano on the free exchange.

Not content only with its call to the country for sacrifice and austerity, the Government began to set its own house in order. During the bad years from 1952 the fiscal policy of the Government itself had been an important factor to increase inflation. Having taken over the major portion of the mining industry at a time when the costs of production exceeded the prices at which the products sold in the world markets, it found itself saddled with the burden of subsidizing essential imports from that industry. It was in effect taxing its own losses in order to finance cheap importation. As prices rose and inflation swelled, the revenues of the Government diminished in purchasing power, while in consequence of the same rise in prices it was under constant pressure from the workers to compensate by increased subsidization. The fiscal policy was in a vicious circle from which there was no escape but continuous budgetary deficits, which were at the same time a cause and a result of inflation. For these deficits were financed by arbitrary expansion of the money supply, which in its turn of course put up the level of prices. In the years 1950 to 1952, although they were heralding the crash, the money supply was increased by little more than 30 per cent a year. From 1952 the rate of increase rose stupendously, culminating in 1956 at over 230 per cent, and from that time returned to more moderate proportions.[1] At the beginning of 1963 a new currency unit was introduced, the new *peso boliviano* being worth 1,000 old bolivianos.

There is no doubt that in 1957 the Government made a determined and well-considered effort to escape from the morass of frustration and futility in which the economy was bogged down. The moderate success which it achieved, with or without the understanding of the populace, augurs well for the future. But optimism must be tempered by the consideration that in the first decade after the revolution little if anything had been practically effected to cure the ills which were the root cause of economic collapse. What has been achieved by the MNR Government by 1962 is a breathing space—no more—and a Ten Year Plan dependent for its realization on substantial aid from without.

THE MINING INDUSTRY

In his *Memorandum sobre los problemas de la industria minera de Bolivia*, written from exile in 1947, Señor Carlos Víctor Aramayo declared that

the sole *raison d'être* of the Bolivian Altiplano is the mining industry. If it were to disappear, there would disappear with it the very basis of the human and economic life of the most important and the most thickly

[1] The index, calculated in December of each year (1952 = 100), was as follows: 1956: 2,337; 1957: 3,431; 1958: 4,010; 1959: 5,226; 1960: 5,647; 1961: 6,494.

populated zone of the Republic and a large part of the population would gradually emigrate to other regions of the country or to foreign parts. . . If it ends, the Altiplano will be gradually depopulated and the other regions of Bolivia will be checked in their progress.

That such statements as this can be made and accepted—that they may even be true—is evidence of the profound change which has come over men's ways of thinking since the Altiplano came under European occupation. By the Indians of old it was a human habitation loved and defended as men everywhere love and defend their homeland and the native population has always remained even excessively attached to the soil. Before the European invasion they had built up an agriculturally based civilization upon the unfriendly plateau and by laboriously clearing, terracing and irrigating the land had wooed it to produce the crops for which the climate is adapted and made it subservient to their needs. Metals were mined as valuable accessories to the culture they had built. In the centuries before the Incas copper was mined and used for practical and decorative purposes. Gold and silver were used for personal adornment and in the service of religious cult. Later it was discovered how to alloy copper with tin and a bronze was produced whose temper and hardness have astonished metallurgists until recent times. And from this bronze, lacking iron, they made tools, implements and weapons.

They used copper, which they call *anta* [says Garcilaso] in place of iron to make weapons of war, cutting knives and the few tools for carpentry which they had, the large pins with which the women used to fasten their dresses, mirrors, the dibbles with which they weeded their plots, and the hammers for the silversmiths. For these reasons copper was valued highly, because it was more useful to everybody than silver or gold, and so they mined it in greater quantity than the others.[1]

They mined copper for their use and advantage, silver and gold because they had mastered the problems of subsistence to a point where they could afford to indulge in luxuries and refinements. But to have suggested to the men of Inca days or before that they lived for the mines rather than the mines for their use would have seemed to them madness and absurdity. And even today, though the white population might leave the Altiplano if deprived of the revenues from its minerals, the Indian would leave it only under bitter compulsion.

[1] Garcilaso Inca de la Vega, *Comentarios reales de los Incas*, bk v, ch. 14. First published Lisbon 1609. Eng. tr. by C. R. Markham (London, 1869–71).

Primitive mining was a triumph of ingenuity, for the inventive faculty of the Andean Indians had not produced such tools as the pick, the drill and the saw, and they had of course no explosives. They had not invented the bellows and for anvils they had only hard stones. It is probable, though not conclusively proved, that smelting was known to them. They mined mainly native copper but also oxychlorides and silicates. They melted the ores in clay crucibles over a wood or charcoal fire, which they blew up with long bronze tubes in place of bellows. Silver being less readily fusible than copper, the silver ores were pounded in stone mortars and mixed with a flux of galena or lead sulphide, which was called *soroche*. The mixture was melted on a bed of wood and charcoal in small furnaces like·a goldsmith's cupel, which were pierced with holes and were called *huairas* or 'ventilators'. These furnaces were fired by night on the summits of the hills in order that the wind entering strongly and regularly through the holes would keep the fire at the proper heat. The lead content was then extracted by subsequent melting. 'It was a beautiful thing', says Garcilaso, 'in those days to see eight, ten, twelve, fifteen thousand furnaces burning on those hills and peaks.'[1] And in his *Historia de la Villa Imperial de Potosí* Nicolás de Martínez Arzanz y Vela, following Cieza de León, says that at night there were so many of these *huairas* on all the hills that they looked like a festal illumination.

Gold was obtained both by mining and by panning the auriferous sands of the rivers, and probably most of the sources of gold in Bolivia were known in Inca times and before. Many place-names throughout Bolivia are compounded from native words for gold, such as Coripata and Coroico in the Yungas from the Quechua root *cori*, gold. At Tipuani, which was exploited commercially until 1950 by the Aramayo mining interests, evidences of Inca mine workings were found in the form of adits and galleries excavated in the sandstone rock and in some of them there still remained the lamps they had used and their wooden tools of hard *chonta*. The site of La Paz was famous for its gold long before the Spanish founded a city there and is described in one of the most interesting accounts of pre-Columbian mining by Pedro Sancho de la Hoz, who was secretary to Pizarro and completed in 1534 a description of the conquest and pacification of Peru.

The mines (of La Paz) [he says] are in the gorge of a river, about half-

---

[1] *Comentarios*, bk viii, ch. 25.

way up the sides. They are made like caves, by whose mouths they enter to scrape the earth, and they scrape it with the horns of deer, and they carry it outside in certain hides sewn into the form of sacks or of wine-skins of sheep-hide.[1] . . The mines go far into the earth, one ten brazas, another twenty and the greatest mine, which is called Guarnacabo, goes into the earth some forty brazas.[2] They have no light, neither are they broader than is necessary for one person to enter crouching down, and until the man who is in the mine comes out, no other can go in. . . There are other mines beyond these, and there are still others scattered about through the land which are like wells a man's height in depth, so that the worker can just throw the earth from below on top of the ground. And when they have dug them so deep that they cannot throw the earth out on top, they leave them and make new wells.[3]

The Incas knew of mercury but had no use for it and forbade its exploitation because of its deleterious effects. The sulphide ver-milion was, however, prized as a dye, which was called *ichma*, and the young women of the nobility used it to paint their faces, draw-ing a thin vermilion line from eyes to temples.

The Incas had large surpluses of copper and of gold and silver, as of all the essential commodities of their culture, and under them Bolivia became an important producer of bronze, silver and gold. But they valued copper above gold for its greater utility and as-signed no artificial value to the precious metals as such. Mining was organized to provide for the needs and delectations of the people; the state did not exist for the sake of mining. The miners and metallurgists were specialists who handed down their craft from father to son. They were obliged to work for two months in the year in lieu of tribute and more was not asked of them because this was enough in a balanced and self-sufficing economy. Then came Pizarro and the Spanish, impelled by the lust for gold. Their object was the conquest of easy wealth and not—at first—the organization of a prosperous colony on a permanent basis. They carried off loot worth millions, wiped out a civilization in the space of a few years and sowed chaos in their train, leaving behind them a record of cruelty and greed, treachery, resolution and in-trepidity which has not been surpassed in the history of the world. Under them mining was no longer an accessory to the well-being

[1] The Spanish referred to the llama as 'sheep'.
[2] The *braza* was a measure of about five feet.
[3] Pedro Sancho de la Hoz, *Relación para S. M. de lo sucedido en la conquista y paci-ficación de estas provincias de la Nueva Castilla* (Lima, 1917). Eng. tr. by P. A. Means (N.Y., 1917).

of an ordered structure of society but an end in itself and the goal to which all else was subordinated for the enrichment of another hemisphere. As Casto Rojas justly says: 'the efficient cause of the exploration and conquest of the Collao, which later formed the Audiencia of Charcas and is now the Republic of Bolivia, was the greed for gold which dominated the Conquistadores and those who followed them later.'[1] The search for precious metals was pursued with ruthless energy and zeal. Indian labour was exploited with short-sighted disregard for the agricultural basis upon which the Inca economy had rested. Whole regions were virtually depopulated and the foundations of society were overturned. A new scale of comparative values was introduced from which to this day Bolivia has not been able wholly to win free.

The Spanish concentrated on the production of gold and silver, disregarding the industrial metals. Copper, which was the most important mineral product of Peru under the Incas, was imported by Spain from Hungary in the Colonial period. The earliest Spanish mining enterprise in Bolivian territory was the exploitation of the silver mines of Porco, in the present Department of Potosí, by Gonzalo Pizarro and Diego Centeno in 1540; and like most of their mines it had been known to the Incas before them. For the Spanish did not need to do their own prospecting but compelled the Indians by bribery and torture to disclose to them the locations of their mines. Of the silver mine of Chaqui, for example, Alonso de Barba says in his *El arte de los metales*: 'its search cost many lives of Indians, who died by their own hands to avoid being compelled to disclose it.'[2] And in this way practically all the deposits known today were known to the Spanish within twenty years of their occupation; for in the Andes most of the deposits are complex and in their early search for silver the Spanish discovered also the industrial metals in which they were not then interested. Tin was regarded as a waste product of silver ores and there are enterprises in Bolivia today engaged in extracting the tin content from the tailings of Colonial silver mines. Antimony was used for the extraction of gold from silver ores and small deposits near Potosí and Chichas were worked for this purpose. Wolfram was not in demand until 1910, but the present deposits at Chorolque, Chocaya and elsewhere were already known and wolfram also had been regarded as a waste product in the extraction of silver. The

---

[1] Casto Rojas, *Historia financiera de Bolivia* (1926).
[2] Alvaro Alonso de Barba, *El arte de los metales* (1640).

quicksilver mine of Huancavelica in Peru was exploited after the use of mercury for amalgamation in the smelting of silver was introduced in 1556. But the main energy of the Colonial administration was turned to the production of silver and gold, and the volume of precious metals exported from the New World during the Colonial period was so great that it not only profoundly modified the economy of Spain but produced a price revolution throughout Europe and created the conditions from which modern capitalist economy was born.

The most important new discovery made in the Colonial period was that of the Cerro Rico of Potosí, which for two centuries maintained the largest output of silver in the world.[1] Luis Peñaloza makes no exaggeration when he says in his *Historia económica de Bolivia* that the discovery of Potosí was 'the most important single event in Colonial economy and mining'. Its influence upon the whole course of Colonial development for good and for bad was incalculable. The only considerable discoveries on Bolivian territory made since that time have been the silver deposit of Caracoles, which was first exploited in 1873, later in the century Patiño's almost equally famous mountain of tin at Catavi, and the Empresa Minera Matilde, near the eastern shores of Lake Titicaca, which has been prepared and quartered by Mauricio Hochschild S.A.M.I. but not yet worked and is thought to be one of the largest and richest lead and zinc mines in the world.[2] In estimating Bolivia's reserves of mineral resources—which are sometimes thought to be running out—it must always be remembered, therefore, that the greater part of the deposits now being worked were known to the Spanish in Colonial days and that of these the greater part were known to the Indians in pre-Spanish times. Such discoveries as have been made since were all made by chance and there has at no time been any systematic attempt to prospect the Bolivian Andes through their whole course.

By the end of the Colonial period the heyday of Bolivian mining

[1] In *The Economy of Latin America* (1950), p. 59, Wendell C. Gordon says: 'The region around Potosí in Bolivia, over a period of 400 years, is said to have produced $U.S. 1,000,000,000 worth of silver; through the years, it has probably been the most important silver-producing region in the world.'

[2] It is stated that there exists a minimum of 3 million tons of gross ore in the parts already explored, which are estimated to contain 540,000 tons of fine zinc, 63,000 tons of lead, 120,000 tons of silver and 12,000 tons of copper. The exploitation of the deposit awaits capitalization of a project to supply the necessary electric power.

was over. Gold mining never fully recovered from the expulsion of the Jesuits in 1767, for they had been its most active and ruthless exploiters. As the eighteenth century neared its end many of the best silver mines had exhausted their richest ores and found themselves working ores of ever lower grade. Many had reached levels from which the water could no longer be expelled without modern pumping apparatus. The Indian insurrection of 1780 left commercial chaos in its train and made still more acute the growing difficulty of obtaining sufficient supplies of cheap native labour. In 1804 Potosí suffered a drought of unusual severity, followed by famine and pestilence. At the beginning of the century smelting too was hampered by a shortage of quicksilver from Huancavelica and Spain. The mills at Potosí were reduced from ninety to thirteen and at Oruro only eight were in operation. The Republic was born in a country disrupted by fifteen years of civil war, financially exhausted, with commerce and industry at a standstill. In 1833 the Government tried to revive the mining industry by reducing taxation and offering other important facilities. But somewhat later in the century silver prices suffered a severe drop in the world markets and from this setback Bolivian silver mining has never recovered. Although silver is still exported, it has never since been mined for its own sake but is produced incidentally to the extraction of other metals. There are said to be more than ten thousand abandoned silver mines in the country, many of them containing considerable quantities of ore which it is no longer economic to recover.

The modern era in Bolivian mining commenced during the later decades of the nineteenth century with the rise to importance of the industrial metals. Those ores which for three centuries had been rejected as dross acquired economic value almost overnight. Bolivia was fortunately helped to take advantage of the new demand for these humbler ores by the introduction of modern methods of mining and concentration, by the construction of the first railways and by the inflow of foreign capital interested in the exploitation of its massive resources. Towards the end of the century tin, which had not been previously exploited in the New World, became a highly quoted metal in consequence of its utilization in the canning industry and the new demand was quickly followed by Patiño's discovery of Catavi, a mountain which was seamed with tin. Since that time tin has consistently accounted for some 80 per cent of Bolivia's mineral exports and Patiño has contributed half the total.[1] But antimony, wolfram, copper, lead, zinc and bismuth have also been exported in varying quantities as the prices and markets changed from year to year. The following table from the official export lists published by the Banco Central de Bolivia shows comparative exports of the various non-ferrous metals between 1939 and 1949 (figures in metric tons of fine metal except gold, which is given in kilograms):[2]

Exports of Non-Ferrous Metals

Year	Tin	Wolfram	Antimony	Lead	Zinc	Copper	Silver	Gold	Others
1939	27,648	2,002	10,060	14,111	7,770	4,056	225	272	261
1940	38,531	2,510	11,753	11,663	12,197	6,660	175	365	21
1941	42,740	2,613	14,872	15,654	6,067	7,274	229	254	23
1942	38,900	3,363	17,643	12,481	10,909	6,376	253	184	289
1943	40,959	4,141	17,974	11,387	21,074	6,011	227	134	29
1944	39,341	4,761	7,448	9,047	16,319	6,170	212	142	6,161
1945	43,169	2,311	5,535	9,508	20,975	6,097	208	98	651
1946	38,221	1,273	6,964	8,434	19,187	6,127	190	88	501
1947	33,789	1,581	10,856	11,311	14,612	6,242	193	247	2,479
1948	37,899	1,491	12,260	25,606	21,100	6,622	235	126	3,081
1949	34,662	1,526	10,275	26,311	17,667	5,074	207	1,009	4,942

In the first quarter of this century Bolivia was the world's largest producer of bismuth. Minor exports of sulphur also took place at the end of the nineteen thirties and in the nineteen forties, but there are still extensive sulphur deposits which have not been exploited. Bolivia has large reserves of high-quality iron ore in the Mutún district near the Brazilian frontier. But owing to difficulties of transport and the lack of fuel for processing on the spot, these deposits have not yet been exploited.

Thus a new era of prosperity set in. But it was—and is—a prosperity lacking stability or assurance, dependent upon the fluctuations of world demand and the level of production elsewhere. For Bolivia has always been at a disadvantage with other mineral-producing countries owing to the inaccessibility of its mines, high operating costs and the long and expensive transport. It is a prosperity which flourishes in time of war and dwindles when the world is at peace.

[1] Bolivia used to supply about 20 per cent of the world's output of tin and antimony.
[2] For the years 1950–61 see below, pp. 152–3.

Bolivia's 'tin belt' follows the line of the eastern Cordillera through its whole length, practically from the Peruvian frontier to the southern limits of the Republic. In this belt tin is ubiquitous and it is also richest in deposits of all subsidiary metals except copper, which is distributed more heavily in the western range. The deposits are nearly always complex and most mines produce three or four different metals. But the veins are not everywhere massive enough for economic exploitation and the majority of the mines are in difficult and inaccessible places, most of them between 14,000 and 17,000 feet above sea level. The exacting work of mining at such altitudes would make it impossible for any country which had not resources of cheap labour. Even so the costs of development, maintenance and transport are unusually high. Conditions have therefore favoured the large mining enterprise. In order to cope with the problems of transport, to construct roads or branch railways, to build an encampment for the workers and to keep them supplied with food and necessaries in barren, wild and untilled regions, a large organization and large resources of capital are needed. Mining has therefore been concentrated mainly on the massive and rich deposits which render such outlay of capital and such large organizations profitable. The small miner is at a heavy disadvantage in Bolivia and almost always works on marginal profits, so that quite small fluctuations of price are apt to force out of operation a high proportion of the smaller undertakings. The need for large undertakings has meant the need for foreign capital. And as is usual in countries whose natural resources are exploited by the help of, and partly for the benefit of, foreign capital there has been constant and growing irritation from the belief that the natural wealth which belongs to the people was leaving the country for the enrichment of foreigners or those who, like Patiño, have made foreigners of themselves. The argument that without the aid of foreign capital Bolivia's resources must have remained largely undeveloped carries little weight in the country and the force of popular resentment, fanned by demagogic leaders, has at last driven the present Government to the expedient of expropriation, whose full consequences remain still to be seen.

Owing partly to the altitude but chiefly to Bolivia's lack of fuel and power, it has hitherto proved impossible to smelt the ores economically in the country and they are exported as concentrates to smelters abroad. As ores nowadays rarely come out with a tin content of more than 2 per cent, and as the mining company pays freightage on the dross as well as the metallic content of its ores, it is obviously out of the question to export the ores in the natural state. Moreover, only a specialist smelter like the British Capper Pass can treat ores of under about 20 per cent. It is therefore necessary to *concentrate* the ores on the spot, that is to raise the percentage of metallic content by washing away part of the dross. Upon the efficiency with which this is done the economy of the mining industry largely depends. Efficiency is measured by the grade of the resultant concentrate, the amount of wastage involved and the operative costs of the mill. The matter is further complicated by the fact that most Bolivian ores, and the resultant concentrates, are complex, containing besides the main metal traces of other metallic content, which in some cases rank as impurities, lowering the value of the concentrate, and in other cases have a small selling value of their own. But in general the higher the grade of the concentrate which is produced at the mill, and the purer it is, the better the market and the smaller the waste freightage paid on the valueless dross content of the export. In the last ten years the grade of Bolivian tin ores has declined by about 40 per cent. In the Patiño mines the ores averaged 1·97 per cent in 1943 and are now[1] less than 1·50 per cent. In the Aramayo mine of Caracoles ores averaged 5·503 per cent in 1943 and are now coming out at less than 2 per cent. The general average for the larger mines is between 1·25 and 2·25 per cent. Many of the small mines produce ores of much higher grade, but as their operating costs are higher and their concentration processes less efficient they are not at an advantage over the larger enterprises. In the Patiño mines material is now being utilized which was abandoned in the stopes in the earlier stages of the mine and by a process of 'block caving' everything is being taken out of the veins, even though the tin content is very low. But the technical process of concentration used in the Patiño mill is so efficient that this poor ore is raised to an average grade of about 60 per cent and is the highest-quality concentrate exported in bulk from Bolivia. From what has been said it will be apparent that tin mining has become a highly technical procedure. The nationalized industry in Bolivia will have to show itself competent not only to extract the ores from the ground but to master the newest developments in scientific methods of concentration, which have hitherto remained the province of foreign technicians,

[1] This refers to the period 1950–2 before the nationalization of the larger mining enterprises.

for only so can the Bolivian industry hold its own in competition with cheaper producers.

The second factor in processing, in addition to the grade of the final concentrate produced, is 'recovery'. For in the process of concentration a certain amount of the tin content of the ores is inevitably washed away with the dross and lost in the refuse or 'tailings' which are discarded. Recovery is measured by the proportion of the tin remaining in the concentrates in relation to the tin lost in the tailings. The recovery at Catavi averages about 78 per cent, which is very high for such low-grade ores, but still means that nearly a quarter of the tin content extracted from the earth is lost. Recovery at other Bolivian mines varies from about 38 per cent at the Bolivian Tin and Tungsten (Patiño Group) at Colabi to 80 per cent at Chorolque and 82 per cent at Caracoles (Compagnie Aramayo de Mines en Bolivie S.A.). Through the whole history of Bolivian tin mining the average recovery can hardly have been more than 50 per cent, for the primitive methods of the early miners, although less efficient at raising the grade, recovered at about 50 or 60 per cent, and few modern processes have gone far above this. Thus there is as much tin now lying in the dumps and tailings throughout the country as has been exported from it.[1] Unfortunately this 'lost tin' is present at such a low percentage that it is not economic to work it up by any known method of concentration. It is the miner's dream to discover some new method by which the very low-grade ores could be concentrated to a level which would be interesting to the smelters and at a commercial cost.

The known reserves of ores economically exploitable by present methods are put at between 75,000 and 100,000 tons of fine tin in the larger mines. The reserve in the smaller mines and unworked deposits is probably greater, though higher operating costs render the exploitation of smaller deposits more problematical. Reserves of ores under 1 per cent are probably fifty or a hundred times as large as this. Yet it is certain that the exploitable ores will continue to decline in average grade and that unless new and ever more efficient methods of concentration are employed—or unless new deposits of high-grade ore are discovered—the Bolivian tin-mining industry is bound to show signs of exhaustion within twenty or twenty-five years.

[1] The tin in one of the Catavi tailing dumps alone is estimated to be worth about $50 million—if it could be recovered.

L

Such then are the main problems in the industry upon which Bolivia still pins its faith. Since the Conquest Bolivia has lived by mining and still lives by mining. Yet it would be rash to assume that the vast natural wealth of minerals which has been exploited has proved an unconditional or unmixed blessing to the country. In his *Economic and Regional Geography of South America* E. W. Shanahan gives the following summary of mining in the Andes, which is particularly applicable to Bolivia.

In no comparable region in the world have such quantities and such a variety of igneous rocks been forced through the crustal formations at such numberless points both in the flanks of the ranges and at their summits; nowhere else have the minerals brought up to the surface been so well preserved from the action of denuding forces as in the Central Andes; but in no other highly mineralized region do most of the ores lie at such high altitudes or in such bare and wild mountain country as they do from Ecuador to Southern Chile. Even within the tropics many of the richer deposits are situated quite near the snowline, sometimes, as in Bolivia, on rugged spurs between the glaciers. To the Incas the gold, silver and copper meant little, and the productive capacity of the soil in crops and pastures very much. Europeans when they came reversed this order of precedence, but in staking so much on the minerals, they were gambling against heavy odds in spite of the abundance of ores on every hand. With characteristic daring the Spaniards tackled the wild and lofty mountains, established lines of communication and transportation across hundreds and even thousands of miles in the continent, faced the shortage of fuel as best they could, and exploited the Indians ruthlessly for labour; but failed either to win for themselves permanent prosperity or to make the Andes more desirable for human settlement than the Incas had done. . . . When all is said and done, however, it is probably true that permanent prosperity of the Andean region depends less on the exploitation of minerals than on agriculture and stock-rearing. . . . The history of mining throughout the Colonial period and until quite recently shows that the industry has been of little benefit to the inhabitants. Mines there in the past have been a transitory source of wealth to all concerned; they have hindered rather than helped the development on sound lines of the countries concerned.

The foregoing account represents the informed assessment of the state of Bolivia's mining industry in about 1950, before the MNR revolution. Subsequent plans and assessments must be appraised against the background of that picture.

The expropriation of the larger mining companies had been a settled policy of the MNR since 1939; and in October 1952, some months only after the revolution, the mining properties of Patiño,

Hochschild and Aramayo, which were together producing more than three-quarters of the country's mineral output, were expropriated by decree[1] and their management was entrusted to a public corporation, the Corporación Minera de Bolivia (Comibol), which, without previous experience of production or marketing technique, became overnight one of the largest mining concerns in the world. By establishing a state monopoly in the export of mineral ores the Government also ensured control over the remaining mineral output and of the foreign exchange earned by all mining exports. As has not infrequently been the case in countries whose natural resources have been developed with the aid of capital from abroad, resentment against 'exploitation' by the foreigner was easily fanned into a political war-cry and the nationalization of the three major mining enterprises was accomplished amidst widespread popular enthusiasm, while many who should have known better welcomed it as a panacea for the country's economic ills. But Bolivia was already a high-cost producer and with the progressive lowering of the average grade of tin ores costs of production increased. The decrease in efficiency which resulted from nationalization and the loss of foreign technical staff, the lack of adequate finance for development and maintenance, the accumulation of redundant labour, and the added burden of higher wages and advanced social legislation to which the MNR were committed turned the mineral industry into an overall liability which has required continuous subsidization since 1952. A vicious circle was created when by the continued use of differential rates of exchange for imports the mineral exports were made to subsidize agricultural and other imports and the mining industry itself was kept short of the foreign-exchange capital necessary to maintain its own efficiency. In consequence the cost of tin production has been consistently above its selling price in the world markets and the nationalized industry has proved a burden on the exchequer, necessitating financial aid from abroad. In a speech addressed to the Central Obrera Boliviana in 1953 the Minister of Mines stated that the cost of tin production in the nationalized mines was $1·03 the pound, whereas the market price was only a fraction over 80 cents. In 1955 the President announced that since the credit financing of the mining industry had been a main cause of the exaggerated inflation from which the country was suffering, it would be necessary to contract foreign experts to help in the reorganization

[1] Ratified by a law of 29 Oct. 1956.

of Comibol. Although tin prices have somewhat ameliorated, the industry has continued to be operated at a loss. In pushing ahead with the nationalization it was very clear that the Government had taken on a heroic task from which even the most courageous might have blenched. Bolivia has needed the mining industry in order to earn foreign exchange. And she has needed financial help from abroad in order to keep the industry going.

In the decade since 1952 mineral output decreased from about 75 per cent to about 60 per cent of total production even while production declined overall. The following table illustrates the extent of the decline in the nationalized mines. The value of mineral exports was reduced both on account of prices in the world markets for non-ferrous metals and because the average grade of the concentrates declined. (According to a statement of the Junta Nacional de Planeamiento 30 per cent of tin concentrates were low-grade on which the cost of processing abroad reached about 45 per cent of the customs value, whereas the processing cost of high-grade concentrates is about 14 per cent.) The following table from the *Boletin Estadistico* shows amounts (in metric tons fine) and values (in $ '000) of the main mineral exports for the years 1950 to 1961.

The Ten Year Plan envisages raising the value of mineral exports from $43 million in 1960 to $76 million in 1966 and $97 million in 1971. This it is hoped to achieve both by increasing the actual volume of production and by raising the standard of concentration, and in the case of tin by the setting up of a smelter to

	Tin		Wolfram		Antimony	
Year	Metric tons fine	$'000	Metric tons fine	$'000	Metric tons fine	$'000
1950	31,714	63,376	1,476	2,940	8,781	2,091
1951	33,664	93,366	1,631	11,348	11,816	7,498
1952	32,472	84,783	2,224	14,221	9,811	4,229
1953	35,371	72,330	2,295	13,746	5,785	1,794
1954	27,919	54,913	2,667	14,156	5,218	1,708
1955	28,369	57,291	3,231	15,674	5,359	1,888
1956	27,273	59,208	2,860	14,425	5,112	1,529
1957	28,242	57,389	2,618	6,387	6,374	1,668
1958	18,013	36,285	1,337	1,198	5,278	1,253
1959	24,193	52,833	1,454	1,319	5,202	1,482
1960	19,715	42,860	1,290	1,484	5,327	1,416
1961	20,827	50,552	1,694	2,325	6,740	2,175
1962	21,837		1,502		6,625	

Year	Lead		Zinc		Copper	
	Metric tons fine	$'000	Metric tons fine	$'000	Metric tons fine	$'000
1950	31,192	10,024	19,570	5,285	4,704	2,158
1951	30,552	11,787	30,535	12,123	4,846	2,734
1952	30,013	11,357	35,619	13,152	4,703	2,919
1953	23,788	7,075	23,974	5,562	4,463	2,901
1954	18,227	5,621	20,398	4,735	3,662	2,373
1955	19,123	6,333	21,327	5,727	3,497	2,673
1956	21,571	7,595	17,071	5,108	4,443	3,956
1957	26,262	8,441	19,666	5,408	3,919	2,557
1958	22,815	5,938	14,222	3,228	2,874	1,520
1959	22,038	4,929	3,393	858	2,693	1,658
1960	21,419	4,843	4,027	1,154	2,271	1,478
1961	20,324	4,124	5,332	1,348	2,081	1,274
1962	18,424		3,648		2,400	

deal with the higher-grade ores locally and so avoid the transport costs on dross. The planned increases for particular metals are as follows (in metric tons fine):

	Tin	Lead	Zinc
1960	19,718	21,419	4,026
1966	33,560	35,200	5,800

The Junta admits that in many cases there are available no definite plans for expansion or concrete projects or even an adequate knowledge of the 'structure of production'. Hence some of its forecasts rest on probable estimates. For antimony, bismuth, wolfram and copper no more than a projected overall total for 1966 is given. The Plan also mentions the exploitation of the lead deposit at Matilde and the iron-ore deposits at Mutún. The Junta estimates that something in the region of $47 million is needed in the first three years for the realization of these projects.

Between 1952 and 1961 the mines were milked dry. The richest and most accessible ores were worked first, nothing was spent on exploration or the development of new veins, depreciation of extraction and concentration machinery was not made good. By 1961 productivity had sunk by about 40 per cent of the level in 1952 and with less efficient concentration the cost of production had increased, so that although in mid-1961 the world price of tin stood high at $1·20 a pound, the cost of production in Bolivia was $1·27 a pound. Comibol was producing at a loss of some $9 million a year, and was without funds even for payment of wages as they fell due. Furthermore it was realized that without prospecting and the opening up of new reserves, the ores currently being worked could not be expected to yield for more than two to five years more. The country was running headlong into bankruptcy with massive unemployment, bloodshed and riot.

In this emergency absolute priority was given to the rehabilitation of the nationalized mines in the Ten Year Plan and the re-capitalization of Comibol. On the basis of a short-term Recovery Plan presented to him in August 1960, Víctor Paz Estenssoro, now in his second term of the Presidency, negotiated a loan from the Inter-American Development Bank and the United States and West German Governments jointly. Negotiations were conducted in the aura of a Soviet counter offer to install tin-smelting plant in Bolivia and advance a loan of $150 million. By the middle of 1961 arrangements for the financing of the Plan—known as Operation Triangle—were agreed and were confirmed by a Supreme Decree of 31 August. The Plan envisages spending $37·75 million in three years on prospecting for new ores, improving the level of recovery of the concentration plant, repair and renewal of extraction and concentration plant, rationalization of labour and the restoration of discipline. The Bank was put in control of the operation and Comibol is to be assisted in the execution of the Plan by an Advisory Group with wide general powers. The aim is that Comibol shall be independent of outside assistance by the end of the third year in consequence of an increase in the gross value of mineral exports; and the loan is made repayable in ten years, payments to start at the end of the third year. During the time the Plan is in operation Comibol has been authorized to suspend payments of compensation to the former mine owners of the nationalized mines and has been exempted from the payment of royalties and import duties.

The preamble to the decree of 31 August 1961 was deliberately outspoken about the situation which had made Operation Triangle a necessary emergency measure. It spoke of the constantly falling production, the poorer quality of the ores remaining to be worked, the low output per capita, the unprofitable level of recovery of the concentration plant and the lack of labour discipline. But it added that since the mines continued to supply three-quarters of the country's exports, their contribution was still essential to the balance of payments and could not be dispensed with without aggravating the economic crisis from which the country was suffering. It added that the insolvency of Comibol and its chronic shortage of funds had had a disastrous effect on national trade and industry to the point where many industrial and commercial undertakings were on the verge of bankruptcy, while the unmet claims of public and private undertakings which supplied services to Comibol totalled $10 million. And it concluded that since the potential yield of still available ores was running out, unless suitable investments were made 'the deterioration of the nationalized mining industry may go to extreme lengths such as will bring about utter national economic disaster with consequent massive unemployment among the workers'. The decree itself contained a number of provisions for restoring labour discipline, eliminating redundancy, rationalizing the systems of payments and bonuses, subsidies and compensation, cutting labour costs and illegalizing wildcat strikes. These cut at the heart of the problem with which the country is faced, for the extravagant demands of an undisciplined and all-powerful labour force have been a major cause of inefficiency since the revolution. The legislation for the nationalization of the mining industry had provided for 'labour control' by giving the labour unions representation on the Board of Comibol and in the management of each of the mines so that the workers should exercise 'administrative, economic and financial' supervision of their activities. These *obreros controles* were given far-reaching powers, including the right of veto; and though it was expressly provided that this power of veto should not extend to technical matters, this limitation was seldom honoured in practice and in many cases the management was completely hamstrung. Redundancy was swollen to an alarming degree by labour legislation prohibiting dismissal. Efficiency had been undermined by strikes, absenteeism, idleness, indiscipline and ever more irresponsible demands. In one case a strike was reported because the workers had not been given a bonus for not striking. By 1960 the labour situation was chaotic.

The provisions for the overhauling of mine labour, including a restriction on the use of the veto, were bitterly contested by the labour leaders and represent the results of a compromise between the conditions imposed by the Inter American Development Bank and the determination of the leaders of the syndicates, from Juan

Lechín downwards, not to renounce the powers they had won. While it would be too optimistic to think that the success of Operation Triangle will stand or fall with the restoration of order and sanity in the labour force, it is certain that if this is not achieved the Plan must fail. The origins of this imbroglio go back to the revolution of 1952 when, as has been explained, the exiled MNR party achieved success through their alliance with the leaders of the syndicates, who brought out the armed mine-workers in their support. From that time they have depended on the support of the organized mine workers to maintain them in power and from the conditions of the revolution which put them in the saddle they have inherited a legacy of undue subservience to shortsighted labour demands. It may be that Operation Triangle will call forth a crucial trial of strength between the MNR Government with its plans for the economic future of the country and the labour organizations which have acquired the taste without the responsibilities of power. On the outcome of this the future of the country may well depend. Unless the provisions for restoring order and discipline among mine labour are implemented, the rest of Operation Triangle will be abortive. And unless the mining industry is put on its feet the remainder of the Ten Year Plan is doomed, for the economy cannot survive to see it through.

PETROLEUM

Against a general background of frustration and gloom the mild boom which took place in the Bolivian petroleum industry during the fifties was a main and almost the only source of jubilation.

Bolivia has an extensive sub-Andine oil belt running northwards from the Argentine frontier at Bermejo in the direction of Santa Cruz and thence turning north-westwards along the piedmont of the Cordillera Real to the frontier with Peru. The area has been imperfectly explored and the amount of reserves is not known, nor the extent to which they could be economically exploited.[1] Since the industry was taken over from the Standard Oil Company in 1937 it remained until 1955 a state monopoly operated through a public corporation, Yacimientos Petrolíferos Fiscales Bolivianos (YPFB). During the forties production was maintained at three

[1] A summary will be found in G. Mariaca, 'Reseña sobre la industria petrolífera de Bolivia', *Boletín, Inst. Sudam. Petróleo* (Montevideo), 1 (1945), No. 5. Since 1955 exploration in many areas has been undertaken by foreign oil companies under concessions.

The Economy

centres in the south-east, Camiri, Sanandita and Bermejo. A refinery was built at Cochabamba with a capacity of 5,000 barrels[1]
a day and one at Sucre with a capacity of 4,000 barrels. A 6⅝-inch
pipeline ran from Camiri to the refinery at Cochabamba and a
4½-inch branch feed connected with Sucre. The line has a capacity
of 8,000 barrels a day. Bolivia had a number of petroleum engineers trained in Mexico and the United States, and when the
writer visited the main oil-production centres of Camiri and Sanandita in 1950, arriving unheralded by lorry from Tarija, he was
excellently impressed by the efficiency and energy which he found
there. But the industry was hampered by shortage of finance for
necessary development; and production, having risen from 60,000
cubic metres in 1947 to 74,000 in 1948 and 108,000 in 1949,
dropped to 83,000 in 1950 and 1951. Internal consumption was
at that time put at about 3,000 barrels a day, so that although processing capacity was adequate to it (except for aviation petrol and
certain heavy oils), output fell short and Bolivia remained an importer of petroleum.[2]

In November 1952 the YPFB brought out a carefully considered
report based on studies made over the last ten years and advocating
investment in fresh exploration, drilling and equipment. The new
Government, despite its acute shortage of finance, went ahead on
the report and new investments in 1953 bore fruit and were amply
justified by a production of 269,000 cubic metres in 1954 rising to
568,000 in the peak year of 1957. A pipeline was constructed from
Sicasica outside Cochabamba to the Pacific port of Arica with
capacity to deliver 7,000 barrels a day for export, and in 1955 a
pipeline from Camiri to Yacuiba on the Argentine frontier came

[1] An American barrel=0·16 cubic metres.
[2] In 1948–9 output of the refineries was as follows (cubic metres):

	Processed	Gasoline	Aviation	Kerosene	Diesel	Fuel
1948	52,645	28,005	69	5,305	4,104	14,109
1949	96,149	53,080	169	6,565	6,472	28,084

Imports in the same years were (cubic metres):

	Crude Petrol	Gasoline	Aviation	Kerosene	Lubricating Oils
1948	67,294	32,585	4,774	3,596	2,458
1949	72,054	14,269	6,107	3,093	1,835

157

into cperation with capacity of 10,000 barrels a day. By the end of the fifties Bolivia had 1,800 kilometres of pipeline. Up to 1954 Bolivia imported petrol and petroleum products to an annual value of about $8 million. By the autumn of 1955 the Government was able to announce that output was adequate for domestic needs and exports exceeded $6 million a year. Although this was over-optimistic, the following statistics reveal that the achievement was no mean one.

Petroleum

('ooo cubic metres)

	Production (crude)	Exports	Internal sales
1952	84	13	95
1953	96	12	115
1954	269	15	212
1955	439	98	259
1956	508	122	316
1957	568	198	289
1958	546	219	288
1959	504	152	283
1960	495	181	303
1961	431	111	308

Source: Official statistics.

The Government recognized that it was without the financial resources to develop the petroleum potential of the country and, reversing earlier exclusionist policy, took steps to attract foreign capital by the offer of concessions on favourable terms. In 1955 a Petroleum Code was published (and ratified by law in November 1956) which divided the country up into exploitation zones and includes the following concessions: a depletion allowance of 27 per cent annually; amortization of capital at the rate of 20 per cent per annum; duty-free importation of machinery and equipment; exemption of petroleum products from export taxes and controls; income tax not in excess of 30 per cent of net profits. Between 1956 and 1961 fourteen oil companies had taken concessions for exploration and development. No startling results have been achieved and the first flush of excitement has abated. While oil is confidently believed to be there, its presence in sufficient concentrations to render extraction economic has still be to proved over a wide area. The YPFB is operating wells in Madrejones which produced

74,000 cubic metres in 1960, and has hopes of finding further deposits in Buena Vista and elsewhere. But while the Bolivian oil industry is certainly a useful adjunct to the economy, it is no longer regarded as the El Dorado which it seemed to the over-confident five years ago.

The Ten Year Plan put forward by the Junta Nacional de Planeamiento envisages stepping up production from 8,000 barrels a day in 1962 to 24,000 barrels in 1966 and 50,000 in 1971. The total investment needed for the whole programme would be $639 million, which the planners calculate would bring in an average profit of $16·7 million a year over a twenty-five-year period and leave still recoverable reserves in the region of 252 million barrels. The amount of foreign aid required is put at $54 million in order to cover the excess of investment over revenues during the first five years, after which the programme would finance itself. But in a project involving the exploitation of as yet untested oil deposits— a matter where the unexpected is even expected to happen— calculations such as this, essential as they are from the point of view of national planning, must be thought of not merely as approximate but as liable to be disproved by the event and wildly wide of the target in either direction.

POWER

The Keenleyside Report, which contained an admirably balanced survey of Bolivia's needs and resources of energy and power at the end of the forties, underlines the importance of this for all sectors of economic development. 'The success of a programme of economic development', it begins, 'depends largely upon the availability of cheap and abundant power, which is needed for the expansion of production in mining, agriculture, and industry, and also for domestic use, in consequence of the raising of popular standards of consumption.'[1]

Bolivia has no coal and has imported coal only for the needs of the railways. There are deposits of peat on the Altiplano and of lignite in the regions of Cochabamba and Tarija, but these have not been realistically surveyed and are unlikely to afford a solution of the major problem. The rural native population of the highlands burn *yareta* and llama dung for domestic purposes and wood is plentiful in the eastern lowlands. The petroleum is predominantly high quality, and weak in crude oils of a heavier base suit-

[1] *UNMTA Report*, p. 80.

able for burning or conversion into electric power. Natural gas exists at Camiri and some other sites; and it was estimated that at Camiri some 2 million cubic metres of natural gas was being wasted each month during the late forties. But hitherto no way of utilizing this economically has been found. For large-scale industrial expansion Bolivia must rely upon hydroelectric power.

In 1947 the total installed capacity for electric power, according to estimates published by the Asociación de Empresas Eléctricas de Bolivia, was 73,476 kw, of which 55,494 was hydroelectric and 17,757 diesel.[1] Of this nearly half was produced by the Bolivian Power Company, a Canadian firm centred in La Paz, and the remainder by mining companies for their own use and by small municipal plants at Cochabamba, Oruro, Potosí, Sucre, Santa Cruz and Tarija. Many towns of the Oriente, including Trinidad and Riberalta, were without electric power. The per capita consumption of electric energy—described by the Report as 'still almost negligible'—amounted to only 66 kwh, while in some industrial countries it exceeds 1,000 kwh. The Mission reported that Bolivia's power-supply industry was in a 'precarious state', and said that shortage of electrical energy and unsatisfactory service were almost universal. The writer can substantiate this from personal observation. Apart from inadequate domestic supplies, there was scarcely a single undertaking, other than the mines which made their own, which was not hampered and inhibited by lack of electrical energy. Electricity was available only in a few larger towns and even there in grossly inadequate quantity. The Report of the United Nations Mission thought it reasonable to assume that demand would increase rapidly in the coming decades and said: 'Even a moderate industrial growth coupled with some rise in popular standards of living, therefore, may easily increase the requirements for electric power several fold during relatively short periods of time' (p. 80).

In 1959 the total consumption of electrical energy in the country was estimated at 455·5 million kwh (compared with 265 million in 1947) and the per capita consumption had risen from 66 to 120 kwh. The latter figure, however, gives a somewhat misleading impression since about 43 per cent of all consumption was accounted for by the mines. In the municipalities of La Paz, Cochabamba and Oruro domestic consumption accounted for 58 per cent and

[1] Total units generated in 1947 were reported as 265 million kwh, and production in 1948 and 1949 was of the same order of magnitude.

industrial for only 19 per cent, so that any expansion of industry would be bound to bring in its train a massive increase of overall demand for electric power outside the self-supplying mining establishments. The Junta Nacional de Planeamiento estimated that the insufficiency of installed capacity in 1959 was already of the order of 30·8 MW.

Bolivia has very massive unutilized resources of hydroelectric power, estimated conservatively by a United States Geological Survey in the forties at a potential of 21 billion kw. The Junta de Planeamiento noted in 1961 that lack of systematic technical studies made it difficult to quantify the possibilities of development in connexion with a plan for economic expansion in the near future. That there are resources beyond the foreseeable needs of the country need not be doubted. But the practicability of their utilization is another matter. The same sort of geophysical difficulties confront any extensive exploitation of hydroelectric resources as have always impeded communications in Bolivia. Most of the major sources of hydroelectric power are far away from possible centres of production. The intervening country must be seen to be believed, and belief comes difficult even then. Apart from the initial costs of installation and the problems of maintenance, the expense (and wastage) involved in carrying electrical energy for vast distances over some of the most mountainous and inaccessible terrain in the world is enough to give pause to the most inconsequential of optimists. Only those who have travelled the country can appreciate the real magnitude of the task. Yet it is certain that if the Ten Year Plan is to prove more than one more pipe-dream, the problem of power must be solved.

The Junta Nacional de Planeamiento noted the difficulty of drawing up plans for immediate development in the absence of systematic technical studies. They do, however, suggest a scheme of construction and electrification over the fifteen years 1961–75, basing it upon the need to satisfy existing deficiencies (estimated at some 30,000 kw), the natural expansion of demand and the special situation expected to be created in the various regions of the country by the Plan for industrial and agricultural development. The scheme envisages the installation throughout the country of capacity for an additional 192,000 kw at a total cost of $58 million.

AGRICULTURE

Something has been said in the course of the foregoing account about both agriculture and factory industry and it is not proposed to go over the same ground again under the detailed headings. The present sections will therefore be limited to general summaries and to certain specific sectors which have not been discussed in detail.

About 2 per cent of Bolivia's land area is estimated to be under cultivation and of this about half is on the relatively unfavourable Altiplano. Some two-thirds of the population live by agriculture.

The land reform initiated in 1952 was followed by a marked decrease in agricultural output and although some improvement was noted after 1958, mainly as a result of new enterprises in the Santa Cruz area, the shortfall was not made good either absolutely or in relation to the increase of population. Imports of agricultural products and foodstuffs continued at about 50 per cent of the total, being estimated at $20 million in 1958 with a deficit of $17 million, after allowing for exports assessed at $3 million.[1] The Ten Year Plan envisages both a marked increase of consumption, incident upon improved standards of living, and the achievement of self-sufficiency by 1971. The aim of the planners is to increase output by 120 per cent between 1958 and 1971; and they base their calculations on an increase of 25 per cent in the number of persons engaged in agricultural pursuits, together with an increase in production per capita of 77 per cent. It is no criticism of the members of the Junta or their advisers to say that such academic lucubrations and paper calculations cannot even be appraised realistically out of relation to the physical and social factors upon which any amelioration of Bolivia's productive capacity depends. Nobody who is familiar with the country can harbour a shadow of doubt that it is theoretically capable of feeding the tiny population many times over. But, for this to happen, economic means of communication between the areas of food production and the markets of consumption must be provided. And secondly, as this is done, adequate man-power must be drafted into the underpopulated valleys and plains. The difficulties attendant on these two prerequisites have already been sufficiently indicated.

Cereals

Over the ten years ending 1945 Bolivian wheat production aver-

[1] *Planeamiento*, Sept. 1961, p. 153.

aged 33,315 tons according to available official statistics. Imports of wheat in the same period averaged 46,724 tons and imports of wheat flour (translated into equivalent tonnage of wheat) averaged 17,596 tons. Home production therefore measured about 34 per cent of consumption. There was no significant variation in these proportions up to 1950. During the forties only about 10 per cent of the wheat grown in Bolivia found its way to the milling industry, which preferred the better-quality imported wheat. Yet the flour mill in La Paz alone had capacity to process the whole of the home production and there were several other flour mills in the provinces.

During the fifties the situation deteriorated. After an artificial boom between 1953 and 1956, the output of wheat flour declined until in 1960 it was only 15 per cent of 1950 (6 million kg. as against 39 million in 1950). Imports of wheat in 1959 (latest figures available at the time of writing) were 14,336 tons and imports of wheat flour were 72,000 tons.

Wheat does not grow on the Altiplano and maize is more at home in the high valleys. Experiment and research on the cultivation of tropical strains of wheat in the lowlands have been proceeding for twenty or thirty years, and there has been a good deal of discussion about the substitution for wheat flour of flour made from maize, rye, yucca and soya. *Uminta*, a cake made from maize flour, is traditional from pre-Inca times and is a delicacy still eaten extensively by the natives.

Livestock

The livestock population of Bolivia was estimated by the Directorate of Statistics in 1948 as follows:[1]

(*Figures in thousands*)

Cattle	1,800	Mules	70
Sheep	4,000	Donkeys	180
Pigs	400	Llamas	1,500
Goats	700	Alpacas	300
Horses	150		

Bolivia's richest reservoir of livestock is provided by the cattle of the eastern lowlands, a reserve far more than adequate to all the

[1] A reliable informant in the Banco Agrícola de Bolivia told the writer at the time that in his opinion these estimates should be reduced by 25 per cent. This is probably true of the first two items, but not in the writer's opinion of the rest.

needs of the country even though the whole population were to become eaters of meat. But it is a reserve which is very difficult to utilize for reasons which have been already explained. The Beni *could*, in the opinion of experts, become a great meat-exporting district. But British and foreign firms interested in the immense natural resources of the Beni have hitherto been deterred by the enormous physical difficulties to be overcome, not least of which are the problems of transport, by the absence of adequate manpower on the spot and by the cost of flood protection, renovation of pasturage and the provision of cold storage plant and abattoirs.

As an alternative to the exploitation of the resources of the northern Oriente, plans have from time to time been formulated for the increase of the livestock population on the highlands.[1] In general cattle do not flourish at the altitude of the Altiplano. But in many of its sheltered valleys, and in the 'high valleys' of Cochabamba, Chuquisaca and Tarija, possibilities exist for increasing the acreage under pasture; and though this involves fairly extensive and costly irrigation works and re-educating the native agricultural worker to new methods, some progress has been made. In 1960, 18,000 head of cattle were slaughtered in La Paz, 26,000 in Cochabamba and only 25,000 in the Beni. Total consumption was 110,000 head. Imports of cattle were insignificant.[2]

The sheep population of the highlands could more easily be increased. Bolivian mutton is good and can to a large extent serve as a substitute for beef. In 1960 consumption of mutton was 109,000 head compared with 110,000 head of beef. At the same time the highland sheep could supply the requirements of the textile industry for wool. Indeed in 1937 home-produced wool supplied 92 per cent of industrial consumption. With the expansion of the industry, 90 per cent of its consumption, or about 700 tons a year, was being supplied by importation in the later forties. By 1959 and 1960 imports of wool had dropped to the order of 200 tons a year. But in these years the output of the industry was only just over 50 per cent (in volume) of what it had been in 1950.

---

[1] Recommendations to this effect were made by H. G. Dion, an FAO specialist who studied the agricultural possibilities of the Altiplano at the request of the Bolivian Government in 1949. See *Agriculture in the Altiplano of Bolivia*, FAO Development Paper No. 4 (1950).

[2] From 8,328 head in 1950 imports of cattle rose to 23,346 head in 1956 and were reduced in 1959 and 1960 to 718 and 296 head respectively.

Tobacco

Various types and qualities of tobacco are produced over large areas of Bolivia, in the Departments of Santa Cruz, the Beni, Pando, Tarija, Cochabamba and Cnuquisaca. The heavy *cayubaba* tobacco of the Beni was at one time well known in world markets.

Bolivia no longer exports tobacco. There is a small local cigarette industry in which about 20 per cent of imported tobacco is combined with home-grown tobacco. It is significant of labour conditions that whereas in 1960 there were 142 persons employed in the manufacture of cigarettes compared with 167 in 1950, output in 1960 was only 59 per cent of that in 1950 (2·2 million packets compared with 3·8 million). Almost equally significant is the graph produced in the *Boletín Estadístico* which demonstrates a remarkable increase by basing production not on quantity but on Boliviano value (Bs. 26,870,030 thousand in 1960 against Bs. 136,752 thousand in 1950). The interpretation of Bolivian statistics almost always makes for mental alertness.

FORESTRY

Bolivia ranks among the most important forested countries in the world. About 40 per cent of the territory, or at a rough estimate 128 million acres, is forested. The number of different species of hardwood exceeds 2,000 and the growth of individual trees is often superlative in quality and dimensions. Softwood is lacking.

Exploitation of these resources is unorganized and desultory and the lumber industry rudimentary. Total production of timber in 1960 and 1961 is put at 4,262,000 and 1,646,000 square feet respectively. Imports for 1960 were put at 339 tons.

Rubber

Bolivia has large reserves of wild rubber in the regions of Amazonian forest. Production rose from 294 tons in 1890 to just under 3,500 tons in 1900 and 1901, decreased in 1902 owing to losses of territory to Brazil, but increased steadily to 1910 with more intensive exploitation. The years 1913–19 were the years of highest output:

Year	1913	1914	1915	1916	1917	1918	1919
Tons	5,143	4,485	5,055	4,917	5,843	4,288	5,347

From this time production declined with the fall in world prices and through the nineteen-thirties it rarely topped 1,000 tons. A new stimulus was given to the industry with the demand created by the Second World War and in 1942 a contract was signed with the Rubber Reserve for the export to the United States at favourable prices of all Bolivian rubber surpluses with the exception of 250 tons a year allowed for exportation to neighbouring countries. Exports to the United States between 1942 and 1946, when the contract ended, averaged 2,546 tons a year, rising to 4,388 tons in 1946. Since 1946 demand has fallen off and the industry has again been in decline.

Bolivian rubber is of the wild variety whose collection over very extended areas of primeval forest is rendered economic only by high selling prices. It is of high elasticity and good quality, but has proved unable to compete with the more cheaply produced plantation rubber.

Exports since 1946 have been (kg.):

1947	930,110	1951	1,936,172	1955	1,376,484	1959	2,234,095
1948	23,900	1952	1,597,896	1956	1,258,554	1960	1,650,577
1949	2,800,082	1953	379,803	1957	1,057,724	1961	1,506,920
1950	1,426,013	1954	671,292	1958	1,072,987		

Resuscitation depending on a change-over from wild to plantation rubber may well be chimerical unless a radical alteration of world conditions were to dry up other more favourably situated sources of supply.

Quina

Bolivian production of quina, which rose to importance in the last century, was, like rubber, unable to compete with the plantation product and of recent years demand has been still further reduced by changes in the method of commercial manufacture of quinine. At present output is limited to supplying the very small local industry for the manufacture of sulphate of quinine. The figures of production are no longer quoted in the *Boletín Estadístico*.

INDUSTRY

The growth of light industry has been at a disadvantage in Bolivia owing to the lack of iron and coal and the continual insufficiency of electrical power. Mass production is impeded by the smallness of the domestic market. It is still to a large extent at the stage of workshop industry and the few factories are small. In 1960 manufacturing industry was estimated to employ only 8 per cent of the working population and its output was put, perhaps generously, at 12 per cent of gross production. As has been said, manufacturing industry was artificially stimulated in the five years between 1952 and 1957 by restrictions on imports and by an unwise currency policy, though a high proportion of the output left the country as clandestine exports. The stabilization of the currency in 1957 dealt a severe blow to industry by reducing purchasing power and therefore diminishing the market of consumption, ending the regime of cheap raw materials, saddling them with redundant labour which, owing to the labour laws then current, could not be dismissed, and rendering export no longer profitable. Indeed from that time local manufacture, particularly of textiles and foodstuffs, had to face severe competition from clandestine imports. In 1960 it was estimated that most manufactories were working at less than half capacity. The Junta de Planeamiento stated that while it had been unable to obtain exact information as to the amount of manufacturing plant idle or uninstalled in the country, this was known to include three saw-mills, two plants for the extraction of edible oils, two yucca mills, a bottle-manufacturing plant, cotton looms, coffee-hulling plant and much miscellaneous equipment. The output of the main industries was estimated to be related to consumption in the following proportions:

Percentage of Consumption

Food processing	35	Cement & glass	87
Textiles	70	Rubber goods	19
Chemistry & pharmaceuticals	19	Metallurgical	3
Leather processing	80	Paper	40
Furniture	80	Construction materials	78

In 1958 national production of flour and bread was 40,000 tons against 120,000 tons of imports; and sugar production was 15,000 tons against something over 33,000 tons of imports.

BIBLIOGRAPHY

Acosta, José de. *Historia natural y moral de las Indias*. Seville, 1590. Eng. tr. by E. G.[rimston], 1604. Reprinted with notes by C. R. Markham (Hakluyt Soc., 1st series, nos. 60–61), London, 1880.

Aguirre Achá, José. *La antigua provincia de Chiquitos*. La Paz, 1923.

Ahlfeld, Frederico. *Los yacimientos minerales de Bolivia*. La Paz, 1941.

—— *Mapa de los yacimientos minerales de Bolivia con una memoria explicativa.* Buenos Aires, 1946.

Alejo, Benjamín. *Historia del arte musical en Bolivia*. La Paz, 1935.

Alviña, Leandro. *La música incaica*. Cuzco, 1919.

Anaya de Urquidi, Mercedes. *Tradiciones y leyendas del folklore boliviano*. La Paz, 1946.

Aponte, José Manuel. *La campaña del Acre*. La Paz, 1907.

Aramayo, Carlos Víctor. *Memorandum sobre los problemas de la industria minera de Bolivia*. Buenos Aires, 1947.

Arcienegas, Germán. *The State of Latin America*. N.Y., 1952.

Arguedas, Alcides. *Pueblo enfermo*. Barcelona, 1917.

—— *Historia general de Bolivia*. La Paz, 1922. French tr. *Histoire générale de la Bolivie*. Paris, 1923.

Arnade, Charles W. 'Una bibliografía selecta de la guerra de la emancipación en Alto-Perú', *Boletín de la Sociedad Geográfica y de Historia 'Potosí'*, xl/12 (1953), 159–69.

—— *The Emergence of the Republic of Bolivia*. Gainesville, Fla., 1957.

—— 'A Selected Bibliography of Bolivian Social Sciences', *Int.-Am: R. of Bibliogr.*, viii/3 (1958).

—— 'The Political Causes of the War of Independence', *J. of Int. Am. Studies*, 11 (1960).

—— 'The Historiography of Colonial and Modern Bolivia', *Hispanic American Historical Review*, Aug. 1962. (Historiographical Series.)

Arosemena, José. *Estudios constitucionales*. La Paz, 1911.

Aspiazu, Agustín. *La meseta de los Andes*. La Paz, 1943.

Avila, Frederico. *El drama de la sangre*. La Paz, 1944.

Avila, M. Beltrán. *Ensayos de crítica histórica*. Oruro, 1924.

Ayala Mercado, Ernesto. *La realidad boliviana*. Cochabamba, 1944.

Bagú, Sergio. *Estructura social de la Colonia*. Buenos Aires, 1952.

Balcazar, Juan Manuel. *Epidemiología boliviana*. La Paz, 1946.

Baldivieso, Pastor. *Campaña del Acre*. La Paz, 1925.

Ballivián y Rojas, Vicente de. *Archivo boliviano. Colección de documentos relativos a la historia de Bolivia durante la época colonial*. Paris, 1872.

Banco Central de Bolivia. *Boletín* and *Suplemento Estadístico* (periodicals), *Memoria* (annual).

Bibliography

Bandelier, A. F. A. *The Islands of Titicaca and Koati.* N.Y., 1910.
Barba, Alvaro Alonso de. *El arte de los metales.* Madrid, 1640.
Baudin, Louis. *L'empire socialiste des Inka.* Paris, 1928.
Benavente, Manuel José. *Sistema musical incaica.* Buenos Aires, 1941.
Bilbao Cáceres, Pío. *El Senado Nacional.* La Paz, 1927.
Blanco G., Carlos. *Resumen de la historia militar de Bolivia.* La Paz, 1931.
Bolivia,[1] Aduana de la Coca. *Estadística General de Exportación de las Provincias Nor y Sud Yungas e Inquisivi.* Periodical.
—— Caja de Seguro y de Ahorro Obrero. *Protección Social.* Periodical.
—— Contraloría General de la República. *Informe anual.*
—— Corporación Boliviana de Fomento. *La Corporación Boliviana de Fomento, sus origenes, su organización y su actividad.* 1943.
—— Dirección General de Economía Rural. *Estudio agro-económico de las provincias Los Andes, Omasuyos e Ingavi.* 1946.
—— Dir. Gen. de Estadística. *Anuario de comercio exterior.*
—— —— *Demografía.* Periodical.
—— —— *Estadística Agropecuaria.* Periodical.
—— —— *Industria Fabril e Manufacturera.* Periodical.
—— —— *Revista Mensual.* Periodical.
—— —— *Transportes y Comunicaciones.* Periodical.
—— Dir. Gen. de Minas y Petróleo. *Memorandum of Tin Mining Industry in Bolivia.* 1950.
—— Ministerio de Agricultura, Ganadería y Colonización. *Revista.* Periodical.
—— Min. de Economía Nacional. *Memoria.* Annual.
—— Min. de Hacienda y Estadística. *Revista de Hacienda.* Periodical.
—— Min. de Relaciones Exteriores. *Las fronteras de Bolivia.* 1941.
—— Subsecretaría de Prensa, Informaciones y Cultura. *El libro blanco de la independencia económica de Bolivia.* 1952.
—— —— *Programa de gobierno.* 1960.
—— Superintendencia de Bancos. *Memoria.* Periodical.
Bravo, Carlos. *La patria boliviana.* La Paz, 1894.
Bulnes, Gonzalo. *Guerra del Pacífico.* Valparaiso, 1912.

Camacho, José María. *Historia de Bolivia.* La Paz, 1904.
Capriles R., Remberto, and Gastón Arduz Eguia. *El problema social en Bolivia.* La Paz, 1941.
Cárdenas, Martín. *Contribuciones a la flora económica de Bolivia.* Cochabamba, 1941.
—— and H. C. Cutler. *Chicha, a Native South American Beer.* Cambridge, Mass., 1947. (Harvard University Botanical Museum Leaflets, xiii/3.)
Cardoza, Efraim. *El cholo en el régimen de las intendencias.* Asunción, 1930.
Carlson, F. A. *Geography of Latin America.* N.Y., 1943.
Carrasco, José. *Estudios constitucionales.* La Paz, 1923.

[1] All the following books and periodicals were published in La Paz.

Bibliography

Chávez Suárez, José. *Historia de Moxos*. La Paz, 1944.
Cleven, N. Andrew N. *The Political Organization of Bolivia*. Washington, 1940.
Coimbra, Juan B. *Siringa*. La Paz, 1946.
Cole, J. P. 'The Cochabamba–Santa Cruz Highway, Bolivia', *Geography*, xliii/202 (Nov. 1958).

Diez de Medina, Eduardo. *Bolivia: breve resumen histórico, físico y político*. La Paz, 1926.
—— *De un siglo al otro. Memorias de un hombre público*. La Paz, 1955.
Diez de Medina, Fernando. *Franz Tamayo*. La Paz, 1944.
—— *Thunupa*. La Paz, 1947.
—— *Literatura boliviana*. La Paz, 1953.
Dion, H. G. *Agriculture in the Altiplano of Bolivia*. Washington, 1950. (FAO Development Paper no. 4.)
Duguid, Julian. *Green Hell*. London, 1931.

Estrada S., Julio, and Ricardo Perales S. *Inmigración y extranjería*. La Paz, 1942.

Fawcett, Col. P. H. *Exploration Fawcett*. London, 1953.
Fellman Velarde, José. *Los imperios andinos*. La Paz, 1961.
Finot, Enrique. *Historia de la pedagogía boliviana*. La Paz, 1917.
—— *Historia de la conquista del Oriente boliviano*. Buenos Aires, 1939.
—— *Historia de la literatura boliviana*. Mexico City, 1943.
—— *Nueva historia de Bolivia*. Buenos Aires, 1946.
Fossati, Humberto. *Monografía de Nor y Sud Yungas*. La Paz, 1948.
Franck, Harry A. *Vagabonding down the Andes*. London, 1919.

Gandia, Enrique de. *Historia del Gran Chaco*. Buenos Aires, 1929.
—— *Historia de Santa Cruz de la Sierra*. Buenos Aires, 1935.
Garcilaso Inca de la Vega. *Comentarios Reales de los Incas*. Buenos Aires, 1943. English tr. *The First Part of the Royal Commentaries of the Incas* (2 vols. Hakluyt Soc. 1st series, nos. 41 and 45). London, 1869, 1871. *The Incas*, tr. and ed. A. Gheerbrant. London, 1963.
Gordon, Wendell C. *The Economy of Latin America*. N.Y., 1950.
Great Britain. Commercial Relations and Exports Department. *Economic and Commercial Conditions in Bolivia, May 1951*. By Hugh John Legg; —— *December 1955*. By Paul Henderson Scott. London, 1957.
Griffin, C. C. *Concerning Latin American Culture*. N.Y., 1940.
Guevara Arze, Walter. *P.M.N.R.A. Exposición de motivos y declaración de principios*. La Paz, 1960.
Guillén Pinto, Alfredo, and Heriberto Guillén Pinto. *Geográfica-atlas escolar de Bolivia*. La Paz, 1926.
—— and Natty Peñaranda de Guillén Pinto. *Mina*. La Paz, 1953.

Bibliography

Gutiérrez, Alberto. *El melgarejismo antes y después de Melgarejo*. La Paz, 1918.

Guzmán, Augusto. *Gesta Valluna*. Cochabamba, 1953.

Guzmán Arze, Humberto. *Selva. Cuentas del trópico*. Cochabamba, n.d.

Handbook of South American Indians. Julian H. Steward ed., 6 vols. Washington, Bureau of Am. Ethnology, Smithsonian Institution, 1946–50.

Hanke, Lewis. *The Imperial City of Potosí*. The Hague, 1956.

Harms Espejo, Carlos. *Bolivia en sus diversas fases principalmente economica*. Santiago, 1922.

Harris, Seymour E., ed. *Economic Problems of Latin America*. N.Y., 1944.

Heath, D. B. 'Land Reform in Bolivia', *Int. Am. Econ. Aff.*, xii/4 (1958–9).

—— 'Commercial Agriculture and Land Reform in the Bolivian Oriente', ibid. xiii/2 (1959–60).

—— 'Land Tenure and Socialization: an Ethno-historical Study from the Bolivian Oriente', ibid. xiii/4 (1959–60).

Hewett, Edgar Lee. *Ancient Andean Life*. N.Y., 1939.

Hughlett, L. J. *Industrialization of Latin America*. N.Y., 1946.

Humphreys, R. A. *Latin American History: a Guide to the Literature in English*. London, OUP for RIIA, 1958.

Instituto de Sociología Boliviana. *Revista*. Sucre. Periodical.

International Financial Statistics (International Monetary Fund). Washington. Monthly.

Isherwood, Christopher. *The Condor and the Cows*. London, 1949.

Iturricha, Agustín. *Historia de Bolivia bajo la administración del mariscal Andrés Santa Cruz*. Sucre, 1924.

Jaimes, J. L. *La Villa Imperial de Potosí*. Buenos Aires, 1905.

James, Preston E. *Latin America*. London, 1950.

Jaúregui Rosquellas, Alfredo. *Geografía general de Bolivia*. La Paz, 1919.

—— *La ciudad de los cuatro nombres*. Sucre, 1924.

—— *Alrededor de la tragedia. Un siglo de vida republicana*. Sucre, 1951.

Joint Bolivian–United States Labor Commission. *Labor Problems in Bolivia*. Montreal, ILO, 1943.

Kirkpatrick, F. A. *Latin America: a Brief History*. Cambridge, 1938.

Kuczynski Godard, Maxine H. *Estudios médicos-sociales en minas de Puno*. Lima, 1945.

La Barre, Weston. *The Aymara Indians of the Lake Titicaca Plateau, Bolivia*. Menasha, Wis., Am. Anthropological Assoc., 1948.

La Paz en su IV centenario. 4 vols. La Paz, 1948.

Lara, Jesús. *Surumi*. Buenos Aires, 1943.

—— *La poesía quechua*. Mexico City, 1947.

171

Bibliography

Lavandez, J. *La colonización en Bolivia durante la primera centuria de su independencia*. La Paz, 1925.

Leavitt, Sturgis E. *A Tentative Bibliography of Bolivian Literature*. Cambridge, Mass., 1933.

Lecuna, Vicente. *Documentos relativos a la creación de Bolivia*. Caracas, 1924.

Leonard, Olen E. *Canton Chullpas: a Socio-economic Study of an Area in the Cochabamba Valley of Bolivia*. Washington, U.S. Dept. of Agriculture, 1948.

—— *Santa Cruz: a Socio-economic Study of an Area in Bolivia*. Washington, U.S. Dept. of Agriculture, 1948.

—— *Bolivia: Land, People and Institutions*. Washington, 1952.

Limpias Saucedo, Manuel. *Los gobernadores de Mojos*. La Paz, 1942.

Linke, Lilo. *Andean Adventure. A Social and Political Study of Colombia, Ecuador and Bolivia*. London, 1945.

McBride, George McCutcheon. *The Agrarian Indian Communities of Highland Bolivia*. N.Y., 1921.

Machicado, Porfirio Díaz. *Ingobernables. Historia de estos últimos tiempos*. Cochabamba, 1951,

—— *Historia de Bolivia*. 5 vols. La Paz, 1954–8.

McQueen, Charles A. *The Bolivian Public Debt*. Washington, 1924.

—— *Bolivian Public Finance*. Washington, 1925.

Mariaca, G. 'Resena sobre la industria petrolífera de Bolivia', *Boletín Inst. Sudam. Petróleo*, i/5 (1945).

Marsh, Margaret A. *The Bankers in Bolivia*. N.Y., 1928.

Martínez Arzanz y Vela, Nicolás de. *Historia de la Villa Imperial de Potosí*. Buenos Aires, 1943.

Martínez y Vela, Bartolomé. *Anales de la Villa Imperial de Potosí*. La Paz, 1939.

Means, Philip A. *Ancient Civilizations of the Andes*. N.Y., 1931.

Mendoza, Jaime. *La universidad de Charcas y la idea revolucionaria: ensayo histórico*. Sucre, 1925.

—— *El macizo boliviano*. La Paz, 1935.

Mercado M., Miguel. *Charcas y el Río de la Plata a través de la historia*. La Paz, 1918.

Monge, Carlos. *Acclimatization in the Andes*. Baltimore, Md., 1948.

—— 'Man, Climate and Changes of Altitude', *Meteorological Monographs*, ii/8 (Oct. 1954).

Montenegro, Carlos. *Nacionalismo y coloniaje*. La Paz, 1943.

Mörner, Magnus. *The Political and Economic Activities of the Jesuits in the La Plata Region. The Hapsburg Era*. Stockholm, 1953.

Morales, José Agustín. *El oro verde de las Yungas*. La Paz, 1938.

Moreno, Gabriel René. *Anales de la prensa boliviana*. Santiago, 1888.

—— *El general Ballivián*, Santiago, 1894.

—— *Ultimos días coloniales en el Alto Perú*. Santiago, 1896–8.

Bibliography

Neiswanger, William A., and James R. Nelson. *Problemas económicas de Bolivia*. La Paz, 1947. (Translation of article contributed to Harris, *Economic Problems of Latin America*, q.v.)

Nelson, Raymond H. *Education in Bolivia*. Washington, 1949 (Federal Security Agency, *Bulletin*, no. 1).

New World Guides to the Latin American Republics, ed. E. P. Hanson, 3rd ed., vol. ii. N.Y., 1950.

O'Connor d'Arlach, Tomás. *Los presidentes de Bolivia desde 1825 hasta 1912*. La Paz, 1918.

Omiste, Modesto. *Crónicas potosinas*. La Paz, 1919.

Orbigny, Alcides d'. *Voyage dans l'Amérique méridionale*. Paris, 1844.

—— *Descripción geográfica, histórica y estadística de Bolivia*. La Paz, 1942.

Ordóñez López, Manuel. *Constitución política de la república de Bolivia: leyes y disposiciones mas usuales*. La Paz, 1917.

Ormachea Zalles, Héctor, in I. L. Kandell, ed. *Education in the Latin American Countries*. N.Y., 1942.

Osborne, H. *Indians of the Andes*. London, 1952.

—— 'Bolivia's New Path', *Geographical Magazine*, xxiii/4 (Aug. 1955).

Otero, Gustavo Adolfo. *Figura y carácter del indio*. La Paz, 1939.

—— *Figuras de la cultura boliviana*. Quito, 1952.

Pan American Union. *A Statement of the Laws of Bolivia in Matters Affecting Business*. 3rd ed. Washington, P.A.U., 1962.

Pando Gutiérrez, Jorge. *Bolivia y el mundo*. La Paz, 1947.

Paredes, Manuel Rigoberto. *Política parlamentaria de Bolivia*. La Paz, 1911.

—— *El arte en la altiplanicie*. La Paz, n.d.

—— *Mitos, supersticiones y supervivencias populares de Bolivia*. La Paz, 1920.

—— *El arte folklórico de Bolivia*. La Paz, 1949.

Paz, Julio. *Historia económica de Bolivia*. La Paz, 1927.

Paz, Luis. *La Corte Suprema de Justicia de Bolivia: su historia y su comentario*. Sucre, 1912.

—— *Constitución política de la Republica de Bolivia: su texto, su historia y su comentario*. Sucre, 1912.

Paz Estenssoro, Víctor. *Mensaje del Presidente de la Republica al H. Congreso Nacional*. 1956.

—— *La Revolución es un proceso que tiene raíces en el pasado*. La Paz, 1961. (Dirección Nacional de Informaciones, Presidencia de la República, pamphlet no. 4.)

Pazos Kanki, Vicente. *Memorias histórico-políticas*. London, 1834; La Paz, 1939.

Peña y Lillo Escóbar, Abel. *Sintesis geográfica de Bolivia*. La Paz, 1947.

Peñaloza, Luis. *Historia económica de Bolivia*. La Paz, 1946.

Pérez Velasco, Daniel. *La mentalidad chola en Bolivia*. La Paz, 1928.

Picón-Salas, Mariano. *De la conquista a la independencia*. Mexico City, 1944.

173

Bibliography

Prada, E. Roberto. *Climas de Bolivia*. La Paz, 1946.

Quesada, Vicente G., *Crónicas potosinas*. Paris, 1890; Potosí, 1950.

Reinaga, Fausto. *Belzú. Precursor de la revolución nacional*. La Paz, 1953.
Revell, Winifred. *Chaco Chapters*. London, 1947.
Reyeros, Rafael A. *Caquiaviri*. La Paz, 1946.
Rippy, J. Fred. 'Bolivia: an Exhibit of the Problems of Economic Development in Retarded Countries', *Int. Am. Econ. Aff.*, x/3 (1956).
Rojas, Casto. *Historia financiera de Bolivia*. La Paz, 1926.
—— *Geografía económica de Bolivia*. La Paz, 1928.
Romero, Gonzalo. *Reflexiones para una interpretación de la historia de Bolivia*. Buenos Aires, 1960.
Royal Institute of International Affairs. *The Republics of South America* (London, 1937).
Ruiz Guinazú, E. *La magistratura indiana*. Buenos Aires, 1916.
Rycroft, W. Stanley, ed. *Indians of the High Andes: Report of the Commission appointed by the Committee on Cooperation in Latin America to study the Indians of the Andean Highland, with a view to establishing a Cooperative Christian Enterprise*. N.Y., 1946.

Saavedra, Bautista. *El ayllu*. La Paz, 1903.
Sanabria Fernández, Hernando. *En busca de El Dorado. La colonización del Oriente boliviano por los cruceños*. Santa Cruz, 1958.
Sánchez Rossel, Alberto. *Tierruca chapaca*. Tarija, 1942.
Sariola, S. 'A Colonisation Experiment in Bolivia', *Rural Sociology*, xxv/1 (Mar. 1960).
Servicio Agrícola Interamericano. *Annual Report*. La Paz, 1957.
Shanahan, E. W. *South America*. London, 1927.
Siles, Hernando. *Derecho parlamentario de Bolivia*. La Paz, 1917.
Siles Zuazo, H. 'Mensaje del Presidente de la República al H. Congreso Nacional'. 1959.
Singewald, J. *Bibliography of Economic Geology of South America*. Geolog. Soc. of Am. Special Papers no. 50, 1943.
Sociedad Geográfica de La Paz. *Boletín*. Periodical.
Solorzano, Juan de. *Política indiana*. Madrid, 1736.
Sotomayor Valdés, R. *Estudio histórico de Bolivia bajo la administración del general D. José María Achá*. Santiago, 1874.
South American Handbook. London, Trade and Travel Publications. Annual.
Suárez, Nicolás. *Anotaciones y documentos sobre la campaña del Alto Acre*. Barcelona, 1928.
Subieta Sagárñaga, Luis. *La mita*. Potosí, 1917.

Tamayo, Franz. *Creación de la pedagogía nacional*. La Paz, 1910.
—— *Tamayo rinde cuenta*. La Paz, 1947.

Bibliography

Thompson, R. W. *Land of To-Morrow*. London, 1937.
Torre Revello, José. *El libro, la imprenta y el periodismo en América*. Buenos Aires, 1940.
Trend, J. B. *Bolívar and the Independence of Spanish America*. London 1946.
Trigo, Bernardo. *Las tejas de mi techo*. La Paz, 1939.
—— *Crónicas y perfiles de mi tierra*. Tarija, 1940.

U.N. Commission of Enquiry on the Coca Leaf. *Report* [E/CN 7/AC. 2/I]. N.Y., 1950.
—— Economic Commission for Latin America. *Economic Survey of Latin America 1948–*. N.Y., 1949–.
—— Interim Co-ordinating Committee for International Commodity Arrangements. *Review of International Commodity Problems*. N.Y., 1949.
—— Technical Assistance Administration. *Report of the U.N. Mission of Technical Assistance to Bolivia*. N.Y., 1951.
U.S. Bureau of the Census. *Bolivia, a Summary of Biostatistics*. Washington, 1945.
Urioste, Ovidio. *Impresiones de viaje*. Cochabamba, n.d.
Urquidi Morales, Arturo. *La comunidad indígena*. Cochabamba, 1941.

Váldez Vicente. *Nueva compilación de leyes del trabajo y de previsión social*. La Paz, 1949.
Valencia Vega, Alipio. *Desarrollo del pensamiento político en Bolivia*. La Paz, 1953.
Vásquez, Edmundo. *El camino abierto*. Arica, 1937.
Vázquez-Machicado, Humberto. 'Los caminos de Santa Cruz de la Sierra', *Revista de Historia de América*, no. 40, 1955.
—— 'La condición del Indio y la legislación del trabajo en Santa Cruz de la Sierra en el siglo xvi', *Universidad de San Carlos* (Guatemala), no. 36, 1956.
—— 'Orígines del mestizaje en Santa Cruz de la Sierra', ibid.
—— José de Mesa, and Teresa Gisbert. *Manual de historia de Bolivia*. La Paz, 1958.
Vega, Carlos. *Panorama de la música popular argentina*. Buenos Aires, 1944.
—— *Los instrumentos musicales aborígenes y criollos de la Argentina*. Buenos Aires, 1946.
Vejarano, Jorge Ricardo. *Orígenes de la independencia suramericana*. Bogotá, 1925.
Vergara Vicuña, Aquiles. *Historia de la Guerra del Chaco*. 7 vols. La Paz, 1940–5.
—— *El mar, nexo de paz entre Bolivia y Chile*. La Paz, 1938.
—— *Bernardino Bilbao Rioja. Vida y hechos*. La Paz, 1948.
Villanueva, Emilio. *Bolivia en el primer centenario de su independencia*. N.Y., 1925.
Violich, Francis. *The Cities of Latin America*. N.Y., 1944.

Bibliography

Walker Martínez, C. *El doctor Linares*. Santiago, 1900.

Weeks, D. 'Bolivia's Agricultural Frontier', *Geographical Review*, xxxvi (1946).

Wilgus, A. Curtis, ed. *Colonial Hispanic America*. Washington, 1936.

Wright, Ch. W. 'Mineral Resources, Production and Trade in Bolivia', *Foreign Minerals Quarterly* (U.S. Bureau of Mines), ii/4 (1939).

Wright, M. R. *Bolivia*. Philadelphia, 1907.

Ybarra, T. *Lands of the Andes, Peru, Bolivia*. N.Y., 1947.

Zon, R. and W. N. Sparhawk. *Forest Resources of the World*. N.Y., 1923.

Zook, David H. *The Conduct of the Chaco War*. N.Y., 1960.

ADDENDUM

Ferguson, J. Halcro. *The Revolutions of Latin America*. London, 1963.

INDEX

Index

land tenure, 71, 73–74
La Paz (Department), 19, 25, 45, 52, 104, 105
La Paz (town), viii, 1, 4, 5, 8, 9, 10, 11, 12, 13, 14, 17, 19, 22, 23, 24, 29, 34, 36, 37, 38, 39, 41, 42, 43, 45, 51, 53, 54, 58, 60, 66, 68, 69, 77, 90, 93, 97, 98, 104, 113, 114, 115, 117, 118, 122, 123, 125, 127, 130, 132, 141–2, 160, 163, 164
La Paz–Guaqui railway, 12, 38
La Plata, 2, 83
Lechín Oquendo, Juan, 66, 68, 69, 81, 156
Lima, 14, 36, 50, 51, 52, 56
Linares, José María, 57–58
Llallagua, 51
llama, 9, 15, 17, 18, 20, 23, 116, 142 n., 159
Lloyd Aereo Boliviano, 37
Loreto, 85, 89

Machacamarca, 39
Madera, 24, 26, 27, 28, 29, 43, 61
Madera–Mamoré railway, 5, 32, 42–43, 61
Madre de Dios, 15, 29
Magdalena, 37
maize, 16, 24, 26, 49, 85, 101, 113, 114, 125, 163
Mamoré, 5, 26 ff., 37, 42, 60, 93
Mapiri, 29
Marbán, Pedro, 85
Matto Grosso, 24, 26, 28, 30
Melgarejo, Mariano, 58, 60
Mendoza, Alonso de, 51
Mennonite, 103
mining, vii, xi, 7, 8, 41, 50–51, 59, 65, 66, 67, 70, 74, 108 n., 111–12, 113, 114, 116, 117, 118, 121, 123, 124, 129, 130, 134, 139–56, 160, 161
Mojos, 26, 27, 45, 52, 83–91, 101, 122
Mollendo, 12, 38, 40, 98, 123
Montepunco, 33 n., 45, 93
Montero, 101
Morales, Agustín, 58–59
Movimiento Nacionalista Revolucionario (MNR), see National Revolutionary Movement
Mururata, 8

Mutún, 145, 153

Nationalization, xi, 39, 65, 71, 129, 147, 148, 150–2
National Revolutionary Movement, 63, 65–71, 78, 81, 100, 117, 129, 132, 139, 147, 150, 156
Nuflo de Chávez, 84, 94
Núñez Cabeza de Vaca, 84
nutrition, 14, 113–16

oil, see petroleum
Olañeta, Pedro Antonio de, 53, 54
Ollagüe, 8, 38, 39
Operation Triangle, 154–6
Orbigny, Alcides d', 2 n., 4, 22, 32, 86
Orinoco, 83
Oropesa, see Cochabamba
Orton, 25, 29
Oruro (Department), 45, 50, 105, 118
Oruro (town), viii, 6, 13, 38, 39, 50, 51, 104, 115, 145, 160

Pacajes, 8
Pacific, War of the, 2, 59–60
Paititi, 83
Pando, 25, 29, 42, 45, 93, 94, 105, 165
Paraguay (country), 2, 16, 27, 28, 51, 52, 61–62, 67, 83, 84, 94
Paraguay (river), 25, 27, 28, 30, 60, 62, 84
Paraná, 28
Parapetí, 27
Partido de Izquierda Revolucionario (PIR), 66
Patiño, 8, 39, 51, 66, 108 n., 144, 145, 147, 148, 150, 151
Paz Estenssoro, Víctor, 66, 68, 69, 70, 81, 129–30, 132, 133 n., 151, 154
Peñaloza, Luis, 57n., 144
Peñaranda, Enrique, 65
Peña y Lillo Escóbar, Abel, 4 n., 5 n.
Peru, 1, 2, 7, 11, 12, 29, 36, 38, 40, 49 n., 50, 51, 52, 53, 54, 55, 56, 57, 58, 59, 63, 84, 94, 96, 98, 99, 141, 143, 144, 147, 156
Peruvian Corporation, ix, 12–13, 38
petroleum, 36, 41, 61, 63, 101, 126, 134, 156–9
Pilcomayo, 19, 24, 27, 61

179

Index